*The Critical Prose of*

# ALEXANDER PUSHKIN

*The Critical Prose of*

# ALEXANDER PUSHKIN

## WITH CRITICAL ESSAYS BY
## FOUR RUSSIAN ROMANTIC POETS

*Edited and Translated by*

## CARL R. PROFFER

INDIANA UNIVERSITY PRESS

*Bloomington  /  London*

*for Ellendea*

# CONTENTS

\* **Asterisks indicate essays for which Pushkin provided no title. The titles
here are the ones assigned by the editors of his** *Complete Collected
Works.*

# PREFACE

**This selection of critical writings by Pushkin was translated**
from Volume Seven of his *Complete Collected Works* (M:AN,
1956–58). It is intended both for the general reader and for
students of Russian literature whose Russian does not yet allow
them the luxury of reading criticism in the original. Intrinsic
interest and merit were the two primary criteria used in making
the selections. I have given special consideration to essays or
notes which show Pushkin's attitudes toward non-Russian
literatures and toward such basic theoretical problems as the
nature of drama and the development of romanticism. The volume also contains examples of Pushkin's polemical articles,
literary mystifications, countercriticisms, and aphorisms written for himself alone—as an attempt to clarify his own thinking. I have tried to avoid items of interest only to specialists.
Where there are two works on the same subject (such as Pushkin's polemic with Bulgarin), I have included only one.

The selections are arranged chronologically. In the case of
unfinished pieces, the date at the end specifies the year of writing; for completed articles, it is the year of publication. The
reader should bear in mind the fact that most of Pushkin's
critical writings were not published in his lifetime. Many of
them survive only in rough drafts and fragments. It should also
be noted that while Pushkin sometimes answered personalities
in print, he avoided printing direct answers to criticisms of his
own works.

As a supplement intended to give the reader a clearer idea
of Russian romanticism and the general literary climate during

the 1820s, I have translated important critical essays and notes by four of Pushkin's contemporaries—all of them poets.

The notes I have provided at the end of each essay or fragment should enable both nonspecialists and graduate students in Russian literature to make their way through Pushkin's topical and literary allusions with minimum difficulty. Many of these notes are based on information in various Academy of Sciences editions of Pushkin's criticism. The notes marked with asterisks in the text are Pushkin's own.

My primary goal in the translation was accuracy—and not that gloss of "readability" which is so easily attained if one makes small cuts and additions, uses improper synonymy, and twists syntactical variety into comfortable clichés. As Vyazemsky wrote, "Either submit to an author when translating him, or don't translate him." This advice is especially applicable to the prose of ideas.

My thanks to J. Thomas Shaw for his critique of the manuscript of this translation, to Edward J. Brown for reading the introduction, to John Houston for help with the French, and to my Muse—who has many names—for inspiration. Of course, the usual reservations apply, except in the last case.

C. R. P.

*Bloomington, Indiana*
*August 3, 1968*

*The Critical Prose of*

ALEXANDER PUSHKIN

# INTRODUCTION

## I · THE BEGINNINGS OF RUSSIAN LITERARY CRITICISM

**It is tempting to begin by saying that Russia had no criticism** before Pushkin. Characteristic is the fact that in *The Messenger of Europe*, founded by Karamzin in 1802 and generally regarded as the first of the important "thick" journals in Russia, there was no special division for criticism until 1810—only four years before Pushkin's first poems appeared in that journal. A decade later Pushkin wrote Bestuzhev-Marlinsky, objecting to his assertion that "we have criticism but no literature," saying:

> Where did you get that idea? It is precisely criticism which we lack. . . . We do not have a single commentary, not a single book of criticism. . . . No, let us say your sentence the other way around: We have literature of a sort, but we have no criticism.[1]

It is clear that there is something solipsistic—and polemical—about the way the writers denied the existence of criticism and the critics the existence of literature. What they meant, of course, was that Russia had *poor* criticism and *poor* literature.

As is usually the case, literature was in better condition than criticism: Derzhavin, Krylov, and Zhukovsky had written a few fine poems. But most of the rest was pyrite for patriots and literary scholars. The poetry was imitative and cacophonous, the plays undramatic, and the prose amateurish.[2] Like Ilya

Murometz, the folk hero who could not walk until he was thirty-three, Russian literature had a long infancy.

"Criticism" was an even more amorphous term then than now. In the few dozen journals which existed between 1800 and 1820, criticism meant reviews of all printed matter whether it be on history, philosophy, pedagogy, agriculture, or finally, *belles-lettres*. There were no books of literary criticism. There were no full-time literary critics. The few critical essays which did appear were usually writen by aristocratic dilettantes, professors of history, or by writers themselves. Little written before the early and mid-1820s is of more than historical interest. Much of the criticism consisted of dry bibliographical or biographical information. One favorite device was the printing of lengthy excerpts interspersed with references to the specific "beauties" of this or that passage. In the manner of our scholarly journals, the quality of paper was noted, typographical and grammatical errors duly listed.

Aristotle's rules were read diligently. For many, Boileau's *Art Poétique*, the "French Koran" as Pushkin called it, was still authoritative; La Harpe's *Lycée, ou Cours de littérature ancienne et moderne* was used to praise or scorn new works. Following the neoclassical tradition which dominated Russian literature during much of the eighteenth century, the majority of Russian "critics" before the 1820s preferred unmixed genres and a legislated hierarchy of values. The growth of sentimentalism around the turn of the century resulted in a few changes —Karamzin and Zhukovsky both practiced a kind of subjective criticism, saying that the taste of sensitive and good men is the most reliable guide.

The two problems which seem to have concerned critics most are of different orders—the literary language and morality in literature. At the beginning of the eighteenth century the written language was a mixture of disparate elements—Church Slavonicisms, bureaucratese, colloquial Russian, complicated by dialectisms and regionalisms, and a mass of undigested borrowings from Dutch, German, English, Italian, and French. Grammar itself might charitably be described as "in a state of transition," and there is no charitable way of describing the vagaries of Russian syntax. In the 1750s Lomonosov proposed a system which fit each canonical genre to a certain style, but it is hard to determine what effect this had on the normalization of the literary language. During the first two decades of the nineteenth century, the main critical polemic arose from the linguistic innovations practiced by Karamzin, the most important popularizer of sentimentalism in Russia. He rejected a variety of archaic words, adopted simplified syntax, defended Gallicisms, and advocated the use of the spoken language of polite society. These changes were opposed by the Society of Lovers of the Russian Word (1811–16), headed by Alexander Shishkov, who, in his "Reflection on Old and New Style," maintained that lexical indigence should be corrected by neologism based on native Slavic roots and the resurrection of archaisms from chronicles and church literature. Although as a schoolboy Pushkin belonged to Arzamas—a rather informal society formed to support Karamzin and parody the solemn Shishkovians—in his poetic practice he soon reacted against the finical, feminine language characteristic of the Karamzin "school." Criticizing the flaccid metaphors and *politesse* of recent elegiac poetry, he maintained that literature needed more of the *muzhik* coarseness. He moved further in this direction as his career progressed. But arguments over acceptable grammatical and lexical items continued even after Pushkin's death; thus Gogol's *Dead Souls* (1842) was violently attacked for lowness of diction.[3]

Underlying the linguistic controversy was a more volatile issue—romanticism. For Russian journalists this was not just a question of changing literary forms. It was a question of morality. Reading was a relatively new thing in Russia, and it was the concern of conservative members of the educated class—mindful of events in France and the rigid precepts of Russian Orthodoxy—that enlightenment not lead to reformation. Speeches on patriotism filled the journals. The task of writers was to teach—in a pleasant way. Poetry, they said, is the language of the gods; it should be elegant and majestic. Reading should be an uplifting experience. Therefore, some critics viewed sentimentalism with alarm. In the early 1780s *The Sorrows of Young Werther* and *Delphine* were regarded as unhealthy reading. Then came Byron, who was plainly pernicious. With its vampirine loves and mutilated mistresses, *l'école frénétique* was proof that the French were as sick as when they murdered their king and invaded Holy Russia. Romanticism was revolution in the literary sphere. Thus criticism was often devoted to discussions of proper and improper subject matter, edifying themes and noxious ones, works which improve man and those which lead him into temptation. The critics who objected to descriptions of ghosts and allusions to adultery were usually the same ones who claimed that no real artist could use base words like *von'*, *njuxat'*, or *korova*[4] in a poem.

The quality of criticism improved during the 1820s and 1830s in spite of many handicaps. Among these were illiteracy, disinterest, and censorship. Few publications lasted more than a few years, and until the 1830s the number of subscribers usually ran between 500 and 1500. Censorship had always been strict, and after the Decembrist Uprising the government published the so-called "cast-iron" code, the 230 paragraphs of which were filled with dangers even for cautious writers. Journals which succeeded with the readers were often closed for violating the Censorship Code; thus in 1832 Ivan Kireevsky's *European* was shut down, followed by Polevoi's *Moscow Telegraph* in 1834, Nadezhdin's *Telescope* and *Chat* in 1836. In 1825 there were only forty-one periodicals in all of Russia, eight of which could be considered literary. When Pushkin died in 1837 there were only six primarily literary periodicals—five in Petersburg, one in Moscow.

Despite the repressive atmosphere, several important articles were written during the 1820s when the conflict between romantic poets and defenders of neoclassicism came into the open and reached a peak of violence. The turning point in this battle came with the publication of Pushkin's "Southern Poems," narrative tales written after the manner of Scott's *Marmion*, Byron's *Corsair* and *Giaour*. Prince Vyazemsky wrote an essay in defense of romanticism and praise of Pushkin's *A Prisoner of the Caucasus*. Thanking him in a letter, Pushkin says:

> Everything that you say about romanticism is charming; you did well in being *the first* to raise your voice for it—the French disease would kill our adolescent literature.[5] [My italics]

Vyazemsky's essay opens with the observation that imprisonment seemed to be the inspiring muse of Russian poetry[6] and it is curious that all of Pushkin's Southern Poems would be variations on this theme: in the first poem a Russian is captured by Circassians; *The Robber Brothers* deals with an unsuccessful escape from prison; *The Fountain of Bakhchisarai* tells the story of a young Polish girl imprisoned in a harem; and the freedom-seeking Aleko, hero of *The Gypsies* (1827), discovers that he is a prisoner of his own selfishness. Pushkin asked Vyazemsky to write an introduction to *The Fountain of Bakhchisarai* and his "In Place of a Foreword" turned out to be one of the most perceptive and vigorous defenses of the romantic trend in literature.[7] Another noteworthy event was the appearance of Orest Somov's essay "On Romantic Poetry" (1823); it has been called "the first formal assessment of the potentials of Romanticism for Russian literature."[8] Wilhelm Küchelbecker's essay "On the Trend of Our Literature, Especially the Lyric, in the Last Decade" (1824) correctly rebuked current Zhukovskians for the mistiness of their vision and the monotony of their elegies, but his opinion of the ode as innately superior was not shared by the best poets. A different view of the problem was presented by Kondraty Ryleev; in his "A Few Thoughts on Poetry" (1825) he attempted to trace the history of the term "romanticism" and argued that the division "classic-romantic" is artificial. Pushkin's unfinished essay "On Classicism and Romanticism" (1824) was a praiseworthy attempt to define what "romanticism" meant,[9] but two years later Vyazemsky could still recommend that "so-called" always be put in front of the word "romanticism."[10]

Yet another indefinite concept complicated the discussions of romanticism during the 1820s. This was *narodnost'*. Prince Vyazemsky was the first to use this term in a literary context; he said "*Narodnyj* equals two French words: *nationale* and *populaire*." "Literature," suggested Vyazemsky, "should be the expression of the character and opinions of a people" *(narod)*. Everyone agreed that *narodnost'* must be a good thing, but they all had different ideas about what its true Russian manifestations were. All too often demands for *narodnost'* were mere chauvinism. Many writers believed that if they took a plot from Russian history, used what they imagined was peasant speech, and described bast-sandals, they were creating a work full of *narodnost'*. Pushkin's note "On Nationalism in Literature" is a characteristically terse corrective statement. Venevitinov's countercritical article "A Critique of an Essay on *Eugene Onegin*" shows similar common sense.[11]

The best criticism of Pushkin's day was written by poets. In the first decades of the nineteenth century, Russian literature was at such an early stage in its evolution that specialized functions had not yet developed. Poets wrote prose, historians wrote criticism, novelists wrote history. Even critics like Nikolai Polevoi and Nikolai Nadezhdin tried their hands at history and short stories. These two, both of whom edited important journals beginning in the late 1820s, differed from previous critics in one respect—they were *raznochintsy*, both by birth and by talent. They mark the advent of professionalism in Russian literary criticism; for them, as for Belinsky, Chernyshevsky, Dobrolyubov, and other successors who were not basically artists, criticism itself was the main occupation. This introduced a new divisive factor into the literary scene. Class animosity was added to the personal animosities which already existed; add to this profit motives, cruelly capricious censorship, political differences, lack of traditions, the imprecision of Russian expository prose, and the general perversity of human logic—and one can see that the moderate accomplishment of Russian criticism in the first quarter of the last century is not without explanation.[12]

# II · PUSHKIN'S CRITICISM

**Pushkin did not scorn criticism. Even though he suffered** attacks on both his poetry and his character, he did not take the easy way out, as so many writers do, and pronounce anathema on all criticism. Some of it, he said, was too ridiculous to merit reply, but the inescapable point is that criticism *does* influence literature and society:

> Beztuzhev's article . . . is awfully immature, but everything of ours which is printed has an effect upon Holy Russia. On the other hand, we should not slight anything, and we should print well-intentioned notes on every article, political or literary, if only there is a little sense in it.[13]

Pushkin believed that good writers have a duty not to leave the field to bad ones. He constantly urged his able friends to contribute to the journals. Pushkin liked the exhilaration of polemic (which he compared to fist-fighting), but more important, he was a patriot; and like his friends he had an inferiority complex about the "insignificance of Russian literature."[14] It could hardly flatter a Russian writer's *amour-propre* when volumes such as *A Miscellany of Russian and Mongolian Literature* were published in the West.[15] Therefore, Pushkin worked to raise the level of criticism. As he wrote:

> The state of criticism by itself shows the degree to which all literature has developed. . . . Scorning criticism only because it is still in its childhood means scorning a youthful literature for not yet having grown up.[16]

If all of the writers who deserve the respect and confidence of the public took it upon themselves to direct public opinion, criticism would soon become what it is not.[17]

Although he was an aristocrat and (as he must have been aware) Russia's greatest poet, Pushkin was willing to do the menial work of literature—to write newspaper reviews of every type of book, to publish and edit a journal, and to answer the attacks of slanderers and the questions of fools.

Although he jotted down notes and worked on critical essays all during his career, his formal published efforts are concentrated in two periods: 1830–31, when Pushkin's friend, the poet Delvig, edited the *Literary Gazette* in Petersburg, and 1836–37, when Pushkin himself founded and edited *The Contemporary*. The forms which Pushkin used for his criticism range from the review and extensive essay to a projected preface, collections of aphorisms, letters to the editor, and, one of his favorites, the brief note—no more than a page in length.

Although multiplicity was forced on any journalist, it was characteristic of Pushkin to deal with a variety of subjects. He discusses the history of the literary language, problems of style, the nature of rhyme, definitions of classical and romantic poetry, problems of translation, literary imitation (with reference to Byron and Scott), the nature of tragedy, and criticism itself. Quite naturally, contemporary Russian literature was his main concern, and we can only regret that Pushkin did not have more notable authors on whom to spend his talents. But his pieces on *The Igor Tale*, Radishchev, Katenin, and Baratynsky are still interesting. Even reviews of Bulgarin, Zagoskin, Pavlov, or the latest almanacs frequently give us insight into Pushkin's mind; and he often uses a third-rate work as an excuse for discussion of theoretical problems or important works of French and English literature. Perhaps the most illuminating category of his criticism is formed by the notes on his own works; the explanations of "The Demon," "Count Nulin," *Boris Godunov*, and the "Refutations of Criticisms" are all fascinating. Pushkin also covers Russian translations of important works from the West

—Gnedich's translation of the *Iliad* and Vyazemsky's translation of *Adolphe*. Of course, a great deal of his criticism deals with writers of other countries—Shakespeare, Scott and Byron, Racine, Molière, Voltaire, Chénier, Musset, Hugo, Sainte-Beuve, and others. His "On Milton and Chateaubriand's Translation of *Paradise Lost*," with its long digressions on Hugo's *Cromwell* and Vigny's *Cinq Mars*, is among the most complex of Pushkin's essays. Besides this, his critical writings include examples of literary polemic; Pushkin excelled in the art of restating an opponent's position in such a way as to make him appear hopelessly simple-minded, a talent he used only in exceptional cases. Finally, there are examples of "mystification"—notably the essay on Joan of Arc's last relative and Voltaire, all of which is a playful fabrication. If there was anything Pushkin disliked in literature or criticism, it was uninterrupted solemnity.

Appropriate as it would be to describe Pushkin's "critical stance" at this point, I hesitate to do so. Blake's remark that to generalize is to be an idiot comes to mind, as does Tolstoy's statement that anyone who wanted to know his ideas on war and peace would have to read *War and Peace*. On basic matters, the reader of Pushkin's criticism needs little assistance. He did not drink the German beer of Schelling—the misty abstractions of idealistic esthetics were alien to his temperament.[18] He shunned ideas not robust enough to bear the strain of lucid expression. He defined his terms clearly and tersely.

Pushkin describes himself as a sceptic in literature: "All of its sects are the same to me, each presenting its profitable and unprofitable side." He refuses to measure new works by old rules. "Wouldn't it be simpler," he suggests, "to follow the romantic school—which is an absence of all rules, but not of all art?" Consequently, when he criticizes dramatic works, for example, he does not take out the familiar Aristotelian ruler, made in France. Unity of characterization is his first concern, not unity of place. He is primarily interested in whether an author can accurately "divine" the many character traits of his heroes, present them in a convincing way, and recreate the proper historical atmosphere. These may seem simple things, but in Pushkin's day such lucid vision was rare.

One of the things which makes Pushkin's criticism so enjoyable to read is the way he avoids the common errors of literary critics—both those of his time and our own. For example, he refuses to compare unlike genres. Of Boileau's characteristic line, "Un sonnet sans défaut vaut seul un long poème," Pushkin asks, "Can one say that a good breakfast is better than bad weather?" He makes fun of those who use the opinions of characters to revile authors. Most important, he refuses to find complexity where there is none. In his critical writings, unlike those who may dismiss him as superficial, Pushkin avoids all cant, jargonizing, turgid theories, and grandiose systems.

Pushkin's critical works seem to suggest a somewhat different attitude toward the place of literature, especially poetry, in society than one gets from his metapoetry and his letters. There is a tendency for Western scholars to see Pushkin as a devotee of "art for art's sake." His remark in a letter to Vyazemsky, that "The aim of poetry is poetry[19] (as Delvig says, if he didn't steal it)" is strong evidence in favor of this. Similarly, in the margin of an essay by Vyazemsky Pushkin comments: "Literature is above morality—or a completely different thing." But his criticism, particularly after 1830, sounds a different note. For example, in a review of Sainte-Beuve, after he has criticized poets who fettered their art to religion or politics—and after saying that he does not understand the word "immorality" the childish way that some journalists do, Pushkin admits:

> Poetry, which by its higher and free nature should not have any goal other than itself, even less should demean itself by using the power of words to shake the eternal truths on which human happiness and greatness are founded, or transform its divine nectar into an inflammatory aphrodisiac compound.[20]

The frequency with which Pushkin returned to the subject of morality in literature indicates that it is impossible to dismiss this remark as a sop to the censors. In "Refutations of Criticism," he says clearly:

> An immoral work is one the aim or effect of which is to subvert the rules on which social happiness or human worth are based. Poems whose aim is to fire the imagination with sensual descriptions debase poetry, turning its divine nectar into an aphrodisiac compound, and its muse into a repulsive Canidia.[21]

I do not wish to imply that Pushkin became a moralist in middle age; he consistently criticizes those who confuse poetry and pedagogy. But what Pushkin says in such places as "Refutations of Criticisms" and "The Memoirs of Samson" suggests that he was not in favor of absolute license. Judging by his comments in "M. E. Lobanov's Opinion about the Spirit of Literature," he believed that proper censorship could be a good thing for society.[22] By its higher nature literature should be free, but Pushkin saw that it was one way of bringing enlightenment to Russia. And one of the things which strikes the reader of letters between writers such as Pushkin, Vyazemsky, A. I. Turgenev, Baratynsky, and Marlinsky is their desire to catch up with the West, to civilize Russia, to provide themselves with the tools—history, philosophy, literature—to build a culture. Pushkin criticizes those who see poetry only as beautiful music produced by rare birds. "The mind cannot be satisfied just by games of harmony and imagination," he writes.[23] "Among us prose is used as poetry-writing is—not as a necessity of life, nor for the expression of a necessary thought, but only as a pleasant manifestation of forms."[24]

And Pushkin's own prose is more than a pleasant manifestation of forms. He *thinks*, and he presents his ideas in rapid-fire succession. Typically, in the piece entitled "On Prose," Pushkin says Voltaire can be considered the best model for a good style:

> Precision and brevity are the most important qualities of prose. It demands ideas—and then more ideas; without them glittering phrases serve no purpose.[25]

The aphoristic character of Pushkin's expository prose is one of the indications that his theory and practice are identical. As an object lesson in brevity, the reader might compare Pushkin's essay on Voltaire to Sainte-Beuve's essay on the same subject.[26] And Pushkin's spare, elegant style is all the more striking when one compares it to the shaggy prose of later critics such as Belinsky or Chernyshevsky. It is the difference between a sculptor who begins with a block of marble and those who get their materials from the scrap heap of the local boiler works. Pushkin's ideas and even his concision come through in translation, but one distinctive feature of his prose which necessarily disappears in an accurate translation is the slight archaic tinge; this is somewhat more marked in his formal criticism than in his fictional prose.

The reader will have to decide the question of how talented Pushkin was as a critic. It is too easy for specialists to make hyperbolic claims about penetration and profundity. I do think that most of Pushkin's critical judgments have stood the test of time well. His low opinion of Victor Hugo's poetry will probably not be shared by the French, and his enthusiasm for Scott seems excessive, but on the whole his evaluations of writers from Shakespeare to Chateaubriand seem sound. His consistent preference for English writers over French ones will probably come as a surprise—particularly in view of the fact that Pushkin's own criticism, including even his metaphors, is often reminiscent of sophisticated French critics of the 1820s and 1830s. But more than most critics, Pushkin displays what he once called "the proportionality and harmony characteristic of human intellect." He has a remarkably clear and sober view of literary problems. He attacks each question directly, avoiding logomachies. His comments on nationalism, drama, characterization, and style seem eminently sensible even today. For the modern reader who has been thoroughly Lubbocked, Leavised, Steinered, and Fryed, the critical writings of Pushkin will be as bracing as the crisp air of the Caucasus.

C. R. P.

## N O T E S

1. *A. S. Pushkin,* Polnoe sobranie sochinenij *(M. 1956–58), X, 145. The letter was written at the end of May or beginning of June, 1825. Pushkin's letters are a valuable source for his candid opinions on literature. One English translation exists:* The Letters of Alexander Pushkin, *ed. and trans. J. Thomas Shaw (Bloomington, Ind., 1963), 3 volumes.*

2. *If one compares what is called Russian "literature" before 1740 to the literatures of Spain, France, Italy, or England, the Russians seem hardly more than barbarians. Rapid progress was made in the second half of the eighteenth century, but the Countess in Pushkin's "Queen of Spades" is surprised to hear there are novels written in Russian, and in 1834 Pushkin could still write an essay entitled "On the Insignificance of Russian Literature." Similarly, when Guizot asked Vyazemsky to send him a résumé of Russian literature without any commentary, Vyazemsky wrote:*

> Je suis effrayé de la nullité de la besogne, qui m'attend. Nous avons beaucoup plus à dire sur ce qui ne se fait pas dans notre monde littéraire, que sur ce qui se fait, et Vous ne nous laissez pas la latitude du négatif, nous devons restés tout court sur le point imperceptible de notre positif. . . . Vous savez bien que tout notre littérature courant et parfois très stagnante se réduit à quelques Journaux et à quelques almanacs. Viennent après productions poétiques, quelques ouvrages scientifiques, élémentaires, et voilà tout.

*He sent this reply in a letter to A. I. Turgenev (April 18, 1828), telling Turgenev: "A bare listing of our books would make a chicken laugh, and all the more so the French roosters."*

3. *From 1815 on, critical polemics often revolved around problems of language and style. Thus Pavel Katenin's translation of*

*Bürger's "Lenore" (1816) was called coarse and compared unfavorably to Zhukovsky's sweet, gentle version. Katenin's version of Racine's* Esther *(1821) was attacked for its archaisms. Pushkin was accused of using low, vulgar diction in* Ruslan and Ludmila *(1821).*

4. *Stink, to sniff, and cow.*

5. *Letter to Vyazemsky, February 6, 1823.*

6. *Zhukovsky's translation of "The Prisoner of Chillon" was published in 1822.*

7. *The first English translation of the foreword appears below, pp. 258–266.*

8. *John Mersereau, Jr.,* Baron Delvig's "Northern Flowers" 1825–32: Literary Almanac of the Pushkin Pléiad *(Carbondale, Ill., 1967), p. 48.*

9. *Two attempts to show what Russian writers meant by the word "romanticism" are: John Mersereau, Jr., "Pushkin's Concept of Romanticism,"* Studies in Romanticism, *III, 1 (1963), 24–41; Carl R. Proffer, "Gogol's Definition of Romanticism,"* Studies in Romanticism, *VI, 2 (1967), 120–27.*

10. *M. I. Gillel'son, "Vjazemskij-kritik,"* Istorija russkoj kritiki, *ed. B. P. Gorodeckij (M. 1958), I, 236.*

11. *In spite of this, arguments about* narodnost' *still go on in Soviet criticism. It is curious how such literary polemics are repeated periodically in various forms. For example, the whole fight over* narodnost' *in the 1820s was repeated in the 1920s in the arguments about "proletarian" literature. In his article "An Answer to Polevoi" (1825) Venevitinov says critics have mistaken* narodnost' *for descriptions of history, customs, beards, etc., but it is an organic thing which exists "in the very feelings of the poet who has been nourished by the spirit of a people." In the 1920s the talented critic Alexander Voronsky chides the noisy poets and prose writers who think that because they have chosen the correct topics (party meetings, factory work, etc.), they have created truly proletarian literature—when in fact they show there has been no "organic assimilation of communism." [A. Voronskij,* Literaturnye portrety *(M. 1929), II, 138–39].*

12. *There are, however, many cases where individual judgments of Russian writers proved more perceptive than the opinions of their French and English contemporaries. Thus, Pushkin praises Musset, who was disliked or hated by most French poets of the nineteenth*

century. *Vyazemsky had high praise for Stendhal when French critics were ignoring or attacking him.*

13. *Letter to Vyazemsky, February 6, 1823.*

14. *See his essay on the subject, below, pp. 162–169.*

15. *In A. I. Turgenev's diary, begun in Göttingen in 1805, he notes that one of his teachers gave him a* Miscellen der Russischen und Mongolischen Litteratur: *"God Almighty! When will they stop putting us with the Mongolians! In the introduction I found a sad truth: Russian literature is richer in translations than in original works."*

16. *Below, p. 102.*

17. *Below, pp. 77–78.*

18. *For example, Pushkin's rather practical definition of "inspiration" (below, p. 43) might be compared to the romantic nonsense written by other poets of his day. He uses no vague metaphors and says nothing about God or the Infinite.*

19. *This statement creates headaches for socialist scholars for whom "art for art's sake" is an obscene formula. The most ridiculous example I know of an effort to mis-define a word is the following editorial parenthesis interpolated by Slonimsky: " 'The aim of poetry is poetry' (i.e. an objective depiction of life, A. S.)."* A. Slonimskij, Masterstvo Pushkina *(M. 1959), p. 253.*

20. *Below, pp. 147–148.*

21. *Below, p. 114.*

22. *Here one must be cautious, because Pushkin did have to get this article past the censorship.*

23. *Below, p. 32.*

24. *Below, p. 59.*

25. *Below, p. 19.*

26. *Charles Sainte-Beuve, "Voltaire and the Président de Brosses,"* Selected Essays, *ed. F. Steegmuller (Garden City, 1964), pp. 145–63.*

# ON PROSE

One day d'Alembert said to La Harpe[1]: "Don't extol Buffon[2] to me. The man writes: 'The Noblest of all the acquisitions of man was this proud, fiery creature!' etc. Why not simply say 'horse'?" La Harpe was surprised by the philosopher's dry reasoning. But d'Alembert was a very intelligent man—and, I confess, I almost agree with his opinion.[3]

I will note in passing that they were talking about Buffon, a great painter of nature whose rich, flowery style will always be a model of descriptive prose; some pictures are painted by a masterful brush. But what can be said about our writers who, considering it plebeian to express the most ordinary things simply, attempt to enliven childish prose with extra words and flaccid metaphors? These fellows never say "friendship" without adding "this sacred feeling the noble flame of which" etc. One must say "early in the morning" and they write: "Barely had the first rays of the rising sun illumined the eastern edges of the azure sкy." Oh, how fresh and new all this is! Is it supposed to be better just because it's longer?

I read some theater-lover's review: "This youthful nurseling of Thalia and Melpomene, generously gifted by Apol. . . ." My God, just put "this good young actress" and continue; be assured no one will notice your expressions, no one will say thanks.

Despicable Zoilus,[4] whose unremitting envy pours out its soporific poison on the laurels of the Russian Parnassus, whose tiresome dullness can compare only with untiring malice. . . . My God, why not simply say "horse"; isn't it shorter, Mr. Editor of a certain journal?

Voltaire can be considered the best model of a sensible style. In his *Micromégas* he ridiculed the excessive refinement of the delicate phrases of Fontenelle, who could never forgive him.[5]

Precision and brevity are the most important qualities of prose. It demands ideas—and then more ideas; without them glittering phrases serve no purpose. Poetry is another matter (although it wouldn't hurt our poets to have a sum of ideas rather more significant than is usually the case with them. Our literature will not move far ahead on reminiscences of past youth.).[6]

[1822, unpublished]

## N O T E S

1. *Jean François de la Harpe (1739–1803)—neoclassical literary theorist whose* Lycée, ou Cours de littérature ancienne et moderne *(Paris, 1799–1805) was Pushkin's textbook at the Tsarskoe Selo Lycée. Citing Cuvier's biography of Buffon from memory, Pushkin substituted La Harpe's name for that of Rivarol.*

2. *George Louis Leclerc, comte de Buffon (1707–88)—Enlightenment naturalist. Pushkin alludes to the smooth, rhythmical, monotonously noble style of his multi-volumed* Histoire naturelle *(1749–78).*

3. *So did Chekhov. In a letter he writes: "It is very difficult to describe the sea. Do you know how I found it described recently in a schoolboy's exercise book? 'The sea is big.' Just that, and no more. It seemed to me quite admirable."*

*Coincidentally, Flaubert said: "Do you remember La Bruyère's advice? 'If you want to say that it is raining, say: —it is raining.'"*

4. *A grammarian and critic of the third or fourth century* B.C., *celebrated for the asperity with which he attacked Homer.*

5. *See the beginning of Chapter Two for a satirical representation of Fontenelle.*

6. *West European sentimentalism had been imported into Russia at the beginning of the nineteenth century. Melancholy elegies bleed-*

*ing with the sorrows of young Werthers and Julies became popular in aristocratic circles.*

# ON FRENCH LITERATURE

**Of all literatures it had the greatest influence on ours.** Lomonosov, following the Germans, followed it. Sumarokov—(Tredyakovsky unwillingly disjoined it by means of his prosody)—Dmitriev, Karamzin, Bogdanovich.[1] Harmful consequences—affectation, timidity, colorlessness. Zhukovsky imitates the Germans, Batyushkov and Baratynsky—Parny. A few write in the Russian manner; of those only Krylov's style is Russian. Prince Vyazemsky had his own style. Katenin—plays in the German manner—his style is his own.

What is French literature? Troubadours. Malherbe is remembered by four lines[2] of the ode to *Duperieu* and the verses of Boileau. Ménard,[3] pure but weak. Racan,[4] Voiture[5]—rubbish. Boileau, Racine, La Fontaine, J. B. Rousseau, Voltaire. Boileau murders French literature, his strange opinions, Voltaire's envy—French literature is distorted—Russians begin to imitate it—Dmitriev, Karamzin, Bogdanovich—how can one imitate it: its stupid prosody—timid, colorless language—eternally uninventive, Rousseau is bad in his odes. Derzhavin.

I won't decide which literature to give preference to, but we have our own language; it's bolder!—customs, history, songs, folk-tales, etc.

[1822, unpublished]

## N O T E S

1. *Most of these names are footnoted below (when Pushkin has more to say about them).*

2. Mais elle était du monde, où les plus belles choses
   On le pire destin:
   Et rose elle a vécu ce que vivent les roses,
   L'espace d'un matin.

3. *François Ménard (1570–1623) or Pierre Ménard (1606–1701)?*

4. *Honorat de Bueil, sire de Racan (1589–1670)—author of* Les Bérgeries, *a pastoral play, and other poetry.*

5. *Vincent Voiture (1597–1648)—L. Cazamian says Voiture's gift was for "finesse, the sharp perception and just rendering of delicate values in the analysis of thought, feeling, or art."*

# A LETTER TO THE EDITOR OF
## *SON OF THE FATHERLAND*

**During the last four years I have happened to be the subject** of comments in the journals. Often inaccurate, often unseemly, some deserved no attention; others it was impossible to answer from afar.[1] The justifications of an author's offended self-esteem could not be interesting to the public; in a new edition I intended, without saying anything, to correct any errors, no matter how they had been pointed out to me; and I have read the occasional flattering praise and approbation with the warmest gratitude, feeling that not just the rather slight merit of my poems gave cause for a noble expression of good-will and cordiality.

Now I am compelled to interrupt my silence. Prince P. A. Vyazemsky, who out of friendship for me undertook the publication of *The Fountain of Bakhchisarai,* appended to it a "Conversation between the Publisher and an Anti-Romantic,"[2] an apparently fictitious conversation—for even if among our printed classicists many resemble the Classicist of the Vyborg Side in the force of their judgments, none of them, it seems to me, express themselves with his wit and politesse.

One of our critics of literature did not like this conversation. In the fifth issue of *The Messenger of Europe,* he printed a second conversation between the Publisher and the Classicist, where, among other things, I read the following:

PUB: So you didn't like my conversation?
CLASS: I confess, it's a pity you printed it with Pushkin's fine poem: I think the author himself will regret this.

The author is very glad that he has a chance to thank Prince Vyazemsky for his fine gift. " A Conversation between the Publisher and a Classicist from the Vyborg Side or from Vasilev Island" was written more for Europe in general than exclusively for Russia, where the opponents of romanticism are too weak and unnoticeable, and are not worth such a brilliant rebuff.

I do not wish and have no right to complain in the other respect, and I accept the praise of the unknown critic with sincere humility.

ALEXANDER PUSHKIN

Odessa
[1824, *Son of the Fatherland*]

## N O T E S

1. *For presumed political unreliability, Pushkin spent the years 1820–24 exiled to the South of Russia.*
2. *Prince Vyazemsky's essay is translated below, pp. 258–266.*

# AN OBJECTION TO
# A. BESTUZHEV'S ESSAY
# "A LOOK AT RUSSIAN
# LITERATURE DURING 1824 AND
# THE BEGINNING OF 1825"

**Bestuzhev[1] suggests that the literature of all nations has** followed the general rules of nature. "What does this mean?" Its first era was an age of "geniuses."

It seems the author wanted to say that every literature has its own gradual development and decline. No.

The author suggests the era "of strong emotions and creations of genius" is its first period. "With time *this circle* (what one?) is restricted. . . . Thirst for novelty seeks untapped sources, and geniuses rush boldly past the crowd in quest of virgin land in the moral and physical worlds; they break their own path." Consequently, a new period begins; but Mr. Bestuzhev fuses them into one and continues: "This era of creation and fullness is followed by an era of mediocrity, surprise, and reckoning. Song writers followed lyric poets, comedy arose after tragedy; but history, criticism, and satire were always the younger branches of literature. It was like this everywhere." No. It is impossible for us to judge about Greek literature—too few of its monuments have reached us. We have no conception of Greek criticism. But we know that Herodotus lived before Aeschylus,[2] the great creator of tragedy. Naevius preceded Horace, Ennius[3] came before Virgil, Catullus before Ovid, Horace before Quintilian; Lucanus[4] and Seneca appeared much later. None of this will fit Mr. Bestuzhev's general definition.

The question arises which of the modern literatures manifests the gradualness arbitrarily defined by Mr. Bestuzhev? Romantic literature began with triolets. The mystères, lays, and fabliaux preceded the creations of Ariosto, Calderón, Dante, Shakespeare. Alfieri,[5] Monti,[6] and Foscolo[7] appeared after the cavalier Marini;[8] Byron, Moore, and Southey after Pope and Addison. In France romantic poetry remained in its childhood for a long time. The best poet of Francis I's time is Marot:[9]

Rima des triolets, fit fleurir la ballade.

Prose was already firmly preponderant: Montaigne, Rabelais were contemporaries of Marot.

The question arises, where do we see even a shadow of the law Mr. Bestuzhev defines?

Do we have criticism? Where is it? Where are our Addisons, La Harpes, Schlegels, Sismondis?[10] What have we analyzed? Whose literary opinions have become national ones; whose criticisms can we cite, use as guides?

But further on Mr. Bestuzhev himself says, "We see many criticisms, anticriticisms, and cross-criticisms, but few sensible criticisms."

[1825, unpublished]

# N O T E S

1. *Alexander Bestuzhev-Marlinsky (1797–1837)—Decembrist, critic, poet. He was most popular as the author of floridly romantic tales about Petersburg society and Caucasian mountain men. The essay to which Pushkin objects appeared in* Polar Star *for 1825.*

2. *Pushkin errs. Herodotus (484?–425* B.C.*), Aeschylus (525–456* B.C.*).*

3. *Naevius (270?–201?* B.C.*) and Ennius (239–169* B.C.*) were among the founders of Latin literature.*

4. *Marcus Annaeus Lucanus (36–95* A.D.*)—Roman poet and prose writer, author of the ten-volume epic* Pharsalia.

5. *Vittorio Alfieri (1749–1803)—nationalistic Italian poet, author of sonnets, odes, and nineteen neoclassical tragedies.*

6. *Vincenzo Monti (1754–1828)—Italian poet, a writer of topical verse.*

7. *Ugo Foscolo (1778–1827)—Italian poet and novelist (and trans-lator of Sterne's* Sentimental Journey). *Contributor to the* Edinburgh Review *during his decade in England.*

8. *Correctly, Giambattista Marino (1569–1625)—Italian poet, foremost of the* settecentisti, *known for dazzling novelties of style.*

9. *Clémont Marot (1496–1543)—French poet noted for his finesse, polish, and triviality.*

10. *Jean Charles Léonard Simonde Sismondi (1773–1842)—Swiss historian, author of the* History of the Italian Republics in the Middle Ages *(16 vols., 1803–18).*

# ON MME. STAËL AND
# ON MR. A. M-V.

**Of all Mme. Staël's works, the book** *Ten Years of Exile* **in** particular should have attracted the attention of Russians. The quick and penetrating glance, the comments striking in their novelty and accuracy, the gratitude and good-will which guided the pen of the author—all do honor to the intellect and feelings of an extraordinary woman. Here is what is said about her in a certain manuscript:[1] "Reading her book *Dix ans d'exil* one can clearly see that, touched by the affectionate reception given by the Russian boyars, she did not say everything that struck her eye.* I dare not reproach the eloquent, noble foreign lady for this; she was the first to render complete justice to the Russian people—who have been the constant subject of ignorant slander

---

* He is talking about Petersburg high society prior to 1812.

by foreign writers." It is precisely this good-will which the author of the manuscript dares not censure that creates the main charm of the part of the book which is devoted to a description of our fatherland. Mme. Staël left Russia as if it were a sacred refuge, a family into which she had been received with trust and cordiality. Fulfilling the duty of a noble heart, she speaks of us with respect and modesty, praises with complete sincerity, censures cautiously, "doesn't take the rubbish out of the hut." Let us, too, be grateful to our celebrated guest: let us respect her illustrious memory as she respected our hospitality. . . .

From Russia Mme. Staël went through the melancholy wastes of Finland to Sweden. Separated from everything dear to her heart at an advanced age, persecuted for seven years by the active despotism of Napoleon, taking tormented interest in the political situation of Europe, she could not, of course, at that time (in the fall of 1812) maintain the lucidity of spirit required for enjoying the beauties of nature. It is no wonder that the lakes, blackened cliffs, and dense forests made her dejected.

Her unfinished notes stop with a gloomy description of Finland. . . .

Mr. A. M., "running through Mme. Staël's little book again, came across" this last fragment and translated it in rather ponderous prose, appending to it the following "notes on Mme. Staël's daydreams": "Not to mention the revelation of frivolous light-mindedness, the absence of perspicacity and total ignorance of the locale which involuntarily strike readers *familiar with the works of the author of the book about Germany*, I was next struck by the narrative itself, which is absolutely like the banal blabbering of those *punctilious little Frenchmen who, not so long ago, appeared in Russia with meagre stores of knowledge and with rich hopes, and were so joyfully received by our generous and sometimes inappropriately good-hearted fellow-countrymen (not, however, our contemporaries in their way of thinking).*"

What style and what *tone!* What relation is there between two pages of Notes from *Delphine, Corinne, A Look at the French Revolution,*[2] etc., and what is there in common between "punctilious (?) little Frenchmen" and the daughter of Necker, persecuted by Napoleon and protected by the Russian Emperor's magnanimity?

"It will really seem strange," continues Mr. A. M., "to anyone who has read the works of Mme. Staël in which she so often becomes expansive etc. how the boundless forests etc. . . . made no other impression on the author of *Corinne* except boredom from the monotony!" Then Mr. A. M. sets up himself as an example: "No, never," says he, "will I forget the agitation of my soul expanding from the insuffusion of such powerful impressions. I will always remember the mornings etc."—There follows a description of northern nature in a style quite distinct from Mme. Staël's prose.

Further on, he advises the late authoress to "question her coach drivers about the exact cause of the fires by means of some interpreter," etc.

The joke about how close the wolves and bears are to Abov University displeased Mr. A. M. exceedingly, but Mr. A. M. himself jested: "Can it be," says he, "that the four hundred students there are educating themselves to be game hunters? In that case she could more precisely have called the academy a dog kennel. Couldn't Mme. Staël find any other *way of seeking out the reasons* retarding the advance of enlightenment than by dressing up as Diana and making the reader scout about the new-fallen snows of Finnish forests with her after bears and wolves, and why look for them in their dens? . . . Finally, from the fright which possessed *the timid soul of our lady*" etc.

One should speak of this *lady* in the courteous language of an educated person. This *lady* was rewarded with the persecution of Napoleon, the trust of monarchs, the respect of Europe—and the very discourteous and not very bright journal article of Mr. A. M.

If you want to be respected, know how to respect others.

St. Ar.[3]

*9 June 1825*
[1825, *The Moscow Telegraph*]

## N O T E S

1. *"An Excerpt from Mme. Staël on Finland, with notes" published in* The Son of the Fatherland. *Written by A. A. Mukhanov, an adjutant to a general in Finland. See Pushkin's letter to Vyazemsky of September 13–15, 1825.*

2. *See below, p. 80.*

3. *Abbreviation for* Staryj Arzamasec, *"An Old Arzamasian." Arzamas was a humorous literary society to which Pushkin belonged when he was younger.*

*The last line of his article is a play on a line from a poem by Vyazemsky.*

# ON M. LEMONTEY'S FOREWORD TO THE TRANSLATION OF I. A. KRYLOV'S FABLES

Lovers[1] of our literature were pleased by Count Orlov's undertaking, even though they guessed that the method of translation, so brilliant and so unsatisfactory, would do some harm to the fables of our inimitable poet.[2] Many awaited M. Lemontey's foreword with great impatience; it is, in fact, noteworthy, though not entirely satisfactory. In general where the author was forced by necessity to write from hearsay, his judgments may sometimes seem erroneous; in contrast, his own surmises and conclusions are surprisingly accurate. It's a pity that the celebrated writer barely touched on subjects about which his opinions would be extremely interesting. You read his essay* with involuntary vexation, as when you listen to the conversation of a very intelligent person who, restrained by concerns of courtesy, too often does not finish his point and too often keeps something to himself.

After he has thrown a cursory glance at the history of our literature, the author says a few words about our language, acknowledges it to be original, doesn't doubt that it is capable of refinement, and, citing the assurances of Russians, assumes that it is rich, mellifluous and abundant in varied turns of phrase.

It was not difficult to justify these opinions. As material for literature, the Slavonic-Russian language has unquestionable superiority over all the European languages: its fate was extremely lucky. In the XIth century, ancient Greek suddenly opened its lexicon and treasure of harmony to it, presented it with the laws of its logical grammar, its beautiful turns of phrase, majestic flow of speech; in a word, it adopted Russian, thus sparing it the slow improvements of time. Already sonorous and expressive by itself, it borrows pliability and regularity from this source. Folk speech had of necessity to separate from the written language; but subsequently they came together, *and such is the medium given to us for the communication of our ideas.*

It is in vain that M. Lemontey thinks the Tartar dominion left rust on the Russian language. An alien language spreads not by fire and sword, but by its own opulence and superiority. What new concepts demanding new words could be brought to us by a nomadic tribe of barbarians who possessed neither literature, nor trade, nor a system of law? Their invasion left no traces in the language of educated Chinese, and our forefathers groaning under the Tartar yoke for the course of two centuries,

* At least in the translation printed in *The Son of the Fatherland.* We haven't had an opportunity to see the French original.

prayed to a Russian God, cursed their threatening rulers, and communicated their complaints to each other in the native tongue. We have seen exactly the same kind of case in modern Greece. What effect does the preservation of their language have on an enslaved people? An examination of this question would lead us too far afield. Whatever the case, barely half a hundred Tartar words were taken into Russian. The Lithuanian wars had no influence on the fate of our language either; it alone remained the untouchable property of our unfortunate fatherland.

During the reign of Peter I, it began to be noticeably distorted by the necessary introduction of Dutch, German, and French words. This fashion spread its influence to writers who at that time were patronized by sovereigns and grandees; fortunately, Lomonosov appeared.

In one comment M. Lemontey speaks of the all-embracing genius of Lomonosov,[3] but he looked at the great fellow-champion of the great Peter from the wrong point of view.

Combining extraordinary strength of will with extraordinary strength of understanding, Lomonosov embraced all branches of enlightenment. The craving for science was the strongest passion of this passion-filled soul. Historian, rhetorician, mechanic, chemist, mineralogist, artist, and poet: he tried everything and understood everything. He is the first to delve into the history of the fatherland, he establishes rules of its standard language, gives laws and models of classical eloquence; with the unfortunate Richman[4] he anticipates the discoveries of Franklin, establishes a factory, sets up the machines himself, presents mosaic works of art, and, finally, reveals the true sources of our poetic language to us.

Poetry is the exclusive passion of the few who are born poets; it embraces and absorbs all the observations, all the efforts, all the impressions of their lives. But if we study Lomonosov's life we will find that the precise sciences were always his main and favorite occupation; writing poetry was sometimes an amusement, but more often it was an exercise required by his position. In vain would we search for fiery bursts of emotion and imagination in our first lyric poet. His style—even, flowery, and picturesque—takes its main merit from a deep knowledge of the Slavonic written language and from a felicitous blending of it with the language of the common people. That is why his versions of the psalms and other powerful and close imitations of the elevated poetry of sacred books are his best works.* They will remain eternal monuments of Russian literature; we will have to learn our poetic language from them for a long time yet, but it is strange to complain that society people don't read Lomonosov, and to demand that a man who died 70 years ago remain a favorite of the public even today. As if the insignificant praises of a fashionable writer were necessary for the fame of the great Lomonosov!

Having mentioned the exclusive use of French in the educated circles of our society, M. Lemontey remarks—just as wittily as accurately—that, because of that, Russian certainly had to preserve a precious simplicity, freshness, and, so to speak, open-heartedness of phrasing. I do not wish to excuse our indifference to the successes of our native literature, but there is no doubt that if our writers lose a great deal of pleasure because of that, at least language and literature win a great deal. Who deflected French literature from the models of classical antiquity? Who powdered and rouged Racine's Melpomene, and even the stern muse of old Corneille? The courtiers of Louis XIV. What put the cold gloss of politeness and wit on all the works of the writers of the eighteenth century? The society of Mme. du Deffand,[5] Boufflers,[6] and d'Epinay,[7] very nice and

* It is curious to see how cleverly Tredyakovsky mocks Lomonosov's "Slavonicisms," how pompously he advises him to take on the "lightness" and "dandyishness of expression characteristic of good company." But it is surprising that in one hemistich Sumarokov stated the true merit of Lomonosov with great precision:

> He is the Malherbe of our country, he is like Pindar![11]
> Enfin Malherbe vint, et, le premier en France, etc.

educated women. But it was not for "the gracious smile of the fair sex"[8] that Milton and Dante wrote.

The severe and just condemnation of French does honor to the dispassionateness of the author. True enlightenment is dispassionate. Citing the fate of his country's prose language as an example, M. Lemontey asserts that our language too should expect "its acceptance in European civilization" not so much from its poets as from its prose writers. The Russian translator was offended by this expression, but if it says *civilization européenne*, the author is probably right.

Let us suppose that Russian poetry has already achieved a high level of development—the enlightenment of the century demands food for thought, the mind cannot be satisfied just by games of harmony and imagination; but science, politics, and philosophy have not yet been expressed in Russian—our metaphysical language[9] does not exist at all. Our prose is still so little developed that even in a simple correspondence we are forced to *create* turns of phrase for the expression of the most ordinary concepts, so that our laziness more willingly expresses itself in an alien language the mechanical forms of which have long been ready and known to all.

Proceeding to several details regarding the life and customs of our Krylov, M. Lemontey said that he doesn't speak any foreign language and only understands French. *Not true!* —the translator sharply objects in his footnote. In fact, Krylov knows the main European languages, and in addition to that he, like Alfieri, has studied ancient Greek for fifty years. In other lands such a characteristic feature of a well-known man would be lauded in all the journals; but in the biographies of our famous writers we content ourselves with a designation of the year of their birth and the details of their rank in civil service, and then we ourselves complain about foreigners' ignorance of everything that concerns us.

In conclusion I will say that we should thank Count Orlov, who chose a truly national poet in order to acquaint Europe with the literature of the north. Of course, no Frenchman would dare to put anyone above La Fontaine; but we, it would seem, can prefer Krylov to him. They will both always remain favorites of their countrymen. Someone has accurately observed that ingenuousness (*naïveté, bonhomie*) is an inborn characteristic of the French people; in contrast, the distinctive feature of our mores is a kind of jolly slyness of mind, mockery, and a picturesque mode of expression: La Fontaine and Krylov are representatives of the spirits of the two peoples.

12 August                                                    N. K.

P. S.  It seemed to me superfluous to note a few obvious errors, excusable for a foreigner—for example the comparison of Krylov and Karamzin (a comparison without any foundation), the alleged unsuitability of our language for perfectly metrical versification, etc.                                    (1825)

[1825, *The Moscow Telegraph*]

# N O T E S

1. *Pierre Eduord Lemontey (1762–1826)—French historian whom Pushkin called "a genius of the nineteenth century" (in a letter to Vyazemsky, July 5, 1824) for his Essai sur l'établissement monarchique de Louis XIV.*

*His introduction was translated in* The Son of the Fatherland *(No. 13–14, 1825) from the Paris edition entitled:* Russian Fables, Selected from the Collection of I. A. Krylov, with Imitations in French and in Italian by Various Authors, and with Two Forewords, in French by M. Lemontey and in Italian by M. Salfia. *Published by M. Orlov, 1825.*

2. *Ivan Andreevich Krylov (1769–1844)—Russia's greatest fabulist, noted for his stupendous wit, laziness, and appetite. (See* Table-Talk.)

3. *Mikhailo Vasilievich Lomonosov (1711–65)—Russia's Renaissance man—scientist, rhetorician, grammarian, prosodist, founder of*

*Moscow University. His poetry is poor, and his neoclassical rules ("On the Use of Church Books in the Russian Language," 1757) for connecting genre and language were of little lasting importance; but he played a major role in introducing syllabo-tonic versification into Russian poetry.*

4. *Georg Wilhelm Richman was one of Lomonosov's fellow scientists. He was killed by lightning while experimenting with atmospheric electricity.*

5. *Marie de Vichy-Chamrond, marquise du Deffand (1697–1789) —among the visitors to her salon were Montesquieu, Fontenelle, La Harpe, and Condorcet.*

6. *Maria Charlotte, comtesse de Boufflers-Rouvrel (1725–1800)— Rousseau was a frequent visitor to her salon.*

7. *Louise d'Epinay (1726–83)—authoress of famous* Mémoires et correspondance *(Paris, 1818) concerning Rousseau, Diderot, Grimm, and others.*

8. *Pushkin cites the silly formula used by A. Kornilovich* (Polar Star, *1824),* Bestuzhev-Marlinsky *(see Pushkin's letter to him, February 8, 1824), and others.*

9. *By "metaphysical language" Pushkin meant not just the phraseology of abstruse philosophy, but the entire realm of language used to express abstract ideas or psychological processes. Elsewhere Pushkin says it is difficult to translate other languages into Russian, because one is forced to create new words and turns of speech constantly. The Russian literary language was at a relatively early stage of development at the beginning of the nineteenth century. It was in the midst of assimilating all the lexical and syntactical features which had been borrowed from French, German, English, and Polish. (See Pushkin's note on the translation of* Adolphe, *below, p. 73.)*

# ON CLASSICAL AND
# ROMANTIC POETRY

**Our critics still have not agreed on a clear difference between** the classical and the romantic. For the inconsistent conception of this subject we are obliged to the French journalists, who usually regard as romanticism everything which seems to them marked with the stamp of dreaminess and German idealism or based on the superstitions and legends of the simple folk: a most imprecise definition. A poem may manifest all these features and still belong to classicism.

If instead of the *form* of a poem we take as a basis only the *spirit* in which it is written we will never disentangle ourselves from definitions.[1] Of course, in its spirit J. B. Rousseau's hymn differs from Pindar's ode, Juvenal's satire from Horace's satire, *Jerusalem Delivered* from the *Aeneid*; however, they all belong to classicism.

We should regard as this type those poems the forms of which were known to the Greeks and Romans and models of which they left us; therefore, here belong: the epic, didactic poem, tragedy, comedy, ode, satire, epistle, heroic poem, eclogue, elegy, epigram, and fable.

But what kinds of poem should be regarded as romantic poetry?

Those which were not known to the ancients and those whose previous forms have changed or have been replaced by others. I do not consider it necessary to talk about the poetry of the Greeks and Romans: every educated European should have a sufficient understanding of the immortal works of majestic antiquity. Let us glance at the origin and gradual development of the poetry of the more modern peoples.

The western empire rapidly headed toward its collapse,

and with it the sciences, literature, and the arts. Finally it fell; enlightenment was extinguished. Ignorance darkened a blood-imbrued Europe. Latin literature barely survived; in the dust of monastery archives monks scraped the verses of Lucretius and Virgil from the parchment and in their place wrote their chronicles and legends on it.

Poetry awakened under the sky of southern France—rhyme echoes in the romance language; this new decoration of verse, at first glance of so little significance, had important influence on the literature of modern peoples. The ear was delighted by the doubled accents of sounds; a difficulty overcome always brings us pleasure—that of loving the proportionality and harmony characteristic of human intellect. The troubadours played with rhyme, invented all possible alterations of verse for it, contrived the most difficult forms: the virelay, ballade, rondeau, sonnet, etc., came into being.

From this came an unavoidable strain in the manner of expression, a kind of affectation completely unknown to the ancients; a trifling wittiness replaced feeling, which cannot express itself in triolets. We find these unfortunate traces in the greatest geniuses of more modern times.

But the intellect is not satisfied with just toys of harmony; the imagination demands scenes and stories. The troubadours turned to new sources of inspiration; they glorified love and war, enlivened the folk legends—the lay, romance, and fabliau were born.

Church festivals and murky conceptions of the ancient tragedy gave rise to the composition of mystery plays (*mystères*). They were almost all written on one model and came under one code of rules, but unfortunately at that time there was no Aristotle to establish unalterable laws of mystery dramaturgy.

Two circumstances had a decisive influence on the spirit of European poetry: the attacks of the Moors and the crusades.

The Moors inspired it with the frenzy and tenderness of love, an attachment to the miraculous, and the luxurious eloquence of the East; knights imparted to it their piety and open-heartedness, their concepts of heroism, and the freedom of morals in the field camps of Gottfried and Richard.

Such was the humble beginning of romantic poetry. If it had stopped with these experiments, the stern judgments of the French critics would be just; but its offshoots blossomed rapidly and sumptuously, and it manifests itself to us as a rival of the ancient muse.

Italy appropriated the epic for herself; half-African Spain took possession of the tragedy and novel; opposite the names of Dante, Ariosto, and Calderón, England proudly displayed the names of Spenser, Milton, and Shakespeare. In Germany (which is rather strange) a new, caustic, witty satire stood out, whose monument was left as Reinicke Fuchs.

In France then poetry was still in its infancy: the best versifier of the time of Francis I

rima des triolets, fit fleurir la ballade.

Prose already had a strong preponderance: Montaigne and Rabelais were contemporaries of Marot.

In Italy and Spain folk poetry already existed prior to the appearance of her geniuses. They traveled along the road already paved: there were long poems before Ariosto's *Orlando*; there were tragedies before the creations of de Vega and Calderón.

In France enlightenment caught poetry in its childhood without any direction, without any strength. Educated minds of the age of Louis XIV rightly despised its insignificance and turned it to ancient models. Boileau promulgated his Koran, and French literature bowed down to him. This pseudoclassical poetry, which was born in the anteroom and never got further than the drawing-room, could not disaccustom itself from a number of congenital habits; and in it we see all the romantic affectation enveloped in strict classical forms.

P.S. However, one should not think that no monuments of

purely romantic poetry were left in France. The tales of La Fontaine and Voltaire and the latter's *Pucelle* carry its stamp on themselves. I am not talking about the multitudinous imitations of either of them (imitations which are for the most part mediocre: it is easier to surpass the geniuses in forgetting all decorum than in poetic merit).

[1825, unpublished]

## N O T E

1. *Here as elsewhere in his literary essays, Pushkin takes what it is now fashionable to call the formalistic approach. For other comments on romanticism see below, "On the Insignificance of Russian Literature." See also John Mersereau, Jr., "Pushkin's Concept of Romanticism,"* Studies in Romanticism, *III, 1 (1963), 24–41.*

# ON THE POEM "THE DEMON"

**I think the critic has erred.**[1] **Many are of the same opinion;** some have even pointed out the person whom Pushkin supposedly wanted to depict in his strange poem. It would seem they are wrong; at least I see another, more moral, aim in "The Demon."

At the best time of life, the heart, which has not yet been made apathetic by experience, is susceptible to the beautiful. It is credulous and tender. Little by little the eternal contradictions of reality engender doubt in it—a tormenting feeling, but one of short duration. After destroying forever the best hopes and poetic predispositions of the soul, it disappears. The great Goethe has reason to call the eternal enemy of humanity *the negating spirit*. And didn't Pushkin want to personify this spirit *of negation or doubt* in his demon, and in a compact tableau he traced its distinguishing features and lamentable influence on the morality of our age.

[1825, unpublished]

### N O T E

1. *The anonymous critic who wrote in* The Son of the Fatherland *(No. 3, 1825): "Pushkin's demon is not an imaginary creation. The author wanted to present a debaucher who tempts inexperienced youth with sensuality and sophistry."*

# ON ANDRÉ CHÉNIER

**André Chénier perished a victim of the French Revolution** when he was 30 years old. For a long time his fame was constituted by a few words said about him by Chateaubriand,[1] two or three fragments, and general regret for the loss of everything else. Finally his works were discovered and published in 1819. One cannot suppress a grievous feeling. . . .

[1825, unpublished]

### N O T E

1. *Chateaubriand discusses Chénier and quotes excerpts from him in a note to Book Three, Chapter Six of* Le Génie du Christianisme *(1802).*

# ON TRAGEDY

**Of all genres the most unrealistic** *(invraisemblable)* **is the** drama, and in drama—the tragedy; because for the most part the spectator must forget time, place, and language; through an effort of imagination he must accept a conventional language of poetry, of fictions. The French writers perceived this and made their capricious rules: action, place, time.[1] Interest being the first law of dramatic art, unity of action must be observed. But place and time are too capricious; they are the source of so much awkwardness, and of constraint in the place of action. Intrigues, confessions of love, governmental conferences, celebrations—everything happens in the same room! Excessive rapidity and compression of events, confidantes . . . *à parte* just as unreasonable, were forced into two scenes and so forth. And all this accomplishes nothing. Wouldn't it be simpler to follow the romantic school—which is an absence of all rules, but not of all art?

Interest is a unity.

The mixture of comic and tragic genres, forcedness, the refinement of colloquial expressions which are sometimes essential.

[1825?, unpublished]

## N O T E

1. *This fragment was written while Pushkin was working on his romantic tragedy,* Boris Godunov. *For other remarks on the classical unities see below,* "*Drafts of a Preface to* Boris Godunov" *and* "*A Letter to the Editor of* The Moscow Messenger."

# ON NATIONALISM IN LITERATURE

**For some time it has been customary among us to talk about** nationalism,[1] to demand nationalism, to complain of the absence of nationalism in works of literature; but no one has thought of defining what he means by the word nationalism.

It seems that one of our critics supposes that nationalism consists in choosing subjects from our country's history.

But it would be foolish to deny Shakespeare the quality of great nationalism in his *Othello, Hamlet, Measure for Measure* and so forth; Vega and Calderón constantly shift to all parts of the world, borrowing the subjects for their tragedies from Italian novellas, from French lays. Ariosto sings Charlemagne, French knights, and a Chinese princess. Racine took his tragedies from ancient history.

However, it is foolish to dispute the quality of great nationalism in all these writers. On the other hand, "what is national in the *Petriada* and *Rossiada*[2] except the names," as Prince Vyazemsky[3] has accurately remarked. Where is the nationalism in Ksenya discussing parental power with a confidante in the middle of Dmitri's camp—in iambic hexameters?

Others see nationalism in words, i.e. they are happy that Russian expressions are used when speaking Russian.

Nationalism in a writer is a quality which can be completely appreciated only by fellow countrymen; for others either it does not exist, or it can even seem a fault. The learned German[4] is exasperated by the politeness of Racine's heroes; the Frenchman[5] laughs seeing Calderón's Coriolanus challenging his opponent to a duel.[6] However, this all bears the stamp of nationalism.

Climate, type of government, and religion give each nation a particular physiognomy which to a greater or lesser extent is reflected in the mirror of poetry. There is a way of thinking and feeling, there is a multitude of customs, beliefs, and habits which belong exclusively to each individual nation.

[1825?, unpublished]

## N O T E S

1. *There is no exact English equivalent of* narodnost'. *Narod means "people" or "nation"; the* prostoj narod *were the peasants, the "simple people," or as I often translate it, the "commonfolk."* Narodnost' *is a quality of belonging to a specific people or nation (and therefore some of the connotations of the English "nationalism" are rather unfortunate).*

*From Pushkin's time until the present, Russian literature has been flooded with arguments over* narodnost'. *Usually these were mere literary chauvinism, but sometimes they were understandable attempts to free Russian literature from the stultifying influence of bad foreign writers.*

2. *Monstrous imitations of the ancient epic by the indefatigable M. M. Kheraskov (1733–1807), whose main distinction in Russian literature is the composition of its longest poem,* Bakhariana *(15,000 lines).*

3. *See below, p. 260.*

4. *August Schlegel.*

5. *Sismondi.*

6. *Pedro Calderón de la Barca (1600–1681). All of the Soviet commentaries incorrectly say this occurs in* Oruzhie ljubvi. *But* Lances de amor y fortuna *is a comedy, and* Coriolanus *does not appear in it.*

# AN OBJECTION TO KÜCHELBECKER'S ESSAY IN *MNEMOSYNE*

**The essays "On the Tendency of Our Literature" and "A** Conversation with Bulgarin" printed in *Mnemosyne* served as the basis for everything that has been said against romantic literature in the last two years.[1]

These essays were written by a learned and intelligent man. Right or wrong, he always requires and gives reasons for his way of thinking and evidence for his judgments—a rather rare thing in our literature.

No one has tried to refute him—either because everyone agreed with him, or because they didn't want to take on an apparently strong and experienced athlete.

In spite of this, many of his judgments are mistaken in all respects. He divides Russian poetry into the lyric and the epic. In the former he includes the works of our old poets, in the latter Zhukovsky[2] and his followers.

Now let us suppose that this division is accurate and see how the critic defines the relative merit of the two types.

\* \* \*

"For example, we. . . ."[3] We quote this opinion because it agrees entirely with our own.

What is power in poetry? Power of invention, structural plan, or style?

*Freedom?* In style, in structure? But what freedom is there in Lomonosov's style, and what plan can one demand in a triumphal ode?

*Inspiration?* This is the disposition of the soul to the most vivid perception of impressions, therefore to the rapid assimilation of ideas, which facilitates their explanation.

Inspiration is necessary in geometry just as it is in poetry. The critic confuses inspiration with rapture.

\* \* \*

No, absolutely not: *rapture* precludes *tranquillity*, an essential condition of the beautiful. *Rapture* does not presuppose power of intellect arranging the parts in their relation to the whole. Rapture is incontinuous, inconstant; consequently it hasn't the power to produce truly great perfection (without which there is no lyric poetry).

Rapture is a tense state of nothing but the imagination. There can be inspiration without rapture, but rapture without inspiration does not exist.

Homer is immeasurably higher than Pindar; the ode, not to mention the elegy, stands among the lower levels of poems. Tragedy, comedy, and satire all require more creativity *(fantaisie)*, imagination—masterful knowledge of nature—than does the ode.

But there is and can be no *plan* in an ode; the plan alone of the *Inferno* is the fruit of high genius. What plan is there in Pindar's Olympian odes, what plan is there in "The Waterfall," Derzhavin's best work?[4]

The *ode* precludes the constant work without which there is nothing truly great.

[1825–26, unpublished]

# N O T E S

1. *Küchelbecker's first essay is translated below, pp. 249–257. Pushkin refers to the statement, "Power, freedom, and inspiration are the three essential conditions for all poetry" and (from "A Conversation with Bulgarin") ". . . he [Horace] was almost never a truly* ecstatic *poet. And what can you call a poet if he is alien to true inspiration?"*

2. *Vasily Andreevich Zhukovsky (1783–1852)—mellifluous but monotonous lyric poet, translator of everything from Bürger's* Lenore *to the* Odyssey. *Zhukovsky is the immediate poetic predecessor of Pushkin, Baratynsky, Delvig, Yazykov, and a host of lesser poets who wrote primarily in the smaller, lyric genres.*

3. *The passage Pushkin probably had in mind is the one beginning, "We all lament. . . ." See below, p. 253.*

4. *Gavril Romanovich Derzhavin (1743–1816)—a more or less neoclassical poet in whose thundering verse Pushkin found more brass than gold. Among the scattered lines which make him Russia's best eighteenth-century poet are those of the ode,* The Waterfall *(1793–94), written under the influence of Ossian.*

# ON THE ALMANAC
## *THE NORTHERN LYRE*

**Almanacs have become the representatives of our literature.** In time its trends and successes will be judged from them. A few pleasant lyric poems, curious prose translations from Eastern languages, and the names of Baratynsky[1] and Vyazemsky guarantee the success of *The Northern Lyre*, the first of the Moscow almanacs.

Of the poems, Tumansky's[2] "Greek Song" and his "To Odessa Friends" stand out because of the harmony and precision of style and reveal indubitable talent. Among the other poets we saw Mr. Muraviev[3] for the first time—and met him with hope and happiness. In that he is our co-worker, we will be silent about Mr. Shevyrev.

Let us note that Mr. Arb. Norov should not have translated Dante, nor Oznobishin André Chénier. We will leave it to the Arabian journalists to defend the honor of their poets translated by Mr. Deliburader[4]—as for us, we find his renderings fine for a Tartar.

The prose essay on Petrarch and Lomonosov[5] could have been interesting and witty. These two great men do in fact bear some resemblance to each other. Both founded the literature of their fatherland, both intended to found their fame on more important occupations, but in spite of themselves are better known as national poets. Separated from each other by time, the circumstances of life, the political situation of their fatherlands, they are alike in their firmness and tirelessness of spirit, striving for enlightenment, and, finally, the respect which they were able to obtain from their fellow countrymen. But Mr. R. profoundly notes that *Petrarch* was in love with Laura, but Lomonosov esteemed Peter and Elizabeth, that Petrarch wrote in Latin, that he wrote the poem *Scipio Africanus*, but Lomonosov wrote no Latin poem. In a curious digression, he tells how an old man came from Spain to Rome to see Titus Livius and that *just such an* old man (but blind besides) came *to see* Petrarch—our Lomonosov cannot offer such a miraculous event. Finally, that Roberto, the King of Naples, once asked Petrarch why he didn't present himself to Philip etc., but that he (Mr. R.) doesn't know what Lomonosov would have said in such a case.

For a long time Mr. R. didn't know why "in our Lomonosov's poetry there is such freshness, such sweetness, not to mention the power, for which he is without doubt obliged to the ancients; but having re-read everything written by him, I found that he knew how and felicitously knew how to transmit very, very much of the Italian to his works, even some of the so-called *concetti*." Dubious.

[1827, unpublished]

## N O T E S

1. *See below, p. 47n1.*
2. *Tumansky, Vasily I. (1800–60)—a once popular, now forgotten, poet.*
3. *A. N. Muraviev—a minor poet and playwright.*
4. *A pseudonym of the talentless D. P. Oznobishin.*
5. *By S. E. Raich, a minor writer.*

# EUGENE BARATYNSKY'S
# POEMS, 1827

**At last the collected poems of Baratynsky[1] have been published**; they were awaited so long and with such impatience.

We hasten to use the opportunity to express our opinion about one of our first-rate poets and (perhaps) one who is still unwillingly given his due by his countrymen.

Baratynsky's first works attracted attention to him. With amazement connoisseurs saw extraordinary grace and maturity in his first efforts.

This precocious development of all poetic abilities perhaps depended on the circumstances, but it already predicted for us that which has now been executed by the poet in such a brilliant manner.

Baratynsky's first works were elegies and in this genre he is pre-eminent. Nowadays it has become fashionable to denigrate elegies, as people used to ridicule odes, but if the flaccid imitators of Lomonosov and Baratynsky are equally unbearable, it does not follow from this that the lyrical[2] and elegiac genres should be excluded from the ranked books of the poetic oligarchy.

And besides, the pure elegy barely exists in Russia. Among the ancients it was distinguished by a special prosody, but sometimes it got off into the idyll, sometimes it entered the tragedy, sometimes it took on a lyrical course (of which in modern times we see examples in Goethe).

[1827, unpublished]

## N O T E S

1. *Eugene A. Baratynsky (1800–1844)—after Pushkin and Lermontov, the most important poet of the period. He began with the lighter forms and romantic tales in verse* (Eda, The Ball, The Concubine). *His later poetry is more intellectual and analytic. It is his heavily philosophical temper to which Pushkin refers in the essay entitled "Baratynsky" (below, pp. 127–129).*

2. *Here "lyrical" applies to odes. Lomonosov decreed that odes should have "lyrical disorder." The poet was supposed to let his imagination "soar."*

# ON BYRON'S DRAMAS

**English critics have disputed Lord Byron's dramatic talent.**
I think they are right. Byron, so original in *Childe-Harold*, in
*The Giaour*, and in *Don Juan*, becomes an imitator as soon as
he enters the dramatic field: in *Manfred* he imitated *Faust*, replacing the commonfolk scenes and sabbaths with others which
in his opinion were more noble; but *Faust* is the greatest creation of poetic spirit, it serves as the representative of modern
poetry, exactly as the *Iliad* serves as a monument of classical
antiquity.

In other tragedies Byron's model was, it would seem, Alfieri.
*Cain* has only the form of a drama; actually its disconnected
scenes and abstract discourses are related to the genre of sceptical poetry of *Childe-Harold*. Byron threw a one-sided glance at
the world and the nature of humanity, then turned away from
them and plunged into himself. He presented us with a phantom
of himself. He created himself a second time, now under the
turban of a renegade, now in the cloak of a corsair, now as a
giaour breathing his last under the schema, now, finally, wandering amid. . . . In the final analysis he comprehended, created,
and depicted a single character (namely, his own); he connected
everything except a few satirical sallies scattered through his
works to this dark, powerful character who is so mysteriously
captivating. But when he began to compose his tragedy, he
doled out one of the component parts of this dark and strong
figure to each character, and in this way he splintered his majestic creation into several petty and insignificant characters.
Byron felt his error and subsequently took up *Faust* anew, imitating it in his *Deformed Transformed* (intending by this means
to improve *le chef d'oeuvre*).

[1827, unpublished]

# FRAGMENTS FROM LETTERS, THOUGHTS, AND NOTES

**True taste consists not in an unreasoning rejection of a certain** word, a certain locution, but in a sense of proportion and conformity.

\* \* \*

A scholar without talent is like the poor mullah who cut up and ate the Koran, thinking he would be filled with the spirit of Mohammed.

\* \* \*

Monotony in a writer shows one-sidedness of intellect, even though it may be a profound one.

\* \* \*

Sterne says that the liveliest of our pleasures ends with a shudder which is almost painful. Unbearable observer! He should have kept it to himself; many people wouldn't have noticed it.[1]

\* \* \*

People complain about the indifference of Russian women to our poetry, suggesting the reason for this is ignorance of our native language; but what woman wouldn't understand the verse of Zhukovsky, Vyazemsky, or Baratynsky? The point is that women are the same everywhere. After giving them subtle minds and the touchiest sensibilities, nature almost totally denied them esthetic sense. Poetry slides across their ears without reaching their souls; they are insensitive to its harmony; notice how they sing fashionable romances, how they distort the most natural verses, ruin the timing, destroy the rhyme. Listen to

their literary opinions, and you will be amazed at the crookedness, and even crudity, of their understanding. . . . Exceptions
are rare.

\* \* \*

The colder, more calculating and cautious we are, the less
we are subject to attacks of ridicule. Egoism can be repulsive,
but it is not ridiculous, for it is eminently sensible. However,
there are people who love themselves with such tenderness, who
are surprised at their own genius with such rapture, who think
about their well-being with such emotion, about their dissatis-
factions with such compassion, that in them egoism has all the
ridiculous side of enthusiasm and sensibility.

\* \* \*

No one more than Baratynsky has feeling in his thoughts
and taste in his feelings.

### EXAMPLES OF IMPOLITENESS

Every day when they get up, the men in a certain Asiatic
nation thank God for not having created them as women.

Mohammed denies the existence of souls in women.

In France, in a land famed for its courtesy, grammar has
solemnly proclaimed the masculine gender the noblest.

A poet surrendered his tragedy to the examination of a certain critic. In the manuscript was this verse:

I am a human and walked[2] on the paths of delusion.

The critic underlined the verse, doubting whether a woman
could be called a human. This recalls the famous decision attributed to Peter I: a woman is not a human, a hen is not a bird,
an ensign is not an officer.

Even people who pass themselves off as the most fervent admirers of the fair sex do not assume that women have intellects
equal to ours; and they publish little textbooks for women as if

for children, adapting them to the weakness of their understanding, etc.

\* \* \*

One day Tredyakovsky[3] came to complain to Shuvalov[4]
about Sumarokov. "Your excellency! Alexander Petrovich hit
me so hard on the right cheek that it still hurts me." —"How is
it, dear fellow," Shuvalov answered him, "that your right cheek
hurts but you are holding your left?" —"Oh, your excellency,
you are right," answered Tredyakovsky, and moved his hand
to the other side. It often happened that Tredyakovsky was
beaten. In the Volynsky file it says that he once demanded an
ode from the court poet Vasily Tredyakovsky for some holiday,
but the ode was not ready, and the fiery state-secretary punished
the negligent versifier with a cane.

\* \* \*

One of our poets used to say proudly: I don't mind if you
find senselessness in my poetry, but you won't find prose. Byron
could not explain some of his poetry. There are two kinds of
senselessness: one comes from a lack of feelings and thoughts—
for which words are substituted—the other from abundance of
feelings and thoughts and a lack of words for their expression.

\* \* \*

"Everything which is beyond geometry is beyond us," said
Pascal. And as a result of this he wrote his philosophical
thoughts!

\* \* \*

*Un sonnet sans défaut vaut seul un long poème.*[5] A good
epigram is better than a bad tragedy . . . what does this mean?
Can one say that a good breakfast is better than bad weather?

\* \* \*

*Tous les genres sont bons, hors le genre ennuyeux.*[6] It was
good to say that for the first time, but how can one solemnly

repeat such a great truth? This joke of Voltaire serves as a basis for the superficial criticism of literary sceptics; but in every case scepticism is only the first step for reasoning. Incidentally, someone[7] has noted that even Voltaire didn't say *également bons.*

\* \* \*

The traveler Ancelot[8] speaks of a certain grammar, not yet published, which sets forth the rules of our language, about a certain Russian novel, still in manuscript form, which has brought fame to its author, and about a certain comedy, still not played and not printed, which is the best of all the Russian theater. In this last case Ancelot may very well be right. An amusing literature!

\* \* \*

L., an aged ladies' man, said: *Moralement je suis toujours physique, mais physiquement je suis devenu moral.*

\* \* \*

Inspiration is the disposition of the soul to the most vivid perception of impressions and assimilation of ideas—and, consequently, the explanation of them. Inspiration is necessary in geometry as it is in poetry.[9]

\* \* \*

Foreigners who assert that in our ancient nobility no concept of honor *(point d'honneur)* existed are very much mistaken. This honor, which consists of readiness to sacrifice everything for the support of some arbitrary rule, is seen—in all the glitter of its madness—in our *mestnichestvo.*[10] The boyars walked to disgrace and to execution submitting their hereditary family feuds to the judgment of the Tsar. The young Fedor, in destroying the proud opposition of the nobles, did what neither the powerful Ivan III, nor his impatient grandson, nor the secretly malicious Godunov could make up their minds to do.

\* \* \*

One not only can, but must be proud of the glory of his ancestors; not to respect it is shameful meanness. Karamzin says: "A rule of the state makes respect for one's ancestors a merit for an educated citizen."[11] Even in their humiliation the Greeks remembered their glorious heritage, and just by this they merited their liberation. Can that which is considered a virtue for an entire nation be a vice in an individual person? This prejudice, sanctioned by the democratic envy of some philosophers, serves only the spread of base egotism. Isn't the unselfish thought that our grandchildren will be respected for the name which we hand down to them the noblest hope of the human heart?

*Mes arrière-neveux me devront cet ombrage!*[12]

\* \* \*

It has been said: *Les sociétés secrètes sont la diplomatie des peuples.* But what people would entrust its rights to secret societies, and what government which respects itself would enter into negotiations with them?

\* \* \*

Byron said that he would never undertake describing a country which he hadn't seen with his own eyes. However, he describes Russia in *Don Juan,* and a few errors in the setting are noticeable. For example, he talks about the mud in the streets of Izmail; Don Juan sets off for Petersburg "in a *kibitka,* an uncomfortable carriage without springs," on "a bad, flinty road." Izmail was taken in the winter, during severe cold.[13] The enemy corpses on the streets were covered by snow, and the victor rode over them surprised at the tidiness of the city: "My God, how clean!" A winter *kibitka* is not uncomfortable, and a winter road is not flinty. There are other mistakes too, more important ones. Byron read a great deal and asked many questions about Russia. It seems he loved it and knew its modern history well. In his poems he often talks about Russia, about our customs. Sardanapalus's dream is reminiscent of the well-known political caricature[14] published in Warsaw during the Suvorov wars. He depicted Peter the Great in the character of Nimrod. In 1813 Byron intended to travel to the Caucasus by way of Persia.

\* \* \*

Cleverness[15] alone does not prove intellect. Idiots and even madmen are sometimes amazingly clever. One might add that cleverness is rarely combined with genius, which is ordinarily artless, or with great character, which is always frank.

\* \* \*

Dear Sir! You don't know spelling and you usually write without sense. I am addressing a very humble request to you: don't pass yourself off as the representative of an educated public and arbiter of the arguments of three literatures. With sincere respect, etc.

\* \* \*

*Coquette, prude.* The word *coquette* has been Russified, but the word *prude* hasn't been translated and still hasn't gone into use. The word designates a woman excessively ticklish in her ideas about honor (feminine)—an untouchable. Such a trait suggests an impurity of imagination disgusting in a woman, especially a young one. It is permissible for a middle-aged woman to know a great deal and to be apprehensive about it, but innocence is the best ornament of youth. In any case *prudery* is either ridiculous or unbearable.

\* \* \*

Some people are not concerned about either the glory or the calamities of their fatherland; they know its history only since the time of Prince Potemkin; they have some concept of the statistics only for the district where their estates are located— nevertheless, they consider themselves patriots because they love fish-and-vegetable soup, and their children run around in red shirts.

\* \* \*

Moscow is a maids' room, and Petersburg is an anteroom.

\* \* \*

One must try to have the majority of voices on one's own side—so don't offend fools.

\* \* \*

The appearance of *The History of the Russian State* (as it should have) made a great deal of noise and produced a strong impression.[16] Three thousand copies sold out in one month, which even Karamzin himself did not expect. Society people rushed to read the history of their fatherland. It was a new discovery for them. Ancient Russia, it seemed, had been found by Karamzin as America by Columbus. For some time nothing else was talked about anywhere. I confess it is impossible to imagine anything more foolish than the society opinions which I happened to hear; they were enough to dissuade anyone from a desire for glory. One lady (a very nice one incidentally), opening the second part in front of me, read aloud: " 'Vladimir adopted Svyatopolk, however he didn't love him. . . .' *However!* Why not *but?* However! Do you sense all the insignificance of your Karamzin?" No one wrote critiques of him in the journals: no one among us is capable of analyzing and evaluating the vast creation of Karamzin. Kachenovsky attacked the foreword.[17] Nikita Muraviev, a young man, intelligent and ardent, wrote a critique of the foreword (the foreword!).[18] In a letter to Vyazemsky, Mikhail Orlov[19] rebuked Karamzin—why didn't he put some brilliant hypothesis about the origin of the Slavs in the beginning of his work? i.e. he demanded not history from the historian, but something else. At dinner a few wits re-wrote the first chapters of Titus Livius in Karamzin's style; but hardly anyone said thanks to a man who had isolated himself in a scholar's study at a time of the most flattering success and who dedicated an entire twelve years of his life to silent and tireless labors. The footnotes to the Russian history bear witness to the vast erudition of Karamzin, acquired by him at an age when for ordinary people the scope of education and knowledge has long ago been circumscribed and the bustle of the civil service has replaced striving toward enlightenment. Many people forgot that Karamzin printed his *History* in Russia, in an autocratic state; that having freed him from the censorship the sovereign, by this sign of confidence, placed upon Karamzin the obligation of all possible modesty and moderation. I repeat that *The History of the Russian State* is not only the creation of a great writer, but also the feat of an honorable man.

\* \* \*

Delvig's idylls amaze me.[20] What power of imagination one must have in order to transport oneself so completely from the nineteenth century to the golden age, and what extraordinary esthetic *sensitivity* in order to divine Greek poetry so well through Latin imitations and German translations, the luxuriance, the mollitude, the charm—more negative than positive—which does not allow anything forced in the feelings, anything subtle or confused in the ideas, anything superfluous or unnatural in the descriptions.

\* \* \*

French literature was born in the anteroom and did not go any further than the drawing-room.

[Written in 1827, published in *Northern Flowers* for 1828]

# N O T E S

1. *The censors emasculated Pushkin's text by removing this observation from* A Sentimental Journey.
2. *The verb is feminine.*
3. *Vasily K. Tredyakovsky (1703–69)—neoclassical poet famed for his ineptitude.*
4. *Ivan I. Shuvalov—a high Russian dignitary.*

5. *This quotation from Boileau's* Art Poétique *was also used by Küchelbecker in a note to his essay (below, p. 251).*

6. *From Voltaire's preface to the comedy* L'Enfant prodigue.

7. *Küchelbecker.*

8. *Jacques Arsène Polycarpe François Ancelot (1794–1854). In his* Six mois en Russie *(Paris, 1827) he refers to Grech's* Grammar, *Bulgarin's* Vyzhigin, *and Griboedov's* Woe from Wit.

9. *Flaubert said: "Poetry is as precise as geometry." [F. Steegmuller,* Flaubert and Madame Bovary *(New York, 1939), p. 330.]*

10. *The old Russian custom of having governmental and court positions filled by heredity rather than merit.*

11. *This is a rough paraphrase of a statement in the preface to Nikolai Karamzin's* History of the Russian State.

12. *Line 21 of La Fontaine's fable "La vieillard et les trois jeunes hommes."*

13. *The taking of Izmail (or Ismail) is described in the eighth and ninth cantos of* Don Juan. *In IX, XXX Byron says:*

And there in a *kibitka* he roll'd on,
    (A cursed sort of carriage without springs,
Which on rough roads leaves scarcely a bone whole). . . .

*And In IX, XXXI:*

At every jolt—and there were many—still
    He turned his eyes on his little charge
As if he wish'd that she should fare less ill
    Than he, in these sad highways left at large
To ruts, and flints. . . .

14. Sardanapalus—*a tragedy by Byron (1821) about the last of the Assyrian kings. Act IV, Scene I, lines 78–164. In his dream Sardanapalus sees a mighty, terrifying, and bloody hunter (cf.* Genesis, *X, 9;* Paradise Lost, *XII, 24). The caricature was published in London in 1795; it showed Suvorov offering Catherine the lopped-off heads of women and children after the taking of Warsaw.*

15. Tonkost' *has several basic meanings: thinness, fineness, delicacy, slenderness, and subtlety. None of these sounds quite right in English, so I have used "cleverness"—although it may err a little on the side of* lukavstvo *(slyness, craftiness). In the Russian text Pushkin illustrates his assertion with fifteen lines of a poem on M. S. Vorontsov.*

16. *Nikolai Mikhailovich Karamzin (1766–1826) published the first eight volumes of his* History of the Russian State *in 1818; four more volumes appeared later (the last one, reaching only 1612, posthumously). Before his* History, *Karamzin was already an extremely influential writer, known for sentimental tales ("Poor Liza"), travel notes* (The Letters of a Russian Traveler), *and light poetry.*

17. *Mikhail T. Kachenovsky (1775–1842)—Professor of History at Moscow University, editor of* The Messenger of Europe *(1805–1830). He wrote a critique of two French translations of Karamzin's foreword.*

18. *Nikita M. Muraviev (1796–1843)—a minor writer, Decembrist author of a projected constitution; his comments on the foreword circulated in manuscript only.*

19. *Mikhail F. Orlov (1788–1842)—a Decembrist, member of the literary society Arzamas.*

20. *Anton Antonovich Delvig (1798–1831)—Lycée classmate of Pushkin, he remained one of Pushkin's closest friends. Delvig was noted for indolence, amiability, and elegant poetry based on classical forms (such as "The Bathing Women" and other idylls). He edited the almanac* Northern Flowers *(1825–31) and founded* The Literary Gazette *in 1830.*

# MATERIALS FOR "FRAGMENTS FROM LETTERS, THOUGHTS, AND NOTES"

### PREFACE

Once my uncle fell ill.[1] A friend visited him. "I'm bored," said my uncle, "I would like to write, but I don't know what about." —"Write whatever you think of," answered his friend, "ideas, literary and political observations, satirical portraits, etc. It's very easy: Seneca and Montaigne wrote like that." The friend left and my uncle followed his advice. In the morning his coffee was badly made, and that made him angry; then he reasoned philosophically that a trifle had disturbed him, and he wrote: "Sometimes absolute trifles disturb us." At that moment a journal was brought to him; he glanced into it and saw an essay on dramatic art written by a champion of romanticism. My uncle, an inveterate classicist, thought a little and wrote: "I prefer Racine and Molière to Shakespeare and Calderón—in spite of the shouting of the modern critics." My uncle wrote a couple dozen more such thoughts and went to bed. The next day he sent them to a journalist who thanked him politely, and my uncle had the pleasure of re-reading his thoughts in print.

\* \* \*

Sumarokov knew Russian better than Lomonov, and his criticisms (regarding grammar) are well-founded. Lomonosov didn't answer—or laughed them off. Sumarokov demanded respect for poetry-writing.

\* \* \*

If everything has already been said, why do you write? To say beautifully that which has already been said simply? A sorry occupation! No, let's not slander human reason, which is as inexhaustible in the combinations of concepts as language is inexhaustible in combinations of words. It is precisely in this sense that Prince Vyazemsky's felicitous jest is entirely accurate; justifying the excess of epithets which makes Russian verse so limp, he said very amusingly that all nouns have been used, and it remains for us to give them new shades of meaning with adjectives. Conscientious people fell thoughtful and started solemnly showing that the verbs and participles and other parts of speech had all been used long ago too.

\* \* \*

Among us prose is used as poetry-writing is—not as a necessity of life, not for the expression of a necessary thought, but only as a pleasant manifestation of forms.

\* \* \*

Abuse men in general, analyze all their vices—not one will consider interceding. But touch upon the fair sex satirically—all women will rise up against you unanimously. They make up *one* nation, one sect.

\* \* \*

One of the reasons for the avidity with which we read the notes of great people is our self-esteem: we are happy if we resemble a notable person in any respect at all—opinions, feelings, habits, even weaknesses and vices. We would probably find more resemblance in the opinions, habits, and weaknesses of totally insignificant people, if they left us their confessions.

\* \* \*

Ks. finds a certain work stupid. —"How do you prove that?" —"My goodness," he assures us ingenuously, "why *I* could have written like that."

\* \* \*

Prince Vyazemsky's prose is extremely lively. He possesses the rare ability to express thoughts originally—fortunately he thinks, which is rather rare among us.

\* \* \*

There are different kinds of boldness. Derzhavin wrote: "Eagle, soaring loftily" when happiness "turned its spinal column to you with menacing laughter, you see, you see how the gleam of a dream went to sleep around you."

The description of the waterfall:

> The diamond mountain pours[2]
> Down from the heights. . . .

Zhukovsky says of God:

In the smoke of Moscow he cloaked himself.[3]

Krylov says of a brave ant that:

He even went out alone against the spider.[4]

Calderón calls streaks of lightning the fiery tongues of the heavens speaking to the earth. Milton says that the flame of Hell only allowed one to make out the eternal darkness of the underworld.[5]

We find these expressions bold because they transmit a clear idea and poetic pictures to us in a powerful and unusual way.

To this day the French are still amazed at Racine's boldness in having used the word *pavé*, pavement.

Et baise avec respect le pavé de tes temples.

And Delille is proud of having used the word *vache*.[6] Literature which submits to such trivial and capricious criticism is despicable. Pitiful is the fate of poets (no matter, incidentally, what their merit) if they are forced to laud themselves for such victories over the prejudices of taste!

There is a higher boldness: the boldness of invention, of creation, where a broad plan is embraced by creative thought—such is the boldness of Shakespeare, Milton, Dante, Goethe in *Faust*, Molière in *Tartuffe*.

\* \* \*

The repetition of a clever *mot* becomes stupidity. How can epigrams be translated? I have in mind not anthological ones in which the poetic charm is developed, not those of Marot into which a lively story is compressed, but that which Boileau defines with the words: *Un bon mot de deux rimes orné*.[7]

[1827, unpublished]

# N O T E S

1. *This section is a parody of Pushkin's Uncle Vasily (himself a minor poet), who published his "Comments on People and Society"*

*in* The Literary Museum *(1827). Among his cutting aphorisms:* "Without fearing the anger of the fashionable romantics, and in spite of Schlegel's stern criticism, I say frankly that I prefer Molière to Goethe and Racine to Schiller."

2. *The quotations are from Derzhavin's "The Grandee," "On Count Zubov's Return from Persia," and "The Waterfall."*

3. *"A Singer in the Kremlin."*

4. *From Krylov's fable, "The Ant."*

5. A dungeon horrible, on all sides round,
  As one great furnace flamed; yet from those flames
  No light; but rather darkness visible
  Served only to discover sights of woe.
  (*Paradise Lost*, I, 61–64.)

6. *Jacques Delille (1738–1813) used the line, "La vache gonfle en paix sa mamelle pendante" in his poem,* L'Homme des champs. *And in a preface to his translation (1770) of Virgil's* Georgics, Delille *praises Racine for introducing new (or old) words, and cites the line from the prologue to* Esther *(1689) in which Racine uses pavé.*

7. *From his* Art Poétique.

# VARIANTS TO "FRAGMENTS FROM LETTERS, THOUGHTS, AND NOTES"

**Rousseau has already remarked that none of the women writers** have gone beyond mediocrity—except Sappho "and one other," says Rousseau, meaning New Héloise, whom he passed off as a nonfictitious person. *Vitam impendere vero.* In general they have ridiculous ideas about the elevated subjects of politics and philosophy! Tender minds are not capable of masculine intensity of thought; at first glance the subjects of the fine arts seem their property, but even here the more you listen in on their literary opinions, the more you will be amazed at the crookedness and even crudity of their understanding. Born with the touchiest sensibilities, they cry over August La Fontaine's[1] mediocre novels and coldly read Racine's eloquent tragedies. Poetry slides across their ears without reaching their souls.

\* \* \*

Apropos or inapropos, some critics—voluntary guardians of the fair sex—usually note when reviewing works that such and such words, expressions, and descriptions will be improper for ladies to read because they are too colloquial, too base. As if a witty fable of Krylov or the descriptions of Scottish taverns in Walter Scott's novels must certainly offend the delicate feeling of a fashionable lady! As if a woman were some ideal being, foreign to everything earthly, and must be horrified by the simple prosaic details of life!

This provincial primness demonstrates little knowledge of society and what is or isn't accepted in it.

Unfortunately, precisely this is too common among us and causes no small harm to our infant and finical literature.

[Date?]

## N O T E

1. *August Heinrich Julius La Fontaine (1758–1831)—a prolific German novelist, not to be confused with the celebrated fabulist.* (*See* Eugene Onegin, *IV, L.*)

# ON OLIN'S TRAGEDY
## *THE CORSAIR*[1]

**None of Lord Byron's works produced such a strong impression** in England as his poem *The Corsair,* in spite of the fact that in

merit it yields to many others: to *The Giaour* in the fiery depiction of passions, to *The Siege of Corinth* and *The Prisoner
of Chillon* in the touching development of the human heart, in
tragic power to *Parisina,* and, finally, to the third and fourth
cantos of *Childe Harold* in the depth of thought and the height
of truly lyrical flight, and to *Don Juan* in amazing Shakespearean variety. *The Corsair* owed its incredible success to the
personality of the main character, who mysteriously reminds us
of the man[2] whose fateful will then ruled one part of Europe,
menacing the other. At least English critics supposed this was
Byron's intention, but it is more likely that even here the poet
brought on stage the character who appears in all his works and
whose countenance he finally took on himself in *Childe Harold.*
However that may be, the poet never expressed his intention:
likening himself to Napoleon pleased his self-esteem.

Byron worried little about the plots of his works, or he
didn't even think about them at all: a few weakly connected
scenes sufficed him for this multitude of thoughts, emotions,
and tableaux. English critics disputed Byron's dramatic talent.
The point is that he comprehended and came to love only one
character (namely, his own); he related everything except a few
satirical sallies scattered through his works to this dark, powerful character who is so mysteriously attractive. But when he
began to compose his tragedy he doled out one of the component parts of this dark and strong figure to each character, and
in this way splintered his majestic creation into several petty
and insignificant characters.

That is why, in spite of great poetic beauties, his tragedies
are in general beneath his genius; and the dramatic part of his
poems (except perhaps only *Parisina*) has no merit whatever.

But what will we think about the writer who takes from the
poem *The Corsair* only a plot worthy of an absurd Spanish tale,
and composes a dramatic trilogy using this plot, replacing the
enchanting, profound poetry of Byron with stilted and deformed prose worthy of our unfortunate imitators of the late
Kotzebue?—That is what Mr. Olin has done in writing his ro-

mantic tragedy *The Corsair*—an imitation of Byron. The question arises: what was it in Byron's poem that struck him—can it really have been the plot? *o miratores! . . .*

[1827, unpublished]

## N O T E S

1. *Valerian Olin (1788–1840), a minor writer and translator, published his tragedy in 1827. In a review of* The Fountain of Bakhchisarai *in 1824 Olin had criticized Pushkin for "lack of plot" (nedostatok plana). The "Russian" word* plan *is difficult to translate. It suggests plot, plan, structural arrangement.*

2. *Napoleon. (Compare V. Nabokov,* EO Commentary, *Vol. II, pp. 357–58.)*

# A LETTER TO THE PUBLISHER OF
## *THE MOSCOW MESSENGER*

I[1] thank you for the interest you have taken in the fate of *Godunov;* your impatience to see it is very flattering to my self-esteem, but now, when through a combination of favorable circumstances the possibility of publishing it is open to me, I foresee new difficulties which I had not suspected before.

Separated from Moscow and Petersburg society since 1820,[2] I could observe the trend of our literature only in the journals. Reading the heated arguments about romanticism, I imagined that we really were bored by the regularity and perfection of classical antiquity and by the pale, monotonous copies of its imitators, that weary taste was demanding other more powerful sensations and was seeking them in the murky but seething springs of a new national poetry. However, it seemed rather strange to me that our youthful literature, which offered no models in any genre, had already managed to dull the taste of the reading public with a few experiments; but, thought I, French literature, which we have all known so closely since childhood, is probably the reason for this phenomenon. I confess honestly that I have been brought up in terror of this most respected public, and I see no shame in pleasing it and following the spirit of the time. This first confession leads to another more important one: so be it, I regret to say that in literature I am a sceptic (not to say anything worse) and that all its sects are the same to me, each presenting its profitable and unprofitable side. Should rituals and forms superstitiously enslave literary conscience? Why shouldn't a writer submit to the accepted customs in the literature of his nation as he submits to the laws of his language? He should be master of his subject in spite of the hindrance of rules, as he is obliged to master the language in spite of grammatical chains.

\* \* \*

Firmly convinced that the old-fashioned forms of our theater demanded transformation, I arranged my tragedy according to the system of Our Father Shakespeare, and to his altar brought him as sacrifices two classical unities, barely preserving the third. Besides this notorious trinity there is a unity which French criticism does not even mention (probably not supposing that its essentiality could be disputed), the unity of style—the fourth essential condition for French tragedy, one which the Spanish, English, and German theaters were spared. You feel that I, too, have followed such a seductive example.

What else is there to say? I exchanged the respected Alexandrine for pentametric blank verse, in a few scenes I even stooped to despicable prose;[3] I didn't divide my tragedy into acts—and I even thought the public would say *thanks very much* to me.

Voluntarily forgoing the advantages presented to me by a system of art justified by experience, established by custom, I attempted to make up for this perceptible shortcoming with a faithful depiction of characters and the time, with the development of historical personages and events—in a word, I wrote a truly romantic tragedy.

Meanwhile, examining more attentively the critical articles found in the journals, I began to suspect that I had cruelly deceived myself in thinking that an aspiration for a romantic transformation had been revealed in our literature. I saw that when using the general term romanticism people meant works bearing the stamp of dejection or dreaminess, that following this arbitrary definition one of the most original writers of our time[4] (one who is not always correct, but who always finds justification in the pleasure of his enchanted readers) had no doubts about including Ozerov in the ranks of the romantic poets, that, finally, our journalistic Aristarchs[5] were unceremoniously putting Dante and Lamartine on the same level, despotically dividing literary Europe into the classic and the romantic, ceding to the first the languages of the Latin South and attributing to the second the German tribes of the North, so that Dante *(il gran padre Alighieri)*, Ariosto, Lope de Vega, Calderón, and Cervantes landed in the classical phalanx to which victory, thanks to this unexpected help provided by the publisher of *The Moscow Telegraph*, will indubitably, it seems, belong.[6]

\* \* \*

All this strongly shook my conviction as an author. I began to suspect that my tragedy was an anachronism.

\* \* \*

Meanwhile, reading the shallow poems which were approvingly termed romantic, I saw in them not traces of the sincere and free movement of romantic poetry, but the finicality of French pseudoclassicism. I soon confirmed this.

In the first volume of *The Moscow Messenger* you read an excerpt from *Boris Godunov*, the scene with the chronicler. The character of Pimen is not my invention. In him I collected characteristics which had captivated me in our old chronicles:

naïveté, touching humility, something both child-like and wise, a devout (one may say) zeal for the power of the Tsar given to him by God, and a total absence of frivolity or bias pervade these precious monuments of times long past, among which the embittered chronicles of Prince Kurbsky stands out from the other chronicles as the stormy life of Ivan's exile stood out from the humble lives of the serene monks.

It seemed to me that this character was at once new and familiar to the Russian heart, that the moving good-naturedness of the ancient chroniclers (so vividly understood by Karamzin and reflected in his immortal work) would embellish the simplicity of my verse and merit the condescending smile of the reader. But what happened? Intelligent people turned their attention to Pimen's political opinions and found them out of date; others doubted that verse without rhyme could be called verse. Mr. Z. suggested exchanging the scene from *Boris Godunov* for pictures from *The Ladies' Journal*. And with that the stern criticism of the most respected public ended.

What follows from this? That Mr. Z. and the public are right, but that Messrs. the journalists are to blame for having led me into temptation with false information. Brought up under the influence of French literature, Russians have become accustomed to the rules asserted by its critics and look unwillingly at anything which does not fit under these laws. Innovations are dangerous, and, it seems, unnecessary.

Do you want to know what else is keeping me from printing my tragedy? Those passages in it which can be interpreted as allegories, hints, *allusions*. Thanks to the French we do not understand how a dramatic author can completely renounce this own way of thinking in order to completely transport himself into the age which is being depicted by him. The Frenchman writes his tragedy with the *Constitutionnel* or with the *Quotidienne* before his eyes in order to make his Scilla,[7] Tiberius,[8] Leonidas[9] declare his opinion of Villelle[10] or Canning[11] in hexametric verses. Because of this ingenious way of doing things, many eloquent journalistic sallies may be heard on the present-day French stage; but true tragedy does not exist. Note that in Corneille you do not find allusions; except for *Esther* and *Véronique* there are none in Racine either. The chronicle of the French theater saw a bold hint at the amusement of Louis XIV's court in *Britannicus*.[12]

> *Il ne dit, il ne fait que ce qu'on lui prescrit* etc.

But is it likely that the clever courtier Racine would dare to make such an abusive comparison of Louis to Nero? Being a true poet, Racine was full of Tacitus, the spirit of Rome, when writing these fine verses;[13] he was depicting decadent Rome and the court of a tyrant, not thinking about Versailles ballets—as Hume or Walpole (I don't remember who) notes about Shakespeare in a similar case. The very boldness of this allusion serves as proof that it did not even enter Racine's mind.

[1828, unpublished]

# N O T E S

1. *This letter was never published. Pushkin wrote it after Shevyrev had praised "Night, A Cell in Chudov Monastery" (a scene from* Godunov) *in his "Review of Russian Literature for 1827."*

*Pushkin's tragedy* Boris Godunov *was written between 1824 and 1825 while he was confined to the family estate Mikhailovskoe. The entire work could not be published for several years.*

2. *The year in which Tsar Alexander exiled Pushkin to the South.*

3. *Compare* Eugene Onegin *(III, XIII): "I shall descend to humble prose." And* Don Juan *(I, CCIV): "If I should condescend to prose."*

4. *Prince Vyazemsky, in a preface to Ozerov's works. Pushkin's marginal notes to this preface show his dislike of elegant nonsense, repetitiousness, and periphrasis.*

5. *Aristarchus of Samothrace (fl. 156* B.C.*)—a critic whose labors were chiefly devoted to annotating the* Iliad *and* Odyssey.

6. *Pushkin refers to Nikolai Polevoi: ". . . classicism and romanticism were fated to divide Europe: the former was fated to Latin*

Europe, the latter to Germanic and Slavic Europe." (The Moscow Telegraph, *No. 8, 1825). Compare Pushkin's letter to Vyazemsky of May 25, 1825.*

7. *A tragedy by Victor-Joseph Etienne Joui (1821).*

8. The Last Day of Tiberius *(1828) by Antoine Vincent Arnault (1766–1834).*

9. *A tragedy by Michel Pichat (1790–1828), a popular writer of melodramas.*

10. *Jean Baptiste Guillaume Villele (1773–1854) served in many important governmental positions, especially during the 1820's.*

11. *George Canning (1770–1827)—British foreign secretary and ambassador.*

12. *Act IV, Scene IV. According to Boileau, when Louis XIV heard these lines he stopped participating in court ballets.*

13. *Cazamian writes:* "Britannicus *is steeped in Tacitus, and the condition of the Roman state . . . is the background of the play." An interesting coincidence.*

# ON POETIC STYLE

**In a mature literature there comes a time when, bored with** monotonous works of art, with the limited sphere of an arbitrarily selective language, intelligent men turn to the fresh imagination of the commonfolk and to the strange colloquialism which had at first been scorned. Thus at one time in France *blasés,* society people, were enraptured by the muse of Vadé;[1] thus nowadays Wordsworth and Coleridge have enthralled the minds of many. But Vadé had neither imagination nor poetic feeling; his witty works contain nothing but gaiety expressed in the street language of peddlers and porters. The works of the English poets, in contrast, are filled with profound feelings and poetic thoughts expressed in the language of the honorable common man.[2] For us, praise God, this time has not yet arrived; the so-called language of the gods is still so new for us that we call anyone who can write ten iambic verses with rhymes a poet. Not only have we not yet thought of making poetic style approach noble simplicity—we try to make prose pompous too; we still do not understand poetry freed from the conventional embellishments of versifying. The experiments of Zhukovsky and Katenin[3] were unsuccessful not in themselves, but in the reaction they produced. Few, extremely few, people understood the merit of the translations from Hebel,[4] and even fewer the force and originality of *The Murderer,* a ballad which can stand beside the best works of Bürger and Southey. What the murderer says when he turns to the moon, the sole witness of his malefaction:

> Look, look you bald-headed . . .

a line filled with truly tragic force, just seemed ridiculous to hasty people who failed to consider that sometimes terror is expressed in laughter. The ghost scene in *Hamlet* is written entirely in a joking, even a low style; but one's hair stands on end from Hamlet's jokes.

[1828, unpublished]

## N O T E S

1. *Jean Joseph Vadé (1720–57)—author of light verse and comedies in which he used the coarse jargon of the fishmarket.*
2. *As Wordsworth wrote in the Preface to the* Lyrical Ballads:

Low and rustic life was generally chosen because in that situation the essential passions of the heart find a better soil in which they can attain their maturity, are less under restraint, and speak a plainer and more emphatic language; because in that situation our momentary feelings exist in a state of greater simplicity, and consequently may be more accurately contemplated. . . . The language too of these men is adopted (purified indeed from what appear to be its real defects, from all lasting and rational causes of dislike and disgust) because such men hourly communicate with the best objects from which the best part of language is originally derived."

*Pushkin would never have said it in such a diffuse manner, but simplicity was one of his most important criteria for poetic diction too. The English romantics' dissatisfaction with eighteenth-century conventions is paralleled by the Russian romantics' break with the Slavonic pomposities of Russian pseudoclassicism.*

3. *Pushkin considered "The Murderer" Katenin's best ballad. See below, "The Works of Pavel Katenin."*

4. *Johann Hebel (1760–1826)—Zhukovsky translated his* Sonntagsfrühe *and several other ballads.*

# ON SHAKESPEARE'S
# *ROMEO AND JULIET*

**Many of the tragedies attributed to Shakespeare do not belong** to him, but were just corrected by him. Although in its style it is completely separated from his well-known devices, the tragedy *Romeo and Juliet* so obviously fits into his dramatic system and bears so many traces of his broad, unencumbered brush that it must be considered a work of Shakespeare. The Italy contemporary to the poet was reflected in it, with its climate, passions, holidays, mollitude, sonnets, with its luxuriant language filled with brilliance and *concetti*. Thus Shakespeare understood poetic locale. After Juliet, after Romeo, those two enchanting creations of Shakespearean grace, Mercutio, a model of the young cavalier of that time, refined, affectionate, noble Mercutio, is the most remarkable character of the entire tragedy. The poet chose him as a representative of the Italians, who were the fashionable people of Europe, the French of the XVIth century.

[1830, *Northern Flowers*]

# ON WALTER SCOTT'S NOVELS

**The main charm of Walter Scott's novels consists in the fact** that we become acquainted with past time—not with the *enflure* of French tragedies, not with the fastidiousness of sentimental novels, not with the *dignité* of history—but in the homespun way which suits our age. *Ce qui me dégoûte c'est ce que. . . .* Here on the other hand *ce qui nous charme dans le roman historique—est absolument ce que nous voyons.*

Shakespeare, Goethe, Walter Scott have no servile partiality for kings and heroes. They do not resemble (as French heroes do) serfs doing imitations of *la dignité et la noblesse. Ils sont familiers dans les circonstances ordinaires de la vie, leur parole n'a rien d'affecté, de théâtral même dans les circonstances solennelles—car les grandes circonstances leur sont familières.*

*On voit que Walter Scott est de la petite société des rois d'Angleterre.*

[1830, unpublished]

# ON THE TRANSLATION OF B. CONSTANT'S NOVEL *ADOLPHE*

**Prince Vyazemsky has translated and will soon publish the** famous novel of Benj. Constant.[1] *Adolphe* is one of those "two or three novels":

> in which the epoch is reflected
> and modern man
> rather correctly represented

with his immortal soul,
selfish and dry,
to dreaming measurelessly given,
with his embittered mind
boiling in empty inaction.[2]

Benj. Constant first brought on the scene the character subsequently popularized by Lord Byron's genius. We await the
appearance of the book with impatience. It will be curious to see
how Prince Vyazemsky's experienced and lively pen has overcome the difficulty of the metaphysical language,[3] always graceful, sophisticated, often inspired. In this respect the translation
will be a genuinely creative work, and an important event in
the history of our literature.

[1830, *The Literary Gazette*]

## N O T E S

1. *After some difficulties with the censorship, Vyazemsky's translation was published in 1831. The dedication begins: "To Alexander
Sergeevich Pushkin. Accept my translation of our favorite novel."*
2. Eugene Onegin, *VII, XXII. Nabokov's translation.*
3. *See Note 9, "On M. Lemontey's Foreword."*

# HOMER'S *ILIAD*, 
# TRANSLATED BY N. GNEDICH[1]

**Finally the translation of the *Iliad* so long and so impatiently**
awaited has been published! When writers spoiled by momentary successes devote themselves for the most part to glittering
trifles, when talent avoids work and fashion scorns the models

of majestic antiquity, when poetry is just a light-minded occupation and not a devoted service—it is with a feeling of deep respect and gratitude that we regard a poet who has proudly devoted the best years of his life exclusively to one work, to unselfish inspiration and the achievement of a single exalted feat. The Russian *Iliad* is before us. We will proceed to study it, in order, with time, to give a report to our readers about a book which should have such an important influence on our national literature.

[1830, *The Literary Gazette*]

### N O T E

1. *Nikolai Ivanovich Gnedich (1784–1853). He had labored over his majestic and sonorous* Iliad *for many years. The complete edition was published in December, 1829.*

## ON CRITICISM

*Criticism in general.* **Criticism is a science.**

Criticism is the science of revealing beauties and shortcomings in works of art and literature.

It is based on a complete knowledge of the rules by which an artist or writer is guided in his works, on a profound study of models, and on an active observation of notable contemporary phenomena.

I won't speak of dispassionateness—in criticism he who is guided by anything except pure love for art descends to the crowd—which is slavishly governed by base, selfish motives.

Where there is no love for art, there is no criticism. "Do you want to be a connoisseur of the arts?" says Winckelman,[1] "Try to love the artist; look for beauties in his creations."

[1830, unpublished]

## N O T E

1. *Johann Joachim Winckelman (1717–68)—German historian of art in his* Abhandlungen von der Empfindung der Schönen.

# A CONVERSATION ABOUT CRITICISM

A. **Have you read NN's criticism in the last number of** *Galatea*?
B. No, I don't read Russian criticism.
A. In vain. Nothing else will give you a better idea of the state of our literature.
B. What! Do you really suppose journal criticism is the final judge of the works of our literature?
A. Not at all. But it gives an idea about the relations of our writers among themselves, about their greater or lesser degree of fame, and finally, about the opinions which dominate the public.
B. I don't need to read *The Telegraph* to know that Pushkin's poems are in fashion and that no one in our country understands romantic poetry. As for the relations of Mr. Raich and Mr. Polevoi, Mr. Kachenovsky and Mr. Bulgarin, that does not interest me in the least. . . .[1]
A. However, it is amusing.
B. You like fist fights?
A. Why not? Our boyars were amused by them. Derzhavin also sang them.[2] I like Prince Vyazemsky in a scrap with some

literary carouser as much as Count Orlov in battle with a coachman. These are features of nationality.

B. You mentioned Prince Vyazemsky. Admit that he is the only one from higher literature who stoops to polemics.

A. If you please. . . . First say what it is you are calling higher literature. . . .

*  *  *

B. The public is rather indifferent to the successes of literature— true criticism does not interest it. Occasionally it looks at a fight between two journalists, listens in passing to the mono- logue of an irritated author—or shrugs its shoulders.

A. Have it your way; but I stop, look, and listen until the end, and applaud the one who has beaten his opponent. If I were the author myself, I would consider it meanness not to an- swer an attack—no matter what kind it might be. What is this aristocratic pride that allows every rogue from the street to fling dirt at you! Look at the English Lord. He is ready to an- swer the polite challenge of a *gentleman* and shoot with Kuchenreiter pistols, or take off his coat and box at the cross- roads with a coachman. That is real bravery. But both in lit- erature and in society life we are too fastidious, too ladylike.

B. Our criticism has no wide circulation; probably the writers of the highest circle don't read Russian journals and don't know whether they are being praised or abused.

A. Excuse me. Pushkin reads every number of *The Messenger of Europe*, where he is abused, which means, in his energetic expression, "to overhear at the doors what is being said about him in the anteroom."

B. That's really curious!

A. At least it is very understandable curiosity!

B. Pushkin answers with epigrams, what more do you need?

A. But satire is not criticism—an epigram is not a refutation. I am worrying about the good of literature, not just my own pleasure. If all the writers who deserve the respect and con- fidence of the public took it upon themselves to direct public opinion, criticism would soon become what it is not. Wouldn't it be interesting, for example, to read Gnedich's opinion of romanticism or Krylov's about present-day elegiac poetry? Wouldn't it be pleasant to see Pushkin analyzing Khomyakov's tragedy?[3] These men are in close contact with each other and probably exchange comments with each other about new works. Why not make us, too, participants in their critical discussions?

[1830, unpublished]

## N O T E S

1. *There had been unseemly polemics between S. Raich (publisher of* Galatea) *and Polevoi* (The Moscow Telegraph), *also between Bulgarin's* Northern Bee *and Kachenovsky's* Messenger of Europe.

2. *In his ode* Felitsa. *Count Orlov was known to enjoy this pastime.*

3. Ermak *by Alexei Stepanovich Khomyakov (1804–60)—poet, publicist, Slavophil theoretician.*

# ON JOURNAL CRITICISM

**In one of our journals it is noted that a** *Literary Gazette* **cannot** exist in our country for an extremely simple reason: *we have no literature.*[1] If this were correct, we would not be in need of criticism; but the works of our literature, however rarely they appear, live, and die, and are not evaluated according to their merit. In our journals criticism is either limited to dry bibliographical information, satirical remarks (more or less witty), general praises between friends, or simply turns into a domestic correspondence between the publisher and his co-workers, the proof-reader etc. "Clear a place for my new essay," says the co-worker. "With pleasure," answers the publisher. And all this is printed.[2] Not long ago there was a reference to *powder* in our journal. "There, now you'll really have powder!" it says in the typesetter's comment, and the publisher himself objects to this:

> Abuse for the mighty prophet,
> Scorn for the weak one.[3]

These family jokes must have their key and, probably, are very amusing—but for us they make no sense as yet.

It will be said that criticism should concern itself solely with works of obvious merit. I don't think so. A certain work is insignificant in itself, but remarkable for its success or influence; and in this respect moral observations are more important than literary observations. Last year several books were printed *(Ivan Vyzhigin*[4] among others) about which criticism could have said much that is instructive and interesting. But where were they analyzed, explicated? Not to mention living writers, Lomonosov, Derzhavin, and Fonvizin,[5] who still await final and dispassionate evaluation. Grandiloquent nicknames, unconditional praises, banal exclamations can no longer satisfy sensible people. However, *The Literary Gazette* was essential for us not so much for the public as for a certain number of writers who, for different reasons, could not appear under their own name in any of the Petersburg or Moscow journals.

[1830, *The Literary Gazette*]

# N O T E S

1. *In "An Epistle from* The Northern Bee *to* The Northern Ant" *(published in No. 3 of* The Northern Bee *for 1830) an anonymous person wrote: "Our literature is an invisible literature. Everyone talks about it, but no one sees it."*

2. *The examples Pushkin gives are from Nadezhdin's editorial remarks in* The Messenger of Europe.

3. From Zhukovsky's "A Singer in the Camp of Russian Warriors."

4. Faddey Bulgarin's novel (1829). See below, "The Triumph of Friendship."

5. Denis Ivanovich Fonvizin (1744–92)—satirical playwright of the neoclassical period. His Brigadir and The Minor are the best Russian prose comedies before Gogol's Inspector General (1836).


# YURY MILOSLAVSKY, OR, THE RUSSIANS IN 1612

**In our time, by the term** *novel* **we mean an historical epoch** developed in a fictional narrative. Walter Scott attracted a whole crowd of imitators.[1] But how far they all are from the Scottish wonder-worker![2] Like Agrippa's[3] pupil, having summoned the demon of the past they didn't know how to control it, and became victims of their own audacity. With a heavy supply of domestic habits, prejudices, and daily impressions, they themselves clamber over into the age into which they want to transport the reader. Under a *béret* topped with feathers you recognize a head combed by your barber; the starched tie of a present-day *dandy* shows through lace collars *à la* Henry IV. Gothic heroines brought up at Madame Campan's[4] and statesmen of the XVIth century read the *Times* and *Journal des débats*. How many incongruities, unnecessary trifles, important omissions! How much refinement! And, above all, how little life![5] However, these bland works are read in Europe. Is it, as Madame de Staël maintained, because people know only the history of their own time,[6] and therefore are incapable of noticing the absurdity of anachronisms in novels? Or because even a weak and inaccurate depiction of the past possesses inexplicable charm for an imagination which has been dulled by the monotonous mottle of the present, the quotidian?

Let us make haste to note that these reproaches are not made apropos of *Yury Miloslavsky*. Mr. Zagoskin really does transport us to 1612. Our good commonfolk, boyars, Cossacks, monks, brawling rascals—all of them are divined, all of them act and feel as they must have acted and felt during the troubled times of Minin[7] and Avraam Palitsyn.[8] How vivid, how interesting the scenes from ancient Russian life are! How much truth and good-hearted gaiety in the depiction of the characters Kirsha, Alexei Burnash, Fedka Khomyak, Pan Kopychinsky, papa Eremei! The events of the novel fit effortlessly into the very broad framework of historical events. The author does not hurry with his story, he pauses over details, and he looks to the side—but he never tires the reader's attention. The dialogue (lively and dramatic wherever it deals with the common-folk) reveals a master of his craft. But the unquestionable talent of Mr. Zagoskin noticeably betrays him when he approaches historical characters. Minin's speech on the Nizhny-Novgorod square is weak; there are no bursts of the commonfolk's eloquence in it. The boyars' council is depicted coldly. Two or three small anachronisms and several oversights in the language and *costume* can also be noticed. [Here Pushkin gives several examples of linguistic errors and anachronisms. C. R. P.] But these minor oversights and others noted in No. 1 of this year's *Moscow Messenger* cannot hurt the brilliant and entirely deserved success of *Yury Miloslavsky*.

[1830, *The Literary Gazette*]

## N O T E S

1. *Mikhail N. Zagoskin (1789–1852), author of* Yury Miloslavsky, *was not the only Russian to take advantage of the popularity of Sir Walter Scott and James Fenimore Cooper. Among the most prolific writers of historical novels were Faddey Bulgarin and Ivan Lazhechnikov.*

2. *Originally Pushkin wrote: "But except for Cooper and Manzoni, how far they all are from the Scottish wonder-worker!"*

3. *Henry Cornelius Agrippa von Nettesheim (1486–1535)—writer, soldier, physician, and occultist on whose legend Southey wrote his "Cornelius Agrippa, a Ballad of a Young Man that Would Read Unlawful Books, and How He Was Punished" (1798) and Goethe his* Der Zauberlehrling.

4. *Jeanne Campan (1752–1822)—confidante of Marie Antoinette, later an educator, author of* De l'éducation des femmes.

5. *In a draft Pushkin says: "One witty lady compared Alfred de Vigny's novel* [Cinq Mars] *to a bad, pale lithograph."*

6. *Chapter Two (Part One) of her* Considérations sur les principaux événements de la révolution française *opens with the statement:*

> Les hommes ne savent guère que l'histoire de leur temps; et l'on diroit, en lisant les déclamations de nos jours, que les huit siècles de la monarchie qui ont précéde la révolution française n'ont été que des temps tranquilles, et que la nation étoit alors sur des roses. [*Oeuvres Complètes de Mme. la Baronne de Staël* (Paris, 1820), XII, 24.]

7. *Kozma Minin (d. 1616)—a butcher—and national hero during the Polish invasion of 1612.*

8. *Avraamy Palitsyn—monk at the Trinity Monastery during the Time of Troubles, one of the leaders of the resistance to the Poles, author of a well-known* Legend *which gives a "history" of the period.*

# ON *THE MEMOIRS OF SAMSON*

**The French journals inform us of the forthcoming publication** of *The Memoirs of Samson, the Executioner of Paris.*[1] This had to be expected. This is what craving for novelty and strong impressions has led us to.

After the scandalous *Confessions* of eighteenth-century

philosophy came political revelations which were no less scandalous. We were not satisfied with seeing famous people in night-caps and bathrobes; we wanted to follow them into their bedrooms and further. When even this bored us there appeared a crowd of dubious people with their disgraceful tales. But we didn't stop with the shameless memoirs of Henrietta Wilson,[2] Casanova,[3] and the Contemporary Lady.[4] We rushed to the scoundrelly confessions of a police spy and an explanation of them by a branded convict. The journals were filled with excerpts from Vidocq.[5] The poet Hugo was not abashed about finding inspiration in them for a novel full of fire and filth.[6] We lacked an executioner among the latest writers. Finally he too has appeared; and, to our shame, let us say that the success of his *Memoirs* seems indubitable.

We do not envy people who, basing their calculations on the immorality of our curiosity, have devoted their pens to a repetition of the tales of the apparently illiterate Samson. But less us confess, too, we who live in an age of confessions: we await the *Memoirs of the Executioner of Paris* with impatience, although with revulsion too. We will see what he has in common with living people. In what animal roar will he express his thoughts? What will this work—which inspired Count Maistre with such a poetic, such a terrifying page[7]—tell us? What will he tell us, this man who during the forty years of his bloody life presided over the last convulsions of so many victims—some famous, some unknown, some holy, and some hateful? All, all of them—his momentary acquaintances—will, in turn, pass before us across the guillotine on which he, the ferocious buffoon, plays his monotonous role. Martyrs, malefactors, heroes—both the royal sufferer and his murderer, Charlotte Corday, the courtesan du Barry, the madman Louvel, the insurgent Berton, the doctor Castaing, who poisoned his friends, and Papavoine, who stabbed children—we will see them again in their last terrible moment.[8] Heads will plop down before us one after the other, each uttering its last word. . . . And having sated our cruel curiosity, the executioner's book will take its place in the libraries to await the learned inquiries of a future historian.

[1830, *The Literary Gazette*]

# N O T E S

1. *This refers to a fraud perpetrated by Balzac and Louis de l'Ain (1789–1852)*: Mémoires pour servir à l'histoire de la Révolution française, *par Sanson, exécuteur des arrêts criminels pendant la Révolution (2 vols., Paris, 1829).*

*Charles Henri Sanson [not Samson as Pushkin has it] was master of the guillotine during the Reign of Terror.*

2. Memoirs of Henrietta Wilson, *written by herself. Paris, 1825.*

3. *Giovanni Jacopo Casanova (de Seingalt),* Mémoires écrits par lui-même *(12 vols., 1826–38).*

4. *Elselina Saint-Elme (1778–1845)—authoress of the scandalous and mendacious* Mémoires d'une contemporaine *(1827).*

5. Mémoires de Vidocq, chef de la police de la sûreté *(Paris, 1828–29, 4 vols.)—another fabrication by Louis l'Héritier de l'Ain.*

6. *In* Le dernier jour d'un condamné. *Incidentally, Hugo mentions Papavoine and Castaing (as Pushkin does at the end of this note).*

7. *In Joseph de Maistre's* Les soirées de Saint-Pétersbourg, Traité sur les sacrifices *(Paris, 1821) there is a short section entitled* Le Bourreau.

8. *Pushkin alludes to: Louis XVI and Danton; Louis Pierre Louvel, who stabbed the Duc de Berry in 1820 [As a young man Pushkin attended the theater displaying a portrait of Louvel with the inscription, "A Lesson to Kings."]; Jean Baptiste Berton, an anti-Bourbon conspirator; Dr. Edmé Samuel Castaing, who poisoned two men over an inheritance; and Louis Auguste Papavoine, who stabbed a little boy and girl in a park. (For a more colorful version of this information, see my source Nabokov,* EO Commentary, *Vol. III, pp. 334–35.) Finally, Soviet scholars note that some of Pushkin's comments on Vidocq were meant and perceived as an allusion to Bulgarin.*

# MORNING-STAR

In this almanac we meet the names of our best-known writers,[1] also the poems of a few ladies—an unexpected decoration, a pleasant novelty in our literature.

But the most remarkable essay in the almanac, the essay which deserves more than the cursory glance of the inattentive reader, is "A Survey of Russian Literature in 1829," a work by Mr. Kireevsky.[2] The author belongs to the young school of Moscow literary men, a school which was founded under the influence of modern German philosophy,[3] and which has already produced Shevyrev,[4] who has earned the approving attention of the great Goethe, and D. Venevitinov,[5] who was so early mourned by the friends of all that is beautiful. A few of Mr. Kireevsky's critical essays were published in *The Moscow Messenger* and attracted the attention of a small number of people who truly appreciate talent. Mr. Kireevsky's "Survey" will probably make a greater impression, not because the ideas in it are more mature (which, incidentally, is unquestionable, in spite of the overly systematic bent of the author's mind), but only because some of his opinions are expressed in a cutting and unusual way.

Setting the success of governmental legislation higher than the glory of military feats, in the beginning of his essay Mr. Kireevsky acknowledges the promulgation of the new Censorship Code[6] as "the most important event for the good of Russia in many years and more important than our brilliant victories beyond the Danube and Ararat, more important than the taking of Erzerum and that glorious shadow which Russian banners cast on the walls of Constantinople." Already he attributes to this Code noticeable movement in the current literature of the past year.

Our journals borrowed more from foreign journals; translations, though for the most part bad ones, transmitted to us more signs of the intellectual life of our neighbors; and therefore imperceptibly all of our literature moved closer to common European life. Even the quarrels in our journals, their indecorous criticisms, their wild tone, their strange personalities, their *non-urban* politenesses—all of this was like the awkward movements of a child just out of tight swaddling clothes: movements essential for the development of strength, for future beauty and health.

At the beginning, examining the character of nineteenth-century literature, Mr. Kireevsky speaks of the writers who in his opinion have defined the spirit of our literature; but first he devotes an eloquent page to the memory of "one who gave the impulse to a half century of enlightenment among our people, who used his entire life for the good of his fatherland," to whom perhaps even Karamzin is obliged for his first enlightenment.

He died not long ago [says Mr. Kireevsky] forgotten by almost everyone, near that Moscow which was the witness and center of his brilliant activity. Now his name[7] is barely familiar to the majority of our contemporaries, and if Karamzin had not spoken of him, perhaps many people reading this essay would be hearing about the deeds of Novikov and his comrades for the first time and would doubt the actuality of events so close to us. Memory of him almost disappeared; those who participated in his work scattered, drowned in the dark worries of personal activity; many are no longer among us, but the deed which they did remains; it lives, it bears fruit and awaits the gratitude of posterity.

Novikov did not spread love for the sciences and desire to read among us—he *created* it. Before him, according to Karamzin, there were two bookstores in Moscow which sold 10,000 rubles worth yearly; within a few years there were twenty, and they sold 200,000 rubles worth of books. Besides that, Novikov started bookstores in other Russian cities—the most remote ones; the works he considered especially important he distributed for almost nothing; he had useful books translated, he expanded the number of participants in his activity, and soon not only all European Russia, but even Siberia began to read. Then our fatherland, though not for long, was a witness of an event almost singular in the annals of our enlightenment: the birth of *public opinion.*

Acknowledging the philanthropic influence of Karamzin for the character of the first period of nineteenth-century literature, the idealism of Zhukovsky for the center of the second, and Pushkin, the poet of reality,[8] as a representative of the third, the author proceeds to a survey of last year's literature.

It seems the XIIth volume of *The History of the Russian State*, the last fruit of great labors, the last feat of a useful life (sacred for every Russian) even surpassed the earlier ones in its power of eloquence, vastness of sweep, accuracy of depiction, clarity, organization of tableaux, and that even glitter, that pure jewel-like firmness of Karamzin's style. In general the merit of this history grows along with the life of the times which have passed. The closer to the present, the more completely the fate of our fatherland opens up before us; the more complex the picture of events, the more trimly it is reflected in the mirror of his imagination, that pure conscience of our people.

Mr. Kireevsky includes the poem *Poltava*[9] among the historical works. "In fact," he says, "of the twenty critiques that have come out on this poem, more than half discussed whether the characters and events described in it really agreed with history. The critics could not have found greater praise for Pushkin." Acknowledging the considerable maturity of talent in the poem, he criticizes its lack of unity of interest, *"the single one of all the unities, the nonobservance of which is not forgiven by the laws of liberal poetics."* This is how he explains the small success which the last, and probably the best, of A. Pushkin's long poems had.

Last year [continues the author] Zhukovsky printed his "Sea," "Song of the Victors," from Schiller, and connected excerpts from the *Iliad*. Here for the first time we have seen in Homer a quality which we did not find in other translations: what is stilted and base in others is simple and noble here; what is soulless and flaccid in others is powerful, masculine, and touching here; here everything is warm, everything is elevated, each word is from the soul; perhaps precisely this is a mistake, if the beautiful can be a mistake.

The author had Kostrov[10] in mind; last year we did not yet have Gnedich's *Iliad* to be proud of.

Zhukovsky's "Sea" reminds one clearly of all his previous poetry. The same sounds, the same feeling, the same charm, the same quality. It seems all the strings of his previous lyre were echoed here in one sincere sound. There is, however, a difference; something more pensive than in his previous poetry.

Of the young poets of the German school, Mr. Kireevsky mentions Shevyrev, Khomyakov, and Tyutchev.[11] The true talent of the first two is unquestionable. But Khomyakov wrote *Ermak*, and this tragedy deserves a separate critical essay.

A profound feeling of heartfelt emotion inspired the young critic with a few touching lines. He speaks about his friend, about "the best of the elect," about the late Venevitinov.

Venevitinov was created to have a strong effect on the enlightenment of his fatherland, to embellish its poetry, and perhaps to be the creator of its philosophy. He who thinks into Venevitinov's works with love (for only love gives up complete comprehension), he who finds traces of a common source in these separate fragments and the unity of the being who inspirits them, he who grasps the profundity of his thoughts which are connected by the well-ordered life of a poetic soul—he will recognize a philosopher who is permeated with the revelations of his century, he will recognize a profound, original poet whose every feeling is illumined by thought, every thought warmed by heart, whose dream is not embellished by art, but is of itself born beautiful, whose best song is his own existence, the free development of his complete, harmonious soul. For nature generously allotted him his own gifts and united their variety by means of balance. Therefore everything beautiful was natural to him, therefore in coming to know himself he found the solution to all the mysteries of art, and it was in his own soul that he read the outline of the higher laws and contemplated the beauty of creation. Because nature was accessible to his mind and to his heart, he could

> Glance into her mysterious breast
> As into the heart of a friend.

Harmony of mind and heart was the distinctive character of his spirit, and his fantasy itself was more a music of thoughts and feelings than a play of imagination. This proves that he was born even more for philosophy than for poetry. His prose works, which are being printed and will soon be published, will also confirm everything we have said.

Here the critic powerfully and wittily demonstrates the predominant use of the German philosophers for those of our writers who, undistinguished by their own personal gift, show even more clearly the merit of something they have acquired which was not their own:

Here two kinds of writer dominate; some follow the French trend, the others the German. What do we meet in the works of the first? We don't find *ideas* in them (for specifically French ideas are already old, and therefore are not ideas but commonplaces: the French themselves borrow them from the Germans and English). But we find *play of words* in them—rarely, extremely rarely, and that accidentally combined with wit, and *jokes*, which are almost always devoid of taste and often devoid of any sense. And can it be otherwise? Wit and taste are developed only in the environment of the best society; and do many of our writers have the good fortune to belong to it?

In contrast, in the works of the writers who are steeped in the reading of German thinkers, we almost always find something worthy of respect, at least a shadow of an idea, at least a striving toward this shadow.

In Prince Vyazemsky Mr. Kireevsky sees proof that true talent glitters everywhere, in any trend, under any influence. "However," says the author, "even Prince Vyazemsky, in spite of his gifts, in spite of the fact that we can call him the wittiest of our writers, is higher where, as in *Dejection*, the voice of the heart is louder than that of the intellect."

The author does not agree with the opinion of the people who assert that the French trend dominates in Baratynsky's works too. He sees in him a self-sufficient, *original* poet.

In order to *hear* all the *nuances* of Baratynsky's lyre, one must have more sensitive hearing and more attention than for other poets. The more we read him, the more that is new (and not noticed at first glance) we discover in him—the sure sign of poetry which is enclosed in its own existence, not accessible to everyone. Are many capable of appreciating fully the merit of his verse even in the artistic respect, the precision of expression, the noble *refinement*? But if the ideal of best society suddenly appeared in some capital unknown to us, in its select circle no other language would be known.

The author correctly puts *Eda*,[12] one of the most original works of elegiac poetry, above *The Evening Ball*,[13] a more glittering poem, but one less elegant, less touching, less freely and profoundly inspired. Defining the character of Baron Delvig's poetry, the critic says:

Every imitation by system has to be cold and soulless. Only an imitation from love can be poetic and even creative. But can we completely forget ourselves in the latter case? And isn't it because we love our model that we find in it traits which correspond to the demands of our spirit? That is why in all successful imitations of the ancients the modern ones always remain modern. I will say more: there is not one truly artistic translation of the ancient classics where there are no traces of this state of the soul—which was foreign to our forefathers' minds. Religious feeling, for which we are obliged to Christianity; romantic love, the gift of Arabs and barbarians; dejection, the child of the North and dependency; all kinds of fanaticism, the unavoidable fruit of the battle of centuries-long disturbances in Europe with attempts at betterment; finally, intellect overcoming feelings, and thence the striving toward unity and concentration. . . .

Discussing several works of our dramatic muse, the author depicts the state of the stage with such humor that though we do not completely share his opinion, we cannot help quoting this original passage:

In general our theater presents a strange contradiction of itself: almost the entire repertoire of our comedies consists of imitations of the French, and in spite of that, precisely the qualities which distinguish the French comedy from all others—taste, decorum, wit, purity of language and everything that belongs to the essentials of good society—all of this is completely alien to our theater. Our stage, instead of being the mirror of our life, serves as a magnifying glass only for our servants' quarters, beyond which our muse does not penetrate. In the servants' quarters she is *at home;* there are her living rooms, study, ballroom, and bathroom; she spends all day there, when she doesn't ride on the back of a carriage to visit the muses of other countries; and in order to depict the Russian Thalia like this one must present her liveried and in boots.

Such is the general character of our original comedies, one still not changed by a few rare exceptions. The reason for this character is partly that from Fonvizin to Griboedov*[14] we haven't had one truly comic talent, and it is well-

* It would seem the author expressed himself incorrectly. Didn't he want to say: *except Fonvizin and Griboedov?*

known that an unusual man, like an unusual idea, always gives a one-sided direction to intellect, that an overweight of strength is balanced only by another strength, that the harm caused by a genius is corrected by the appearance of another who counterbalances it.

However, one could point out to our comic writers that in choosing *such* a direction they are acting imprudently. . . . They should not chase after the simple folk, and no matter how base their language, how rich their outspoken jokes in improprieties, how coarse their farces at which the gallery guffaws, they will never achieve their real ideal and any cab-driver will kill all their comedies with one word.

Enumerating the translations which have appeared in 1829, the author notes that predominantly six foreign poets share the love of our writers: Goethe, Schiller, Shakespeare, Byron, Moore, and Mickiewicz.

Passing over a few more or less noteworthy works which are not in the sphere of pure literature, the author turns to works in the narrative genre. Last year was rich in them, but unquestionably *Ivan Vyzhigin,* because of its extraordinary success, was most worth attention. Two editions were sold out in less than one year; the third is being prepared. Mr. Kireevsky pronounces a severe and cutting sentence on it,* without, however, explaining satisfactorily the unbelievable success of Mr. Bulgarin's moralistic-satirical novel.

It is noteworthy [says Mr. Kireevsky] that last year about 100,000 copies of the Russian alphabet were published, about 60,000 copies of the Slavic alphabet, 60,000 copies of the catechism, about 15,000 copies of the French alphabet, and in general textbooks sold almost a third more last year than in the previous one. That is what we need, what we lack, what the public justly demands.

We hasten to finish this already too lengthy summary. Mr. Kireevsky, mentioning the journals briefly, the spirit of their

* Cf. *Morning-Star.* "A Review of Russian Literature," p. 73.

polemics, the almanacs, the translations of a few well-known works, ends his essay with the following sad rumination:

> But if we examine our literature in relation to the literatures of other countries, if an enlightened European, having opened before us all the intellectual treasures of his country, asks us, "Where is your literature? What works can you take pride in before Europe?" What will we answer him?
>
> We will point out to him *The History of the Russian State*, we will present him a few odes of Derzhavin, a few poems of Zhukovsky and Pushkin, a few of Krylov's fables, a few scenes from Fonvizin and Griboedov—and where will we find a work of European merit?
>
> Let us be dispassionate and confess that we still do not have a complete reflecton of the intellectual life of the nation, we do not have a literature. But let us be comforted: we do have the good, the promise of all the others—we have the hope and the idea of the great destiny of our fatherland!

We smiled reading this melancholy epilogue. But let us point out to Mr. Kireevsky that where a twenty-three-year-old critic could write such an interesting, such an eloquent "Survey of Literature," there is literature—and the time of its maturity is no longer far off.

[1830, *The Literary Gazette*]

## N O T E S

1. *The almanac contained new poems by Pushkin himself (and his Uncle Vasily), Vyazemsky, Delvig, Baratynsky, Venevitinov, Shevyrev, and Yazykov.*

2. *Ivan V. Kireevsky (1806–56)—a critic who progressed from literary journalism and the German beer of Schelling (to borrow a metaphor from Vyazemsky) to the Orthodox kvass of Slavophilism. With his brother Peter and Khomyakov, he become one of the most important anti-Westernizers.*

3. *A friendly society called "The Lovers of Wisdom" was estab-lished in Moscow by V. F. Odoevsky (a short-story writer and mu-sicologist), professors Pogodin and Shevyrev, the young poets Venevitinov and Khomyakov, and Kireevsky himself. Together these future Slavophils explored the mists and myths of German idealistic philosophy.*

4. *Stepan P. Shevyrev (1806–64)—a bad poet, an often sensitive critic and historian of Russian literature, professor at Moscow Uni-versity, a Slavophil, later a close friend of Gogol.*

*Goethe had written a letter to Shevyrev thanking him for his analysis of an excerpt from* Faust. *The letter was published in* The Moscow Messenger *(No. 11, 1828).*

5. *Dmitri Venevitinov (1805–27)—a poet, critic, translator, and philosopher. See below, notes to his essay on* Eugene Onegin.

6. *The New Censorship Code of April 22, 1828 was less stringent than that established in 1826 after the Decembrist uprising, but it would seem that Pushkin is not enthusiastic.*

7. *Nikolai Ivanovich Novikov (1744–1818)—editor and writer of satirical journals such as* The Drone *(1769–70) and* The Painter *(1772–73) which Catherine II shut down for suggesting the truth. His selfless zeal for enlightenment led him into publishing, and be-tween 1775 and 1789 his presses turned out more books than had been published in Russia since printing was invented. In 1791, as part of the reaction to the French Revolution, Catherine had him arrested; and he remained in prison until she died.*

8. *Pushkin substituted this expression; Kireevsky speaks only of a period "of striving toward a better reality."*

9. *A romantic narrative poem in three cantos about Kochubey, Mazepa, and the Battle of Poltava, written October 3–16, 1828. (See below, "Refutations of Criticisms.")*

10. *Ermil I. Kostrov—an earlier translator of the* Iliad.

11. *Fyodor I. Tyutchev (1803–73)—a pantheistic lyric poet.*

12. *Eugene Baratynsky's narrative poem about the seduction of a sweet young Finn by a callow Russian officer.*

13. *An early title of Baratynsky's long poem,* The Ball *(1828).*

14. *Alexander Sergeevich Griboedov (1795–1829)—author of* Woe from Wit *(written 1822–25), Russia's best comedy in verse.*

# ON PRINCE VYAZEMSKY'S ESSAYS

**Several journals accused of impropriety in their polemics have** pointed to Prince Vyazemsky as the initiator of the abuse which predominates in our literature. A dishonest charge. Prince Vyazemsky's critical essays bear the stamp of a subtle, observant, and original intellect. Often you don't agree with his thoughts, but they make you think. Even where his opinions clearly contradict ideas we have come to accept, he draws one along involuntarily by his extraordinary force of *argument* and by the adroitness of the sophism itself. His epigrammatic critiques may seem offensive to an author's self-esteem, but Prince Vyazemsky can boldly say that he has never insulted the personalities of his opponents; but they always transgress the border of literary criticism and constantly, intending to attack the writer, cause indignation among society people and ordinary citizens. But should one be indignant at them? We don't think so. In them there is excusable ignorance of the rules of courtesy rather than reprehensible intent. A sense of courtesy depends on education and other circumstances. Society people have their own way of thinking, their own prejudices, which are incomprehensible to other castes. How would you explain the duel of two French officers to a peaceful Aleutian? Their touchiness would seem extremely strange to him, and he would be quite right.

Proof that our journals never intended to go beyond the boundaries of decorum is their good-hearted surprise at such accusations and their unanimous indication of the one whose works most of all bear the stamp of an aristocratic intellect and a subtle knowledge of social courtesies.

[1830, *The Literary Gazette*]

# DRAFTS OF A PREFACE
## TO *BORIS GODUNOV*

I

**Since**[1] **you really must have it, here is my tragedy—but I** demand that before reading it you peruse the last volume of Karamzin.[2] It is filled with good pleasantries and subtle allusions to the history of that time, like our underpinnings of Kiev and Kamenka. One must understand them—that is *sine qua non*.

On the example of Shakespeare I limited myself to developing an epoch and historical characters without searching for theatrical effects, romantic pathos etc. . . . Its style is mixed. —It is gross and low where I was obliged to have plebeian and coarse characters intervene; as for the gross indecencies—pay no attention to them: this was written as it came to me and will disappear with the first revision. A tragedy without love attracted my imagination. But apart from love entering a great deal into the romantic and passionate character of my adventurer, I made Dmitri fall in love with Marina in order to make the strange character of the latter stand out better. It is barely outlined in Karamzin. But certainly she was an odd and pretty woman. She had only one passion and that was ambition, but with such a degree of energy, of fury, that it is difficult to imagine it. Look how after having sampled royalty, drunk on a dream, she prostitutes herself to one adventurer after another —shares now the disgusting bed of a Jew, now the tent of a Cossack, always ready to give herself to whoever can show her a faint hope of a throne which no longer exists. Look at her brave war, poverty, shame, at the same time negotiating with the King of Poland like one crowned head to another, and then end her most stormy and most extraordinary existence so miserably. I have only one scene for her, but I will return to her if

God lets me live long enough. She upsets me like a violent emotion. She is horribly Polish, as Mme. Lubomirska's cousin said.[3]

Gavrila Pushkin is one of my ancestors; I have depicted him as I found him in history and in my family papers. He had great talents—man of war, man of court, man of conspiracy above all. It was he and Pleshcheev who assured the success of the Pretender by an unheard-of audacity. Afterward I have found him again in Moscow—one of the seven chiefs who defended it in 1612—then in 1616 sitting alongside Kozma Minin in the Duma, then as voevoda of Nizhny, then among the deputies who crowned Romanov, then ambassador. He was everything, even an arsonist, as is proved by an official document which I found in Pogoreloe Gorodishche—the town which he had burned (in order to punish it for I don't know what) in the manner of the proconsuls of the *Convention Nationale.*

I intend to return to Shuisky also.[4] In the historical account he shows a singular mixture of audacity, flexibility, and strength of character. Lackey of Godunov, he is one of the first boyars to go over to Dmitri's side. He is the first who conspires, and note this, he is the one who risks himself; he is the one who vociferates, who accuses, who after being chief becomes a soldier in the front ranks. He is about to lose his head, Dmitri pardons him when he's already on the scaffold, he exiles him, and with the thoughtless generosity that characterizes this amiable adventurer, he recalls him to his court, and covers him with gifts and honors. What does Shuisky do—he who has come so close to the hatchet and the block? He has nothing more important to do than to conspire anew, to succeed, to have himself elected Tsar, to fall and during his fall to preserve more dignity and strength of spirit than he had ever had in his entire life.

There is much of Henri IV in Dmitri. Like him he is brave, generous, and boastful, like him indifferent to religion—both abjure their faith for a political cause, both love pleasures and war, both devote themselves to chimerical projects, both are victims of conspiracies. . . . But Henri IV didn't have a Ksenya on his conscience—it is true that this horrible accusation hasn't been proved and, as for me, I make a point of not believing it.

Griboedov has criticized the character of Job; it is true the patriarch was a man of great intellect—through absent-mindedness I made a fool of him.

In writing my *Godunov* I have reflected on tragedy, and if I undertake a preface I will make a scandal. It is perhaps the most misunderstood genre. People have tried to base its laws on verisimilitude, and it is precisely this which the nature of the drama excludes; without even mentioning time and place, etc., what kind of verisimilitude is there in a room divided into two parts, one of which is occupied by two thousand people supposedly not visible to those who are on the stage?

(2) *The language.* For example, La Harpe's Philoctète,[5] after listening to a tirade of Pyrrhus, says in good French: *Hélas, j'entends les doux sons de la langue grecque.* Isn't all this an unverisimilitude of convention? The true geniuses of the tragedy never concerned themselves about any verisimilitude except that of character and situation. Look how boldly Corneille acted in *Le Cid:* "So, you want the rule of twenty-four hours? So be it." And then he piles up the events of four months for you. Nothing is more ridiculous than these small changes of accepted rules. Alfieri was strongly struck by the ridiculousness of the *aside;* he suppresses it and then lengthens the monologue. Such puerility!

My letter is considerably longer than I wanted to make it. Please keep it, for I will have need of it if the devil drags me into writing a preface.

January 30, 1829                    St. Petersburg

## II

It is with repugnance that I have decided to publish my tragedy, and although in general I have always been rather indifferent to the success or failure of my works, I confess the failure of *Boris Godunov* would hurt me—and I am almost certain of it. Like Montaigne, I can say of my work: *C'est une oeuvre de bonne foi.*[6]

Written by me during strict solitude, far from society which cools one's enthusiasm, this tragedy is a fruit of constant labor which brought me everything that a writer is permitted to enjoy: animated, inspired work; the inner conviction that I had made every effort; finally, the approval of a small number of chosen people.

My tragedy is already known to almost all of those whose opinions I value. The only one[7] who has been missing among my listeners is he to whom I am obliged for the idea of my tragedy, whose genius inspirited and supported me, whose approval I imagined as the sweetest reward—and was the only thing that distracted me during my solitary labor.

### III

The study of Shakespeare, Karamzin, and our old chronicles gave me the idea of clothing in dramatic forms one of the most dramatic epochs of modern history. Not disturbed by any other influence, I imitated Shakespeare in his broad and free depiction of characters, in the simple and careless combination of plots; I followed Karamzin in the clear development of events; I tried to guess the way of thinking and the language of the time from the chronicles. Rich sources! Whether I was able to make the best use of them, I don't know—but at least my labors were zealous and conscientious.

For a long time I could not decide to print my drama. Until now my self-esteem has been little disturbed by the good or bad reception of my poems, by the benignant or severe decision of the journals about some tale in verse. The too flattering critics did not blind me. Reading the most insulting analyses I tried to guess the critic's opinion, to understand with all possible dispassionateness precisely what his objection was. And if I never answered them, it did not stem from scorn, but solely from the conviction that for our literature *il est indifférent* that such and such a chapter of *Onegin* is better or worse than another. But I frankly confess that the failure of my drama would distress me, for I am firmly convinced that national laws[8] of the Shakespearean drama are appropriate for our theater—not the court convention of Racine's tragedies—and that every unsuccessful experiment can delay the reform of our stage. (A. S. Khomyakov's *Ermak* is more a lyric work than a dramatic one. It owes its success to the beautiful verse in which it is written.)

I will proceed to explanations of a few particulars. The line which I have used (iambic pentameter) is ordinarily accepted by the English and Germans. The first example of it we find in our country is, I think, in *The Argives*;[9] A. Zhandr uses it predominantly in the fragment of his fine tragedy written in free verse.[10] I have preserved the caesura of French pentameter in the second foot, and I think, erred in this, by voluntarily depriving my line of the variety peculiar to it. There are coarse jokes, scenes of the commonfolk. It is good if the poet can avoid them (the poet should not be vulgar of his own free will), but if not, he has no need of trying to replace them with something else.

Finding in history one of my ancestors who played an important role in this unfortunate epoch, I introduced him onto the stage without thinking about the delicacy of propriety, *con amore*—but without any aristocratic haughtiness. Of all my imitations of Byron, aristocratic haughtiness was the most ridiculous. The new gentry makes up our aristocracy; the ancient gentry has gone into decline, its rights have been equalized with the rights of other classes, the great estates have been splintered, destroyed, and no one, not even the descendants themselves etc. In the eyes of the judicious rabble, belonging to the old aristocracy does not present any advantages, and an isolated show of respect for the glory of one's ancestors can only draw censure for eccentricity or senseless imitation of foreigners.

[1829–30, unpublished]

## N O T E S

1. *The first fragment was originally written as a letter to N. N. Raevsky in 1825; but this draft, written in French, was dated January 30, 1829. The other fragments, written in Russian, were set down in 1830.*

2. *Volume XI of* The History of the Russian State.

3. *The cousin was Carolina Sobanskaya, whom Pushkin met in Petersburg in 1828.*

4. *Pushkin planned plays entitled* Vasily Shuisky *and* Dmitri and Marina.

5. *In his tragedy* Philoctète *(1783).*

6. *The opening of Montaigne's* Essays *is:* "C'est ici une livre de bonne foi, lecteur."

7. *Karamzin.*

8. *Narodnyj—national, folk, popular, of the people (see notes to "On Nationalism in Literature"). Pushkin means that Shakespeare's plays were English in spirit and enjoyed by people from many classes (not just courtiers).*

9. *A tragedy by Wilhelm Küchelbecker.*

10. *Andrei A. Zhandr published a translation of Act I of Jean de Rotrou's* Venceslas *in 1825.*

# REFUTATIONS OF CRITICISMS

## I

**Being a Russian writer, I have always considered it a duty to** follow current literature, and I have always read criticisms which I occasioned with particular attention. I honestly admit that praise touched me as a clear and apparently sincere sign of good-will and friendliness. I dare say that reading the most hostile critiques I always tried to enter into my critic's way of thinking and follow his judgments without refuting them with egotistic impatience, but wishing to agree to them with all possible authorial self-effacement. Unfortunately, I noticed that for the most part we did not understand each other. As for critical articles written with the sole aim of offending me in any way possible, I will say only that they angered me very much, at least in the first moments, and that therefore their writers may be content, assured that their labors were not lost. If during sixteen years of my life as an author I never answered a single criticism (I'm not talking about the abuse), this occurred, of course, not from scorn.

The state of criticism by itself shows the degree to which all literature has developed. The critiques of *The Messenger of Europe* and the condemnations of *The Northern Bee* are enough for us. We still have no need of Schlegels or even La Harpes. Scorning criticism only because it is still in its childhood means scorning a youthful literature for not yet having grown up. This would be unjust. But just as our literature can proudly exhibit to Europe Karamzin's *History*, a few of Derzhavin's odes, a few of Krylov's fables, Zhukovsky's paean to 1812,[1] a few flowers of northern elegiac poetry—so our criticism can present a few isolated essays filled with lucid ideas, profound views, and fine wit. But they have appeared in isolation, at a distance from each other; and they still haven't acquired weight and constant influence. Their time has still not arrived.

I haven't answered my critics because I lacked the desire, good humor, or pedantry either, nor because I supposed these critics had no influence on the reading public. But, I confess, I was ashamed to repeat banal or grade-school truths to refute them, to discourse on grammar, rhetoric, and the alphabet, and, what is most embarrassing of all, to justify myself where there were no accusations, to say pompously:

Et moi je vous soutiens que mes vers sont très bons[2]

or, for lack of anything to do, to go squabble before the public and try to make it laugh (for which I have not the slightest proclivity). For example, one of my critics—a good and well-intentioned man, incidentally—analyzing *Poltava*, I think, presented a few excerpts and in place of any criticism, asserted that such verses in themselves "poorly recommend themselves."[3] What could I answer him to this? And almost all of his comrades behaved the same way. Our critics usually say: this is good because it is excellent, but that is bad because it is rotten. There is no way you will lure them out of this position.

One other reason, and the main one: laziness. I could never get angered enough at the senselessness or the unscrupulousness to take up a pen and start objecting. Presently, in the unbearable hours of quarantine incarceration, having neither books nor a comrade with me, to pass the time I got the idea of writing a refutation of all the criticisms which I could recall and my own remarks on my own works. I dare assure my reader (if the Lord sends me a reader), that never in my life could I have thought up an occupation more stupid than this.

\* \* \*

In general *Ruslan and Ludmila* was received favorably.[4] Except for one article in *The Messenger of Europe* in which it was abused in an extremely groundless way, and the extremely pointed "questions" baring the weakness of the poem's structure, there seems not to have been a bad word said about it. No one even noticed that it is cold. They accused it of immorality for a few slightly sensual descriptions, for verses which I deleted in the second edition:

> Oh, terrible sight! The decrepit wizard
> Caresses with a wrinkled hand, etc.

for the introduction to I don't remember which canto:

> In vain you have hidden in the shadow, etc.

and for the parody of *Twelve Sleeping Maidens;*[5] for the latter I could well be reproved for a lack of esthetic feeling. It was inexcusable (especially at my age) to parody a pure, poetic creation to please the rabble. The other rebukes were rather empty. Is there even one passage in *Ruslan* which—in the license of the drollery—could be compared with the pranks of, for example, Ariosto, about whom I was constantly reminded? And the passage which I deleted was a very, very toned down imitation of Ariosto (*Orlando,* canto V, o. VIII).

\* \* \*

*A Prisoner of the Caucasus* was the first unsuccessful study of a character whom it was difficult for me to cope with; thanks to a few elegiac and descriptive verses, it was received better than anything else I have written.[6] But Nikolai and Alexander Raevsky and I laughed to our hearts' content at it.[7]

\* \* \*

*The Fountain of Bakhchisarai* is weaker than the *Prisoner* and, like it, echoes the reading of Byron, over whom I had gone out of my mind.[8] The scene of Zarema with Maria has dramatic merit. I don't think it was criticized. A. Raevsky roared at the following verses:

> Often in fateful battles
> He would raise his saber—and with a swing
> Suddenly remained motionless,
> Look madly around,
> Turned pale, etc.

Young writers in general do not know how to depict the physical movements of passions. Their heroes always tremble, laugh wildly, gnash their teeth, and so forth. All this is ridiculous, like a melodrama.

\* \* \*

I don't recall who remarked to me that it was improbable that robbers chained to each other could swim across a river. This entire event was real and happened in 1820 during my stay in Ekaterinoslav.[9]

\* \* \*

Our critics left me at peace for a long time. This does them honor: I was far from being in favorable circumstances. From habit they kept supposing I was a very young man. As I recall, the first hostile articles began to appear after the publication of the fourth and fifth cantos of *Eugene Onegin*. The critique of these chapters printed in the *Athenaeum* surprised me by its good tone, good style, and the strangeness of its quibbles. The most ordinary rhetorical figures and tropes stopped the critic: can one say "the glass bubbles" instead of "the wine bubbles in the glass," "the fireplace smokes" instead of "steam comes out of the fireplace"? Aren't "jealous suspicion" and "faithless ice" too bold? What do you think this would mean:

> . . . the children
> Resonantly cut the ice with skates.

The critic guessed, however, that this means: "the children run across the ice on skates." Instead of:

> On red feet a heavy goose
> (Intending to swim on the breast of the waters)
> Steps carefully on the ice.

The critic read:

> On red feet a heavy goose
> Intended to swim—

and accurately noted that one can't swim on red feet.

A few cases of poetic license: the accusative and not the genitive case after the negative particle *ne: vremjan* instead of *vremen* ["times"] (as for example in Batyushkov:[10]

> Now ancient Rus and the customs
> of Vladimir's times) *[vremjan]*

caused my critic great consternation. Most of all he was irritated by the line:

> *Ljudskuju molv' i konskij top*
> [People's talk and horses' clattering]

"Do we who have learned from the old grammars express ourselves like this, can one mangle the Russian language like this?"

Later this line was cruelly ridiculed in *The Messenger of Europe* too. *Molv'* [talk] is an indigenous Russian word. *Top* [clatter] instead of *topot* is just as often used as *sip* [hiss] instead of *sipen'e*. (As in the old Russian poem: "He let out a hiss *[sip]* like a snake.) Therefore *xlop* [clapping] instead of *xlopan'e* is not at all contrary to the spirit of the Russian language.

Besides, this entire line is not mine, but was taken whole from a Russian folk-tale:

> *I vysel on za vrata gradskie, i uslysal konskij top i ljudskuju molv'.* [And he emerged from the city gates, and he heard horses' clatter and people's talk.] *Bova Korolevich*

The study of ancient songs, folk-tales, etc. is essential for a complete knowledge of the qualities of the Russian language. It is in vain that our critics scorn them.

The line:

> *Dva veka ssorit' ne xocu*
> [I do not wish to argue for two centuries]

seemed incorrect to the critic. What does grammar say? That an active verb governed by a negative particle requires not the accusative, but the genitive case. For example: Ja *ne* pisu *stixov* [I don't write verse.]. But in my line of verse the verb *ssorit'* [to argue] is governed not by the particle *ne*, but by the verb *xocu* [I wish]. *Ergo,* the rule doesn't fit here. Let's take, for example, the following sentence: Ja *ne* mogu vam pozvolit' nacat' pisat' . . . *stixi* [I can't allow you to begin writing verse]—and, of course, not *stixov*. Can it be the electric force of the negative particle is supposed to pass through this whole chain of verbs and reverberate in the noun? I think not.

\* \* \*

It is now sixteen years since I began publishing, and the critics have pointed out five grammatical errors (real ones) in my poetry:

1. ostanovljal vzor na otdalennye gromady

2. na *teme* gor (temeni)
3. *voil* vmesto vyl
4. byl otkazan, vmesto *emu otkazali*
5. *igumenu* vmesto *igumnu*.

I was always sincerely grateful to them and always corrected the place that had been pointed out. I write prose considerable less correctly, and I speak still worse, almost as Mr. —— writes.

\* \* \*

The spoken language of the simple folk (who don't read foreign books and, thank God, don't express their thoughts in French as we do) is also worth the deepest studies. Alfieri studied Italian in a Florentine bazaar; it wouldn't be bad for us to occasionally listen to the Moscow candle-mongers. They speak an amazingly pure and correct language.

\* \* \*

Spies are like the letter "ъ." They are necessary only in a few cases, and even there one can get along without them—but they've gotten used to poking in everywhere.

\* \* \*

The omitted stanzas repeatedly gave rise to reproaches. There is no reason to be surprised that there are stanzas which I could not or did not want to print in *Eugene Onegin*. But, being omitted, they interrupt the connection of the story, and therefore the place where they belonged is designated. It would have been better to replace these stanzas with other ones or to rewrite and fuse together the ones which I did keep. But sorry, I'm too lazy for that. I humbly confess also that there are two omitted stanzas in *Don Juan*.

\* \* \*

In the journal which he started to publish, Mr. Fedorov, examining the 4th and 5th chapters rather favorably, pointed out to me, however, that in the description of autumn several of my lines in a row begin with the particle *Uz* [already], which he called "*uz*'s," but which is called *anaphora* in rhetoric. He also condemned the word *korova* [cow] and reprimanded me for calling noble and, apparently, high-ranking misses *devconki* [girls] (which of course is impolite), while calling a simple country lass *deva* [maiden]:

> V izbuske raspevaja, deva
> Prjadet . . .
> [Singing in a hut, the maiden spins . . .]

\* \* \*

No critique was written on the sixth canto; even in *The Messenger of Europe* the Latin misprint wasn't noticed. Apropos: since I left the Lycée I haven't opened a Latin book and have completely forgotten Latin. Life is short; there's no time to re-read. Remarkable books crowd one upon the other, and today no one writes them in Latin. In the fourteenth century, on the other hand, Latin was essential and was justly regarded as the first sign of an educated man.

\* \* \*

I ran through the criticism of the seventh canto in *The Northern Bee* when I was visiting someone and at a moment when I wasn't in the mood for *Onegin*. . . . I noticed only very well written verses and a rather amusing joke about the beetle. In my work it is said:

> It was evening. The sky grew dark. Waters
> Flowed quietly. A beetle buzzed.

The critic was gladdened by the appearance of this new personage and expected from him a character better sustained than the others. It seems, however, that there was not a single sensible observation or critical thought. I didn't read any other criticisms, for, really, I wasn't in the mood for them.

N.B. The criticism in *The Northern Bee* was ascribed to Mr. Bulgarin in vain: (1) the poetry in it is too good, (2) the prose is too weak, (3) Mr. Bulgarin wouldn't say that the description of Moscow is taken from *Ivan Vyzhigin*, because Mr. Bulgarin doesn't say that the tragedy *Boris Godunov* is taken from his novel.[11]

\* \* \*

The jokes of our critics sometimes amaze one by their naïveté. Here's a true anecdote: one of our younger comrades in the Lycée (he should not be remembered just for this joke), a good lad, but rather simple and last in every class, one day composed two little verses well-known to the entire Lycée:

> *Xa xa xa, xi xi xi*
> *Del'vig piset stixi.*
> [Ha ha ha, he, he he
> Delvig writes poetry.]

What was it like for us, Delvig and I, to find the following joke in the first issue of the pompous *Messenger of Europe* for 1830: "The almanac *Northern Flowers* is divided in prose and poetry—he, he!" Imagine how gladdened we were by our old acquaintance. That's not all. This "he, he" apparently seemed so ingenious that it was reprinted with great praise in *The Northern Bee*: "he, he, as *The Messenger of Europe* said with such wit" etc.

\* \* \*

Speaking of Delvig in an eloquent and thought-filled survey of our literature, young Kireevsky employed this refined expression: "His ancient muse is sometimes covered by the padded jacket of modern despondency." An amusing expression, of course. Why not simply have said: "Sometimes the despondency of modern poetry is echoed in Delvig's verse."—Our journalists, against whom Mr. Kireevsky reacted rather discourteously, were gladdened; they picked up this padded jacket, ripped it to shreds, and for a year now they have been sporting it, trying to make their public laugh. Let's suppose one and the same joke succeeds for them every time—what profit do they get from that! The public has almost nothing to do with literature, and the small number of those who love it ultimately believes not in a joke which is unceasingly repeated, but in the opinions of sensible criticism and dispassionateness which are constantly, if slowly, clearing a path.

## II

Of *The Gypsies*[12] one lady remarked that there is only one honorable person in the entire poem, and that's the bear. The late Ryleev was indignant that Aleko should lead a bear and collect money from a gawking public besides. Vyazemsky repeated the same remark. (Ryleev asked me to make at least a blacksmith of Aleko, which would have been far nobler.) Best of all would have been to make him a civil servant of the eighth class or a landowner, not a gypsy. True, in that case there would have been no poem at all, *ma tanto meglio*.

\* \* \*

My tragedy will probably have no success.[13] The journals are infuriated with me. I no longer have the main attraction for the public—a literary name which is young and novel. Besides, the main scenes have already been printed or distorted in other people's *imitations*. Opening Mr. Bulgarin's historical novel at random I found that in his work Prince V. Shuisky comes to announce the appearance of the Pretender to the Tsar. In my work Boris Godunov talks alone with Basmanov about the destruction of the *mestnichestvo*—in Mr. Bulgarin's the same thing. All of this is dramatic invention, not a historical story.

\* \* \*

Among other literary accusations, I was rebuked for the overly dear price of *Eugene Onegin*, and terrible greediness was seen in this. It is all right for someone who has never in his life sold his works or whose works have never been sold to say this, but how could the publishers of *The Northern Bee* repeat this fine accusation? The price is fixed not by the writer, but by the booksellers. With respect to poems, the number of those who want them is limited. They are the ones who pay five rubles for a seat in the theater. The booksellers who have bought an entire edition for, let us suppose, a ruble a copy could nevertheless sell it for five rubles. True, in that case the author could undertake a second, cheap edition, but then the bookseller himself could lower his price and thus doom the new edition. These business deals are very well known to us bourgeois writers. We know that the cheapness of a book does not prove the unselfishness of the author, but either the great demand for it or the total stoppage of sales. I ask: which is more profitable—to print 20,000 copies of one book and sell them for 50 kopeks apiece, or to print 200 copies and sell them for 50 rubles?

The price of the last edition of Krylov's fables, who is in all respects our most national poet *(le plus national et le plus populaire)*, does not contradict what we have said. Fables (like novels) are read by the writer, the merchant, the society person, the lady, the maid, and children. But only lovers of poetry read a lyric poem. And are there many of them?

\* \* \*

We've gotten so used to reading childish criticism that it doesn't even amuse us.[14] But what would we say, for example, on reading the following critique of Racine's *Phaedra* (if, unfortunately, a Russian wrote it in our time):

> There is nothing more repulsive than the subject the author has chosen. A married woman, the mother of a family, fallen in love with a young dolt, her husband's step-son (!!!!). What indecency! She is not ashamed to confess her lewd passion to his face (!!!!). That's not all. Using the stupid gullibility of her husband for evil, the fury tells a vile cock-and-bull story about the innocent Hippolyte, one which we daren't even explain—out of re-

spect for our feminine readers!!! The wretched, evil old man, without checking the details, without analyzing the matter, curses his very own son (!!)—after which Hippolyte is crushed by horses (!!!); Phaedra poisons herself, her vile confidante drowns herself and—period. And that's what writers write without blushing, writers who etc. (here there are personalities and abuse); that's the kind of lewdness our literature has got to, a bloodthirsty lewd witch with warts on her face!

—I refer the critics to their own conscience. Isn't this the way, though with a more flowery style, that critics dismantle works every day[15]—true, not ones equal in merit to Racine's works, but surely not a bit less reprehensible than them in a moral respect? We ask: should one and can one answer such criticisms seriously, even if they were written in Latin and their friends call this profundity?

If *The Minor*, that single monument of national satire, *The Minor* which once enraptured Catherine and all her brilliant court, if *The Minor* appeared in our time, ridiculing Fonvizin's spelling in our journals, they would comment with horror that Prostakova curses Palashka[16] calling her a "rascal" and a "daughter of a dog," and compares herself with a "bitch"(!!). "What will ladies say!" the critic would exclaim, "why this comedy could end up in ladies' hands!" —Awful, really! What a delicate and fastidious language these gentlemen must use with ladies!

But our ladies (God be their judge) don't listen to them and don't read them, but they do read that coarse W. Scott, who simply doesn't know how to replace simple colloquialism with simple-mindedness.

## III

*Count Nulin* caused me a great deal of trouble.[17] It was found (if I may say it) obscene—in the journals, of course—in society it was favorably received—and none of the journalists wanted to stand up for it. A young man dares to enter a young woman's bedroom at night and gets a slap in the face from her! How awful! How dare one write such repulsive filth? The author asks what Petersburg ladies would have done in Natalya Pavlovna's place: what impudence! Apropos of my poor tale (written, be it said in passing, in the most sober and decent manner), all of classical antiquity and all of European literature was raised against me! I believe in the bashfulness of my critics; I believe that *Count Nulin* really does seem reprehensible to them. But how can one bring up the ancients when speaking of decency? Can it be they know only by name the authors of the comic tales of Ariosto, Boccaccio, La Fontaine, Casti,[18] Spenser, Chaucer, Wieland,[19] Byron? Can it be that they haven't at least read Bogdanovich[20] and Dmitriev?[21] What unhappy pedant will dare to rebuke *Dushenka* for immorality and indecency? What gloomy fool will start pompously condemning "The Fashionable Wife," that charming model of a light, comic story? And the erotic poems of Derzhavin, the great, innocent Derzhavin? But now we will put aside inequality of poetic merit. *Count Nulin* must yield to them in both the license and the verve of the jests.

These critics found a strange way to judge the degree of morality of any poem. One of them has a 15-year old niece, another has a 15-year old female acquaintance—and everything which by the determination of their parents they are still not permitted to read is declared indecent, immoral, and obscene etc.! As if literature exists only for 16-year old girls. The prudent instructor probably doesn't let them—or even their brothers—have the complete collected works of a single classical poet, especially an ancient one. Readers, selected passages, and such like are published for that. But the public is not a 15-year old maiden and not a 13-year old boy. It, thank God, can safely read itself the tales of the good La Fontaine and the eclogues of the good Virgil, and everything that the critics themselves read when by themselves, if our critics read anything besides the galley-proofs of their own journals.

All these gentlemen so touchy about decency recall Tartuffe shyly placing the handkerchief on Dorine's open bosom, and deserve the maid's amusing objection:

> Vous êtes donc bien tendre à la tentation
> Et la chair sur vos sens fait grande impression!
> Certes, je ne sais pas quelle chaleur vous monte:
> Mais à convoîter, moi, je ne suis point si prompte,
> Et je vous verrais nu, du haut jusques en bas
> Que toute votre peau ne me tenterait pas.

\* \* \*

In *The Messenger of Europe* they spoke indignantly about the comparison of Nulin to a tomcat snatching *[capcarapst-vujuscij]* a female cat (an amusing verb: *capcarapstvuju, capcarapstvues', capcarapstvuet*). Actually, there is no such comparison anywhere in *Count Nulin*, just as there is no such verb; but even if there were, so what?

\* \* \*

An immoral work is one the aim or effect of which is to subvert the rules on which social happiness or human worth are based. Poems whose aim is to fire the imagination with sensual descriptions debase poetry, turning its divine nectar into an aphrodisiac compound, and its muse into a repulsive Canidia.[22] But a joke inspired by sincere gaiety and the momentary play of imagination can seem immoral only to those who have a childish or obscure concept of morality; they confuse it with moralizing and see in literature only a pedagogical occupation.

\* \* \*

Apropos: I began to write at 13 and to print at almost the same time. There is much I would like to destroy as unworthy even of my talent, whatever it may be. There is other work which is heavy on my conscience, like a rebuke. . . .[23] At least I don't have to answer for the re-printing of the sins of my adolescence, and all the less other people's pranks. In the almanac published by Mr. Fedorov, among some verses of mine—found God knows where—there is printed an *Idyll* written in the style of the plagiarist of Mr. Panaev's poetry. In the preface to some journal Mr. Bestuzhev thanks some Mr. An. for making the poems available, explaining that not all were worth printing.

This Mr. An. had no right to dispose of my poems, to re-write them his own way, and to send to Mr. Bestuzhev's alma-nac, along with his own works, poetry which I had condemned to oblivion or which was not written for print (for example, "She is dear, I'll say between us") or which it was excusable for me to write at 18, but inexcusable to acknowledge publicly at a more mature and prudent age (for example, "Epistle to Yuriev").

\* \* \*

Re-reading the most abusive critiques I find them so amus-ing that I do not understand how I could have been vexed by them; it seems that if I wanted to ridicule them, I could think of nothing better than to reprint them without any comment. How-ever, I have noted that among us the stupidest invective gains weight from the magic influence of printing. To us the "printed page still seems sacred."[24] We still think: how can this be stupid or incorrect, why, it's printed!

\* \* \*

*Habent sua fata libelli.*[25] *Poltava* had no success. It probably wasn't worth it; but I was spoiled by the reception given my earlier—and much weaker—works; besides, it is a completely original work, and I will bet on that.

Our critics[26] tried to explain the reason for my failure to me —and here's how.

First, they informed me that no one had ever seen a woman fall in love with an old man, and that therefore Maria's love for the old hetman (N.B. proven historically) could not exist.

> Well, what about you, Cheston?
> Though I know, I don't believe.[27]

I couldn't be satisfied by this explanation; love is the most capricious passion. I won't even speak of ugliness and stupidity, which are daily preferred to youth, intellect, and beauty. Remember the mythological legends of Ovid's *Metamorphoses*—Leda, Filira,[28] Pasiphaë,[29] Pygmalion—and admit that all these fictions are not foreign to poetry. And Othello, the old Negro who captivated Desdemona with the stories of his travels and battles? . . . And Myrrha, who inspired the Italian with one of his best tragedies? . . .[30]

Maria (or Matrena), they told me, was carried away by vanity, but not love: it is a great honor for the daughter of a supreme judge to be the concubine of a hetman! Next they told me that my Mazeppa was an "evil and stupid old man." That I depicted Mazeppa as evil I confess: I do not find him good, especially at the moment when he is arranging for the execution of the father of the girl whom he has seduced. And the stupidity of a man shows up either in his acts or in his words: in my poem Mazeppa acts exactly as in history, and his speeches explain his historical character. It was pointed out to me that my Mazeppa was too malevolent, that a Ukrainian hetman is not a schoolboy and wouldn't want vengeance for a slap in the face or having his moustache pulled. Again history is rejected by literary criticism —again "Though I know, I don't believe!" Mazeppa, educated in Europe at a time when concepts of noble honor were at their highest level of power—Mazeppa could long remember the Moscow Tsar's insult and take revenge on him when the occasion arose. In this trait is his entire character—secretive, cruel, consistent. Pulling a Polak or Cossack by the moustache was just the same as grabbing a Russian by the beard. As I recall, for all the insults which he had suffered, Khmelnitzky—by the sentence of the *Rzecz pospolita*—received as retribution the chopped-off moustache of his enemy (cf. *The Konisky Chronicle*).

In my poem, foreseeing failure, the old hetman, alone with his confidante, curses the young Charles, and calls him, as I recall, a little brat and madcap. The critics solemnly reproached *me* for a groundless opinion of the Swedish king. Somewhere in my work it is said Mazeppa was not attached to anyone: the critics cited the hetman's *own words,* assuring Maria that he loved her "more than glory, more than power." How can one answer such criticisms?

The words "moustache," "screech," "get up," "Mazeppa," and "it's time" *[usy, vizzat', vstavaj, Mazepa, ogo, pora]* seemed to the critics *low,* barge-haulers' expressions. What are you going to do!

In *The Messenger of Europe* it was noted that the title of the poem was erroneous, and that I probably didn't call it Mazeppa so as not to recall Byron. Correct, but there was another reason for this too—the epigraph. Thus, in the manuscript *The Fountain of Bakhchisarai* was called *The Harem,* but the melancholy epigraph (which is, of course, better than the whole poem) seduced me.

However, apropos of *Poltava* the critics referred to Byron's *Mazeppa*—but how they understood that! Byron knew Mazeppa only from Voltaire's *History of Charles XII.* He was struck only by the picture of a man attached to a wild horse and plunging across the steppes. A poetic picture, of course, and then look what he made of it. But don't try to find either Mazeppa or Charles there—or the dark, hateful, tormenting character who appears in almost all Byron's works, but who (to the misfortune of one of my critics), as if on purpose, is not in *Mazeppa.* Byron didn't even think about them; he exhibited a row of pictures, one more striking than the next—and that's all. But what a fiery creation! What a broad, quick brush! If the story of the seduced daughter and executed father had fallen under his pen, probably no one would dare to touch this horrifying subject after him.

\* \* \*

Reading these lines in *Voynarovsky*[31] for the first time:

> The wife of the sufferer Kochubey
> And their daughter who had been seduced,

I was amazed how the poet could pass over such a horrifying situation.

It is neither wise nor magnanimous to burden historical characters with fictitious horrors. Slander, even in poems, has always seemed to me unpraiseworthy. But it would be even more unforgivable to omit such a striking historical feature in a description of Mazeppa! Not a single kind, benevolent emotion! Not a single consolatory feature! Seduction, enmity, treason, slyness, cowardice, ferocity. . . . Delvig was surprised that I could work with such a subject. Strong characters and a deep, tragic shadow cast across all these horrors—that is what fascinated me. I wrote *Poltava* in a few days; I couldn't have worked on it any longer—I would have given the whole thing up.[32]

\* \* \*

It was said officially in one newspaper that I am a bourgeois in the nobility.[33] It would be more accurate to say a nobleman in the bourgeoisie. My family is one of the most ancient of the nobility. We descend from the Prussian Radshi, or Rachi, a nobleman (an honorable man, says the chronicler), who came to Russia during the rule of Saint Alexander Yaroslavich Nevsky (cf. *The Russian Chronicler* and *The History of the Russian State*). The Pushkins, Musin-Pushkins, Bobrishchev-Pushkins, Buturlins, Myatlevs, Povodovs, and others were descended from him. Karamzin mentions just the Musin-Pushkins (out of courtesy to the late Count Alexei Ivanovich). Among the small number of noble families which survived the bloody disfavors of Ivan Vasilevich, the historiographer names the Pushkins. During the reign of Boris Godunov the Pushkins were persecuted and offended in an obvious manner in the quarrels with the *mestnichestvo*. G. G. Pushkin, the same who appears in my tragedy, belongs in the number of the most remarkable personages of that epoch—which is so rich in historical characters. During the interregnum another Pushkin, heading a separate army, was alone with Izmailov in "doing his task honorably" (in Karamzin's words). Four Pushkins signed the electoral letter at the election of the Romanovs as Tsars, and one of them, a high official, signed the Zemsky Sobor act to do away with the *mestnichestvo* (which does him little honor). During Peter's reign they were in the opposition, and one of them, the *stolnik*[34] Fedor Alexeevich, was mixed up in Tsikler's plot and was executed along with him and Sokovnin. My great-grandfather was married to the youngest daughter of Admiral Count Golovin, the first Andreevsky cavalier etc. in Russia. He died very young and in prison—having stabbed his wife (in a fit of jealousy or madness) when she was in labor. His only son, my grandfather Lev Alexandrovich, remained faithful to Peter III during the revolt of 1762; he did not want to swear allegiance to Catherine and was put in a fortress along with Izmailov (a strange fate for these names!). Cf. Ruhlière[35] and Castéra.[36] In two years he was released by Catherine's order and always enjoyed her respect. He never entered the service again and lived in Moscow and on his estates.

If being a nobleman of ancient descent means I am imitating an English poet, it is extremely involuntary imitation. But what is there in common between a lord's attachment to his feudal properties and unselfish respect for dead forefathers whose past fame can provide us with neither rank nor patronage? Because now our nobility is made up for the most part of new families who began their existence when the Emperors were already ruling.

But no matter whom I descended from—from *raznochintsy*[37] who entered the nobility, or from a historical family of boyars, one of the most ancient Russian families, from ancestors whose name is found on almost every page of our history—the nature of my ideas would in no way depend on this; and though up until now I have not revealed it anywhere, and it is no one's business—nevertheless, I have not the slightest intention of renouncing it.

No matter what the nature of my ideas was, I would never share democratic hate for the nobility with anyone. It has always seemed to me an essential and natural class for a great and cultured people. Looking around myself and reading our old chronicles, I was sorry to see how the ancient noble families were destroyed, how the remaining ones are falling into decline and disappearing, how new families, new historical names which have taken the place of the former ones, are already falling into decline unprotected by anything, and how a noble name, progressively more and more debased, finally became a subject of gossip and the laughing-stock of the *raznochintsy* who became nobles, and even of idle buffoons!

An educated Frenchman or Englishman values the line of an old chronicle in which the name of his ancestor is mentioned, an honorable knight who fell in such-and-such a battle or in such-and-such a year returning from Palestine; but the Kalmuks have neither a nobility nor a history. Savagery, baseness, and ignorance do not respect the past; they grovel before the present. And among us, some descendants of Rurik value their second uncle's star more than the history of their house, i.e. the history of the fatherland. And people consider this a merit in him! Of course there is merit higher than nobility of family, to be specific: personal merit. But I have seen Suvorov's[38] genealogical tree, written by himself; Suvorov did not scorn his noble descent.

The names Minin and Lomonosov together outweigh, perhaps, all our ancient genealogies. But would it be ridiculous for their descendants to be proud of these names?

*Note.* Let us be just: Mr. Polevoi[39] cannot be reproached for base servility before nobles; on the contrary, we are prepared to accuse him of youthful arrogance which respects neither age, nor rank, nor glory, and which insults both the memory of the dead and relations to the living.

\* \* \*

In another newspaper they declared that my looks are very unprepossessing, and that my portraits are too flattering. I did not answer this personality, although it hurt me deeply.

\* \* \*

Some say: what business is it of the critic or the reader whether I am good or bad-looking, an ancient nobleman or a *raznochinets,* good or evil, whether I have good legs or don't even bow with them, whether I play cards and so forth. My future biographer, should God send me a biographer, will not worry about this. And the critic's and reader's business is my book—and that's all. A superficial judgment, I think. The attacks on writers and the defenses to which they give rise are basically an important step toward the publicity of debates about so-called public figures *(hommes publics),* toward one of the main prerequisites of highly cultured societies. In this respect, even writers who justly deserve our scorn, vilifiers and slanderers, are of real use: little by little respect for the personal honor of a citizen forms, and the might of public opinion increases—might on which the purity of morals of an enlightened people is founded.

In this way the brigade of scholars and writers, no matter what kind they are, is always in the vanguard of all enlightenment's raids and education's sieges. They should not faint-heartedly be indignant that they are eternally destined to bear the first shots and all the adversities, all the dangers.

[1830, unpublished]

## N O T E S

1. *"A Singer in the Camp of Russian Warriors" (1812).*
2. *Molière's* Misanthrope, *Act I, Scene II.*
3. *S. Raich said this of* Onegin *in* Galatea *(No. 14, 1830).*

4. Ruslan and Ludmila *(1820)—Pushkin's first long (six cantos) poem started a polemic to which historians of literature have attributed considerably more significance than Pushkin did. The erotic "jokes" or pranks which he mentions seem very tame now—such things as the "Russian" bogatyr Ratmir being given a bath by twelve tremulous maidens. Pushkin interrupts the scene at the crucial point.*

5. *A long poem by Zhukovsky.*

6. *The hero of* A Prisoner of the Caucasus *(1822) is one of the many dejected descendants of René, Adolphe, Childe Harold, and other more fiery Byronic creations.*

7. *Alexander N. and Nikolai N. Raevsky—During his exile to the South, Pushkin met the family of General Nikolai Raevsky; his two sons became fairly close friends of Pushkin.*

8. *The Fountain of Bakhchisarai (written 1821–23, published 1824)—a loosely-constructed narrative poem (the story of a Polish maiden's imprisonment in the harem of Khan Girey) which echoes such Byronic exotica as* The Giaour, The Corsair, *and* The Bride of Abydos.

*Zhirmunsky's* Byron and Pushkin *(Leningrad, 1924) is the most complete study on this subject.*

9. *The incident occurs in the unfinished poem* Robber Brothers *(written in 1821–22), a fragment of which was printed in 1825.*

10. *Konstantin N. Batyushkov (1778–1855)—a dulcet-tongued elegiac poet whose mature style often resembles that of the early Pushkin.*

11. *Of course, Pushkin knew it was Bulgarin's criticism* (The Northern Bee, *No. 35 and No. 39, 1830).*

*Bulgarin had secretly served as censor of the MS of* Boris Godunov *(at a time when Tsar Nikolai was supposedly Pushkin's personal censor). He recommended that it be made into a novel in the manner of Walter Scott. The MS was proscribed. Bulgarin then wrote his* Vyzhigin, *borrowing from the play he had underhandedly kept out of print.*

12. *A narrative and dramatic poem written in 1824–25 (published in full in 1827). Aleko, the sullen and world-weary hero, abandons the empty sophistication of the North to join a band of Bessarabian gypsies. A trained bear provides Aleko's income.*

13. Boris Godunov.

14. *In the variants Pushkin wrote: "Not long ago one of our critics, comparing Shakespeare and Byron, counted on his fingers— where are there more corpses, in the tragedy of one or the tale of the other. That is what he supposed the essential difference between them to be. The opinion of our critics about morality and decency is very amazingly amusing if you examine it. Do you want to know how Racine's* Phaedra *would be criticized here?"*

15. *This review of* Phaedra *is a parody of Nadezhdin's critique of* Count Nulin *and Baratynsky's* The Ball.
*But the parody has a second application which Soviet Pushkinologists have never noted. It is aimed at Voltaire as well. In the third part of his lengthy* Dissertation sur la tragédie, *the preface to* Sémiramis *(1748), Voltaire wrote of* Hamlet:

> C'est une pièce grossière et barbare, qui ne serait pas supportée par la plus vile populace de la France et de l'Italie. Hamlet y devient fou au second acte, et sa maîtresse devient folle au troisième; le prince tue le père de sa maîtresse, feignant de tuer un rat, et l'héroïne se jette dans la rivière. On fait sa fosse sur le théâtre; des fossoyeurs disent des quolibets dignes d'eux, en tenant dans leurs mains des têtes de morts; le prince Hamlet répond à leurs grossièretés abominables par des folies non moins dégoûtantes. Pendant ce temps-là, un des acteurs fait la conquête de la Pologne. Hamlet, sa mère, et son beau-père, bouvent ensemble sur le théâtre: on chante à table, on s'y querelle, on se bat, on se tue. On croirait que cet ouvrage est le fruit de l'imagination d'un sauvage ivre.

*Pushkin uses this drunken savage in "The Last of Joan of Arc's Relatives." See below, p. 227.*

16. *Eremeevna, not Palashka.*

17. Count Nulin *was published with Baratynsky's* The Ball *in 1828. Both were attacked by Nikolai Nadezhdin in* The Messenger of Europe. *(See below, "A Remark about* Count Nulin.*")*

18. *Giovanni Battista Casti (1724–1803)—Italian-born poet. His travels in Russia helped inspire his* Poema Tataro *(1803) describing the court of Catherine II. His licentious* Animali Parlanti *may also have appealed to Pushkin.*

19. *Wieland, see below, p. 171.*

20. *Ippolit F. Bogdanovich (1743–1803)—a poet. His best-known work was a burlesque entitled* Dushenka.

21. *Ivan I. Dmitriev (1760–1837)—a bad poet of the older generation whom it was customary to treat politely in print. "The Fashionable Wife" is his work.*

22. *A Neapolitan, beloved by Horace. When she deserted him, he held her up to contempt (in the* Epodes*) as an old sorceress who could by a rhomb unsphere the moon.*

23. *Pushkin probably had in mind his* Gavriiliada *(1821), a charmingly blasphemous narrative, and* Tsar Nikita and His Forty Daughters *(1825). The latter has since been translated and published (slightly censored) as a* Playboy *ribald classic.*

24. *A slightly altered quotation from a satire by Dmitriev.*

25. *A line from the poet and prosodist Terentianus Maurus (3rd century* A.D.*).*

26. *Bulgarin and Nadezhdin.*

27. *From* The Braggart, *a neoclassical comedy by Yakov Knyazhnin (1742–91).*

28. *Philyra—lover of Kronos, she was changed into a horse during intercourse and gave birth to the centaur. Then she became a linden tree.*

29. *Pasiphaë—wife of Minos, lover of his bull, mother of the Minotaur.*

30. *Count Alfieri wrote his strictly neoclassical* Mirra *(1791) on this theme.*

31. *A narrative poem (1825) by Kondraty Ryleev. This was one of Ryleev's* dumy *(historical songs) which Pushkin suggested derived from the German* dumm *rather than the Ukrainian* duma *(thought).*

32. *Pushkin began* Poltava *on April 5, 1828, completed the first canto on October 3, the second October 9, and the third October 16.*

33. *In* The Northern Bee *(No. 94, 1830). Bulgarin made several slanderous remarks about Pushkin and the aristocratic writers of* The Literary Gazette, *telling an anecdote about how "a Negro was bought for a bottle of rum."*

34. *A court rank below boyar in pre-seventeenth century Russia.*

35. *Claude Carloman de Rulhière (1735–91)—author of* Histoire de Pologne *and* Anecdotes sur la révolution de Russie en 1762, *etc.*

36. *Jean Castéra—author of* Histoire de Cathérine II, impératrice de la Russie.

37. *Men from various non-noble backgrounds (sons of merchants, clerks, priests, etc.).*

38. *Alexander Suvorov (1730–1800)—Russia's most eccentric and celebrated general.*

39. *Nikolai A. Polevoi (1796–1846)—journalist, writer, historian, editor of* The Moscow Telegraph.

# ON ALFRED DE MUSSET

**While the mellifluous but monotonous Lamartine was preparing** pious new "Meditations" under the meritorious title *Harmonies réligieuses,* while the influential Victor Hugo was publishing his brilliant though strained "Eastern Poems" *(Les Orientales),* while the poor sceptic Delorme[1] was being resurrected in the guise of a reforming neophyte, and strictness of morality and decorum was promulgated in a mandate to all of French literature, suddenly a new poet appeared with a little book of tales and songs and created a terrible scandal.[2] Musset, it seems, took upon himself the obligation of singing only mortal sins, murders, and fornication. In vividness, the voluptuous scenes with which his poems are filled perhaps eclipse the most explicit descriptions of the late Parny.[3] He doesn't even think about morality, he ridicules didacticism—and, unfortunately, in an extremely attractive way. He stands on as little ceremony as possible with the solemn Alexandrine; he fractures and mangles it so that it's a horror and pity. He sings the moon[4] in verses that no one would have dared, except perhaps a poet of the blissfully simple XVI century, when neither Boileau nor Messrs. La Harpe, Hoffman, and Colnet[5] yet existed. And how was the young prankster received? He should have been terrified. You would expect to see the indignation of the journals and all the ferules raised against him. Not at all. The candid prank of the amiable rake was so surprising, so pleasing, that not only did the critics not abuse him, but they took it upon themselves to justify him; they declared that the "Spanish Tales" prove nothing, that one may describe robbers and murderers without even having the aim of explaining how unpraiseworthy their craft is—and still be a good and honorable man, that a twenty-year old poet may be forgiven vivid scenes of pleasures, that when reading his poetry his family probably would not share the horror of the newspapers and see a monster in him, that, in one word, poetry is fantasy and has nothing in common with the prosaic truth of life. Glory to God! It ought to have been thus long ago, dear sirs. Isn't it strange to resurrect in the XIXth century the finickiness and hypocrisy once ridiculed by Molière and treat the public as grown-ups treat children, not to permit it to read the books which you yourself enjoy, and to paste didacticism onto everything, whether apropos or inapropos? The public thinks this ludicrous, and surely it will no longer say thanks to its guardians.

As we have already said, the Italian and Spanish tales are characterized by extraordinary vividness. Of these, I think *Porcia*[6] has the most merit: the night rendezvous scene, the portrait of the jealous man whose hair has suddenly turned grey, the conversation of the two lovers on the sea—all this is charming. The dramatic sketch *Les Marrons du feu* promises France a romantic tragedian. And in the story *Mardoche*[7] Musset is the first of the French poets to grasp the tone of Byron's comic verses—which is not at all a joke. If we are going to understand the words of Horace as the English poet* understood them, we will agree with his opinion: it is difficult to express ordinary subjects properly.

[1830, unpublished]

# N O T E S

1. *A poet invented by Sainte-Beuve. See below, p. 140.*

2. *Musset's first collection of poems was entitled* Contes d'Espagne et d'Italie *(1830).*

* In the epigraph to *Don Juan*:

*Difficile est proprie communia dicere.*

*Communia* means not ordinary subjects, but ones *common to all* (he is talking about tragic subjects which are well-known to everyone, common —in contrast to invented subjects. Cf. *ad Pisones*). The subject of *Don Juan* belongs exclusively to Byron.

3. *Evariste Désiré Desforges, Chevalier de Parny (1753–1814). His mildly salacious Anacreontic strain appealed to Pushkin.*

4. *Musset's* Ballade à la lune *begins:*

> C'était dans la nuit brune,
> Sur le clocher jauni,
>     La lune,
> Comme un point sur un i.

5. *François B. Hoffman (1760–1828) and Charles Colnet de Ravel (1768–1832).*

6. *One of the Italian tales, some 450 Alexandrines.*

7. *A comic tale (with rhymes such as:* mots si doux—*I love you) which Musset wrote when his publisher told him 500 more lines would make possible a volume in octavo for* Contes d'Espagne et d'Italie.

# BARATYNSKY

**Baratynsky is among our finest poets. He is original in Russia** because he thinks. He would be original anywhere else, because he thinks in his own way, correctly and independently, while at the same time he feels strongly and profoundly. The harmony of his verse, freshness of style, liveliness and precision of expression have to strike anyone who is even a little endowed with taste and feeling. Besides the charming elegies and small poems which everyone knows by heart and are constantly being imitated so unsuccessfully, Baratynsky has written two tales which would win him fame in Europe, but in Russia were noticed only by connoisseurs.[1] The first, youthful works of Baratynsky were at one time received with rapture. The latest ones, which are more mature and closer to perfection, have had less success with the public. Let us try to explain the reasons.

This very maturity and process of perfecting his works must be considered the first reason. The ideas, feelings of an eighteen-year-old poet are still close and akin to everyone; young readers accept him, and with ecstasy they recognize in his works their own feelings and thoughts, expressed clearly, vividly, and harmoniously. But the years pass, the young poet matures, his talent grows, his ideas get more elevated, his feelings change. His songs are no longer the same. But the readers are the same and perhaps have just gotten colder in heart and more indifferent to the poetry of life. The poet is separated from them and little by little is completely isolated. He creates for himself, and if he occasionally publishes his works he meets coldness, inattention, and he finds a response to his sounds only in the hearts of a few admirers of poetry who are isolated, forgotten in society like him.

The second reason is the absence of criticism and public opinion. In Russia literature is not a national demand. Writers become well-known due to extraneous circumstances. The public is little interested in them. The class of readers is limited, and they are governed by journals which judge literature as they do political economy, and about political economy as they do music, i.e. randomly, by hearsay, without any basic rules and information, but for the most part by personal considerations. While he was the object of their ill-will, Baratynsky never defended himself, never answered a single journal article. It's true that it is rather difficult to justify oneself where there has been no accusation, and that, on the other hand, it is rather easy to scorn childish malice and street-corner sneers; nevertheless their judgments have definite effect.

The third reason: Baratynsky's epigrams—masterful, model epigrams—have not spared the rulers of the Russian Parnassus. Not only did our poet never descend to journal polemic and not once did he compete with our Aristarchs, in spite of the extraordinary force of his dialectic, but he could not keep himself from strongly expressing his opinion in these small satires which are so amusing and stinging. We dare not reproach him for them. It would be too great a pity if they did not exist.*

* The epigram defined by the legislator of French poetics:

Un bon mot de deux rimes orné,

This unconcern about the fate of his works, this unchanging indifference to success and praise, not only with regard to journalists, but also with regard to the public, is quite remarkable. Never did he try meanly to gratify the ruling taste and demands of momentary fashion; never did he resort to charlatanism, exaggeration to produce a big effect; never did he ignore thankless labor, which is rarely noticed, the labor of fine finishing and etching; never did he trail on the heels of the genius who captivated his age, picking up whatever he had dropped; he went on his own road, alone and independent. It is time for him to occupy a rank which belongs to him and stand beside Zhukovsky and above the singer of Penates and Tavrida.[2]

[1830, unpublished]

### N O T E S

1. *The two tales were* Eda *and* The Ball.
2. *The singer of Penates and Tavrida was Konstantin Batyushkov.*

# ON NATIONAL DRAMA AND ON
# *MARFA POSADNITSA*

**Although**[1] **since the time of Kant and Lessing esthetics has** developed with such clarity and breadth, we still remain with the concepts of the ponderous pedant Gottsched;[2] we still keep repeating that the *Beautiful* is an imitation of refined nature, and

---

soon grows old, and while it has a more vivid effect the first time—like every *bon mot*, it loses all its force with repetition. Contrariwise, in Baratynsky's less restricted epigram, satirical thought takes now a fairy-tale turn, now a dramatic one, and develops more freely, forcefully. Having smiled at it as a *bon mot*, we re-read it with pleasure as a work of art.

that the main value of art is *usefulness*. Why do we like painted statues less than purely marble or bronze ones? Why does the poet prefer to express his thoughts in verse? And what usefulness is there in Titian's Venus or Apollo Belvedere?

Verisimilitude is still considered the main condition and basis of dramatic art. What if it were proved to us that it is precisely dramatic art which excludes verisimilitude? Reading a poem or novel, we can often forget ourselves and suppose that the event being described is not fiction, but true. In an ode or elegy we can think that the poet was depicting his real emotions in real circumstances. But where is the verisimilitude in a building divided into two parts, one of which is filled with spectators who have agreed, etc. . . . .

\* \* \*

Even if we are going to suppose verisimilitude to be in a strict adherence to place, time, costume, and colors, we will see that the greatest dramatic writers have not submitted to this rule. In Shakespeare, Roman lictors retain the customs of London aldermen. In Calderón the brave Coriolanus challenges a consul to a duel and throws a glove at him. In Racine the half-Scythian Hippolyte speaks the language of a young, well-educated marquis. Corneille's Romans are essentially either Spanish knights or Gascon barons, and Corneille's Clytemnestra is accompanied by Swedish guards.[3] For all that, Calderón, Shakespeare, and Racine stand on an inaccessible summit, and their works are the perpetual subject of our studies and raptures. . . .

What kind of verisimilitude should we demand of a dramatic writer? For the resolution of this question let us first examine what drama is and what its purpose is.

Drama was born on the public square and was an entertainment for the people. The people, like children, demand interest, action. The drama presents to them a strange, unusual event. The people demand strong sensations; even an execution is a spectacle for them. Laughter, pity, and horror[4] are the three basic strings of our imagination which are moved by dramatic magic. But laughter quickly weakens, and it is impossible to base complete dramatic action on it alone. The ancient trage-dians ignored this mainspring. Folk satire possessed only this—and took on dramatic form more as parody.

Thus comedy, which advanced so much with time, was born. Let us note that high comedy is not based solely on laughter, but on the development of characters, and that not infrequently it comes close to tragedy.

Tragedy exhibited primarily heinous malefactions, super-natural sufferings, even physical ones (for example, Philoctetes, Oedipus, Lear). But custom dulls perception; imagination gets accustomed to murders and executions, it soon views them in-differently; but the depiction of passions and effusions of human souls are always new for it, always interesting, grand, and instructive. Drama began to manipulate the human soul and passions.

Truth of passions, verisimilitude of feelings in the proffered circumstances—that is what our intellect demands from the dramatic writer.

Drama left the public square and was transferred to palaces at the demand of an educated, select society. Poets moved to court. However, drama remains true to its original purpose—acting on the crowd, on the multitude, satisfying its curiosity. But at this point drama left a universally understandable lan-guage and assumed a fashionable, selected, refined idiom.

Hence the important difference between folk drama[5] (Shakespeare) and court drama (Racine). The creator of the folk tragedy was better educated than his spectators; he knew this and gave them his free-sweeping works with certainty of his own loftiness and the gratitude of the public (which he feels is implicit). At court, on the other hand, the poet felt himself lower than his public. The spectators were better educated than he—at least, he and they thought so. He did not devote himself freely and boldly to his fictions. He tried to divine the demands of the refined taste of people who were alien to him in status.

He feared insulting such-and-such a high rank, offending such-and-such of his haughty spectators—hence the finicality, the ridiculous pomposity which became proverbial *(un héros, un roi de comédie)*, the custom of viewing people of high status with a kind of servility and giving them a strange, inhuman manner of expression. In Racine, for example, Nero does not say simply: *"Je serai caché dans ce cabinet,"* but, *"Caché près de ces lieux je vous verrai, Madame."*[6] Agamemnon wakes up his confidant and says to him grandiloquently:

> Oui, c'est Agamemnon, c'est ton roi qui t'éveille.
> Viens, reconnais la voix qui frappe ton oreille.[7]

We have become accustomed to this; it seems to us it ought to be thus. But we must admit that we don't think it strange if the heroes in Shakespeare's tragedies talk like stablemen, because we feel that the aristocrats should express simple ideas as simple people do.

\* \* \*

It is not my purpose and I do not dare designate the good and bad points of this or that tragedy, to develop basic differences between the systems of Racine and Shakespeare, Calderón, and Goethe. I make haste to survey the history of dramatic art in Russia.

In our country drama has never been a demand of the common people. Rostovsky's mystery plays,[8] the tragedies of Tsarevna Sophia Alexeevna[9] were presented at the royal court and in the chambers of high-ranking boyars, and they were an unusual festival, not a normal entertainment. The first troupes which appeared in Russia did not attract the common people; they did not understand dramatic art and were not accustomed to its conventions. Sumarokov appeared, the most unfortunate of imitators. His tragedies, replete with absurdities, written in a barbaric effeminate language, pleased Elizaveta's court as a novelty, as an imitation of Parisian entertainments. These cold, flaccid works could not have any influence on the likes of the common people. Ozerov felt this. He attempted to give us a national tragedy[10] and imagined that for this it would be enough if he chose a subject from national history, forgetting that the poet of France took all the subjects for his tragedies from Roman, Greek, and Hebrew history, and that the most national tragedies of Shakespeare were borrowed by him from Italian novellas.

We still had no tragedy after *Dmitri Donskoy*, after *Pozharsky*,[11] works of immature talent. Katenin's *Andromache*[12] (perhaps the best work of our Melpomene in strength of true feelings, in truly magic spirit) still did not awaken the stage, emptied after Semenova, from its sleep.

The idealized *Ermak*,[13] a lyrical work of fiery young inspiration, is not a dramatic work. Everything in it is alien to our manners and spirit, everything—even the enchanting charm of the poetry itself.

Comedy was more fortunate. We have two dramatic satires.[14]

Why is it we do not have a national tragedy? It wouldn't hurt to decide whether or not it can exist. We saw that national tragedy was born in the public square, that it developed, and only afterward was called to aristocratic society. In our country it would be the other way around. We would want to lower the Sumarokovian court tragedy to the public square—but what obstacles!

Can our tragedy, which was developed on the example of the Racinian tragedy, become disaccustomed to its aristocratic habits? How is it to shift from its measured, pompous, and fastidious dialogue to the coarse frankness of our national passions, to the public square's license of statement? How is it to suddenly stand away from servility, how is it to get along without the rules to which it has become accustomed—unless there is a forcible accommodation of everything Russian to everything European; where, from whom will it learn an idiom understandable to the common people? What are the basic passions of this people, what are the strings of its heart, where will it find accord—in a word, where are the spectators, where is the public?

Instead of a public it will meet the same small limited circle and offend that circle's haughty customs *(dédaigneux)*; instead of accord, responsiveness, and applause it will hear trivial, captious criticism. Insuperable barriers will rise up before it; in order for it to set up its scaffolding it would be necessary to change and subvert the habits, manners, and ideas of whole centuries.

Before us, however, is an attempt at a national tragedy. . . .

\* \* \*

Before we start our critique of *Marfa Posadnitsa*, let us thank the unknown author for the conscientiousness of his work, a guarantee of his true talent. He wrote his tragedy not from considerations of self-love craving momentary success, not to please the general mass of readers, who are not only not prepared for romantic drama, but who are even absolutely hostile to it.\* He wrote his tragedy as a consequence of strong inner conviction, totally devoting himself to independent inspiration, isolating himself in his work. In the current state of our literature nothing truly worthy of attention can be produced without this self-sacrifice.

\* \* \*

The purpose of the author of *Marfa Posadnitsa* was to develop an important historical event—the fall of Novgorod—which decided the question of one ruler in Russia. History presented him with two great characters. First, Ivan, already sketched in all his cold and terrible greatness by Karamzin; second, Novgorod, the traits of which had to be divined. As dispassionate as fate, the dramatic poet had to depict the rebuff to perishing liberty as a carefully considered blow which set

---

\* We are not speaking of the journals whose sentences have decisive influence not only on the public, but even on the writers who, although they scorn them, are afraid of printed sneers and abuse.

Russia on her huge foundation—and he was served well by a study of the truth which was as honest as it was profound and conscientious, and by the vividness of his youthful, fiery imagination. He had to avoid being clever or tending to one side, sacrificing the other. It was the people of past days, their minds, their prejudices which had to speak in the tragedy—not the author, not his political opinions, nor his secret or open bias. It was not his task to justify or accuse, to prompt the speeches. It was his task to resurrect a past age in all its truth. Did the author of *Marfa Posadnitsa* fulfill these primary essential conditions?

We answer: he did, and if not everywhere, it was not his desire, nor his conviction, nor his conscience which betrayed him, but human nature—always imperfect.

Ivan is everywhere in the tragedy. His thought activates the entire machine, all the passions, all the mainsprings. In the first scene, Novgorod learns about his power-loving pretensions and about the unexpected campaign. The indignation, terror, difference of opinion, and confusion produced by this news already give an idea of his power. He has still not appeared, but already at this point we, like Marfa, feel his presence. The poet transfers us to the Muscovite bivouac amid the dissatisfied princes, amid the boyars and voevodas. Here too the thought of Ivan dominates and rules all thoughts, all passions. Here we see the power of his domination, the subdued rebelliousness of the independent princes, the terror cast on them by Ivan, the blind faith in his omnipotence. The princes freely and clearly understand his action, they foresee and declare elevated plans; the Novgorod emissaries await him. Ivan appears. His speech to the emissaries does not weaken the concept of him which the poet has succeeded in instilling. Cold, firm resolution, strong accusations, feigned magnanimity, a crafty statement of offenses. We really hear Ivan, we recognize the mighty intelligence of his ideas about the country, we hear the spirit of his age. Novgorod answers him in the person of its emissaries. What a scene! What historical accuracy! How the diplomacy of a Russian free city is divined! Ivan doesn't worry about whether they are right or not. He prescribes his final terms; meanwhile he is preparing for a decisive battle. But it is not with arms alone that the cautious Ivan acts. Treachery aids power. It seems to us that the scene between Ivan and the fictitious Boretsky does not hold up. The poet did not want to debase the Novgorod traitor completely—hence the insolence of his speeches and Ivan's undramatic (i.e. unrealistic) condescension. It will be said, "He is patient because he needs Boretsky." True, but Boretsky would not dare forget himself to his face, and the traitor would no longer speak the free language of a Novgorodian. But how fully, how calmly Ivan develops his ideas on how the nation should be governed! And, let us note, the candor—that is the best flattery of a ruler and the only one worthy of him. Ivan's last speech:

> Russian boyars,
> Leaders, princes, etc.

does not seem to us in the spirit of Ivan's reign. He does not need to fire their zeal, he wouldn't explain the reasons for his actions to them. "Enough words," he would tell them, "tomorrow's the battle, be ready."

Having learned his intentions, his thoughts, his mighty will, we part with Ivan, and we see him again when, as conqueror, he is silently entering Novgorod, which has been betrayed to him. His dispositions, transmitted to us by history, are preserved in the tragedy too, without fanciful additions, without explications. Marfa predicts family misfortunes for him and the demise of his dynasty. He answers:

> May what pleases the Lord come to pass!
> Having done my great deed I am at peace.

Such is the depiction of Ivan, a depiction which agrees with history, which holds up almost everywhere. In it the tragedian is not below his subject. He understands it clearly, correctly;

he knows it intimately and presents it to us without exaggeration, without nonsense, without charlatanism.

[1830, unpublished]

# N O T E S

1. *By Mikhail P. Pogodin (1800–75), professor of history at Moscow University, antiquarian, publicist, editor of* The Muscovite, *zealous Slavophil. The play was not published until 1832; Pushkin wrote his essay on the basis of the MS.*

2. *Johann Christoph Gottsched (1700–66)—professor, critic, and dramatist. With Breitinger and Bodmer, one of the dictators of German literary taste.*

3. *Pushkin has confused this with the fifth act of Racine's* Iphigénie en Aulide.

4. Uzhas *means horror or terror, but Pushkin probably had Aristotle's cathartic "pity" and "fear" in mind.*

5. Narodnaja drama—*folk, popular, national drama.*

6. Britannicus, *Act III, Scene 2.*

7. *The opening lines of* Iphigénie en Aulide.

8. *Dmitri, Metropolitan of Rostov—at Kiev's Mohila Academy he, like Feofan Prokopovich, wrote "school dramas."*

9. *Sophia Alexeevna—clever and cruel predecessor of Peter the Great on the Russian throne. She dabbled in literature.*

10. Dmitri Donskoy.

11. *A tragedy (1807) by one M. V. Kryukovsky.*

12. *Katenin's old-fashioned play was finished in 1818, published in 1827. —At a play in 1822, Katenin (a former Guards Colonel) hissed an actress he didn't like, and Count Miloradovich, the Governor-General of Petersburg, forbade his attending the theater there again.*

13. *Khomyakov's play.*

14. *Fonvizin's* The Minor *and Griboedov's* Woe from Wit.

# A REMARK ABOUT *COUNT NULIN*

**At the end of 1825 I was in the country. Re-reading** *Lucrece,* **a** rather weak poem by Shakespeare, I thought: what if it had occurred to Lucrece to give Tarquin a slap in the face? Perhaps it would have cooled his venturousness and he would have been forced to retreat in shame? Lucrece would not have cut her throat. Publius[1] wouldn't have gone insane, Brutus wouldn't have driven out the Caesars, and the world and the history of the world would be different.

Thus, for the republic, the consuls, the dictators, Catos, and Caesar we are indebted to a scandalous incident like one which happened not long ago in my neighborhood in the Novorzhevsky district.[2]

The thought of parodying history and Shakespeare presented itself. I could not resist the double temptation, and in two mornings I wrote the tale.

I have the habit of putting the year and date on my papers. *Count Nulin* was written the 13th and 14th of December. There are strange coincidences.[3]

[1830, unpublished]

## N O T E S

1. *Publius Valerius is mentioned only in the Argument of the poem. Perhaps Pushkin meant Collatine, as he is stunned by Lucrece's suicide (lines 1771–92).*

2. *Pushkin's rakish friend, Alexei Vulf, was courting a priest's wife rather hotly.*

3. *The Decembrist uprising took place on the fourteenth.*

# A REVIEW OF REVIEWS

**Some of our writers see Russian journals as representatives of** national enlightenment and directors of popular opinion, etc., and as a consequence of this they demand for them the kind of respect enjoyed by the *Journal des débats* and *Edinburgh Review*.

Define the meaning of words, said Descartes. In the sense accepted in Europe, a journal is the echo of an entire party; they are periodical pamphlets published by people well-known for their knowledge and talents. Each has its own political tendency, its influence on the order of things. The writing class is a breeding-ground for politicians; they know this, and intending to win popular opinion, they are afraid to lower themselves in the eyes of the public by unconscientiousness, instability, greed, or arrogance. Because of the great competition, ignorance or mediocrity cannot possess a monopoly of the journals, and a person without true talent will not survive *l'épreuve* of publication. Look who it is that publishes these opposing journals in France and in England. In the former it is Chateaubriand, Martignac,[1] Peyrronet[2]—in the latter Gifford, Jeffrey,[3] Pitt. What has this in common with our journals and journalists? I refer the matter to the private conscience of our literary people. I ask what right *The Northern Bee* has to govern the popular opinion of the Russian public, what voice the *Northern Mercury*[4] should have.

[1831, unpublished]

## N O T E S

1. *Jean-Batiste Martignac (1778–1832) held numerous important political offices.*

2. *Charles Peyrronet (1778–1854)—French publicist and politician.*

3. *Francis Jeffrey, Lord Jeffrey—Scottish judge, critic, founder and editor of the* Edinburgh Review *from 1802–1829.*

4. *A journal published in 1830–32 by M. A. Bestuzhev-Ryumin.*


## VIE, POÉSIES ET PENSÉES DE JOSEPH DELORME, PARIS 1829

## LES CONSOLATIONS, POESIES PAR SAINTE-BEUVE, PARIS 1830

**About two years ago a small book published under the title** *Vie, poésies et pensées de J. Delorme* attracted the attention of the critics and public in Paris.[1] In place of a preface, the life of the young poet, who died (as was asserted) in poverty and obscurity, was described in a romantic style. The friends of the deceased presented the poetry and thoughts found in his papers to the public, excusing the shortcomings and errors of Delorme himself by his youth, the unhealthy condition of his spirit, and his physical sufferings. There turned out to be an unusual talent in the poetry, one sharply reflected in the strange choice of subjects. Never in any language had naked spleen been expressed with such dry precision, never had the errors of a pitiful youth abandoned to the whim of passions been uttered with such disillusionment. Gazing at a stream shaded by the dark branches of trees, Delorme thinks about suicide in the following manner:

> Pour qui veut se noyer, la place est bien choisie.
> On n'aurait qu'à venir, un jour de fantaisie,
> A cacher ses habits au pied de ce bouleau,
> Et, comme pour un bain, à descendre dans l'eau:
> Non pas en furieux, la tête la première;
> Mais s'asseoir, regarder; d'un rayon de lumière
> Dans le feuillage et l'eau suivre le long reflet;

Puis, quand on sentirait ses esprits au complet,
Qu'on aurait froid, alors, sans plus traîner la fête,
Pour ne plus la lever, plonger avant la tête,
C'est là mon plus doux voeu, quand je pense à mourir.
J'ai toujours été seul à pleurer, à souffrir;
Sans un coeur près du mien j'ai passé sur la terre;
Ainsi que j'ai vécu, mourons avec mystère,
Sans fracas, sans clameurs, sans voisins assemblés.
L'alouette, en mourant, se cache dans les blés;
Le rossignol, qui sent défaillir son ramage,
Et la bise arriver, et tomber son plumage,
Passe invisible à tous, comme un écho du bois:
Ainsi je veux passer. Seulement, un . . . deux mois,
Peut-être un an après, un jour . . . une soirée,
Quelque pâtre inquiet d'une chèvre égarée,
Un chasseur descendu vers la source, et voyant
Son chien qui s'y lançait sortir en aboyant,
Regardera: la lune avec lui qui regarde
Eclairera ce corps d'une lueur blafarde;
Et soudain il fuira jusqu'au hameau, tout droit.
De grand matin venus, quelques gens de l'endroit
Tirant par les cheveux ce corps méconnaissable,
Cette chair en lambeaux, ces os chargés de sable,
Mêlant des quolibets à quelques sots récits,
Deviseront longtemps sur mes restes noircis,
Et les brouetteront enfin au cimetière;
Vite on clouera le tout dans quelque vieille bière
Qu'un prêtre aspergera d'eau bénite trois fois;
Et je serai laissé sans nom, sans croix de bois!

A son is born to his friend Victor Hugo: Delorme greets him:

Mon ami, vous voilà père d'un nouveau-né;
C'est un garçon encor: le ciel vous l'a donné
Beau, frais, souriant d'aise à cette vie amère;
A peine il a coûté quelque plainte à sa mère.
Il est nuit; je vous vois . . . à doux bruit, le sommeil
Sur un sein blanc qui dort a pris l'enfant vermeil,
Et vous, père, veillant contre la cheminée,
Recueilli dans vous-même, et la tête inclinée,

Vous vous tournez souvent pour revoir, ô douceur!
Le nouveau-né, la mère et le frère et la soeur
Comme un pasteur joyeux de ses toisons nouvelles,
Ou comme un maître, au soir, qui compte ses javelles.
A cette heure si grave, en ce calme profond,
Qui sait, hors vous, l'abîme où votre coeur se fond,
Ami? qui sait vos pleurs, vos muettes caresses;
Les trésors du génie épanchés en tendresses;
L'aigle plus gémissant que la colombe au nid;
Les torrents ruisselants du rocher de granit,
Et, comme sous les feux d'un été de Norvège,
Au penchant des glaciers mille fontes de neige?
Vivez, soyez heureux, et chantez-nous un jour
Ces secrets plus qu'humains d'un ineffable amour!

—Moi, pendant ce temps-là, je veille aussi, je veille,
Non près des rideaux bleus de l'enfance vermeille,
Près du lit nuptial arrosé de parfum,
Mais près d'un froid grabat, sur le corps d'un défunt.
C'est un voisin, vieillard goutteux, mort de la pierre;
Ses nièces m'on requis, je veille à leur prière.
Seul, je m'y suis assis dès neuf heures du soir.
A la tête du lit une croix en bois noir,
Avec un Christ en os, pose entre deux chandelles
Sur une chaise; auprès, le buis cher aux fidèles
Trempe dans une assiette, et je vois sous les draps
Le mort en long, pieds joints, et croisant les deux bras.
Oh! si, du moins, ce mort m'avait durant sa vie
Eté longtemps connu! s'il me prenait envie
De baiser ce front jaune une dernière fois!
En regardant toujours ces plis raides et droits,
Si je voyais enfin remuer quelque chose,
Bouger comme le pied d'un vivant qui repose,
Et la flamme bleuir! si j'entendais crier
Le bois du lit!... ou bien si je pouvais prier!
Mais rien: nul effroi saint; pas de souvenir tendre;
Je regarde sans voir, j'écoute sans entendre,
Chaque heure sonne lente, et lorsque, par trop las
De ce calme abattant et de ces rêves plats,

Pour respirer un peu je vais à la fenêtre
(Car au ciel de minuit le croissant vient de naître),
Voilà, soudain, qu'au toit lointain d'une maison,
Non pas vers l'orient, s'embrase l'horizon,
Et j'entends résonner, pour toute mélodie,
Des aboiements de chiens hurlant dans l'incendie.

Among these sick confessions, these dreams of sad weaknesses, and tasteless imitations of the long-ago ridiculed poetry
of old Ronsard, we find—with amazement—poems filled with
freshness and purity. For example, what melancholy charm in
the description of his muse!

Non, ma Muse n'est pas l'odalisque brillante
Qui danse les seins nus, à la voix sémillante,
Aux noirs cheveux luisants, aux longs yeux de houri;
Elle n'est ni la jeune et vermeille Péri,
Dont l'aile radieuse éclipserait la queue
D'un beau paon, ni la fée à l'aile blanche et bleue,
Ces deux rivales soeurs, qui, dès qu'il a dit *oui*,
Ouvrent mondes et cieux à l'enfant ébloui.
Elle n'est pas non plus, ô ma Muse adorée!
Elle n'est pas la vierge ou la veuve éplorée,
Qui d'un cloître désert, d'une tour sans vassaux,
Solitaire habitante, erre sous les arceaux,
Disant un nom; descend aux tombes féodales;
A genoux, de velours inonde au loin les dalles,
Et le front sur un marbre, épanche avec des pleurs
L'hymne mélodieux de ses nobles malheurs.

Non;—mais, quand seule au bois votre douleur chemine,
Avez-vous vu, là-bas, dans un fond, la chaumine
Sous l'arbre mort; auprès, un ravin est creusé;
Une fille en tout temps y lave un linge usé.
Peut-être à votre vue elle a baissé la tête,
Car, bien pauvre qu'elle est, sa naissance est honnête.
Elle eût pu, comme une autre, en de plus heureux jours
S'épanouir au monde et fleurir aux amours;
Voler en char; passer aux bals, aux promenades;
Respirer au balcon parfums et sérénades;

Ou, de sa harpe d'or éveillant cent rivaux,
Ne voir rien qu'un sourire entre tant de bravos.
Mais le ciel dès l'abord s'est obscurci sur elle,
Et l'arbuste en naissant fut atteint de la grêle;
Elle file, elle coud, et garde à la maison
Un père vieux, aveugle et privé de raison.

It is true that he terminates this charming picture with a clinical description of tuberculosis; his muse spits blood:

. . . une toux déchirante
La prend dans sa chanson, pousse en sifflant un cri,
Et lance les glaviers de son poumon meurtri.

In our opinion one may consider the following elegy worthy of standing beside the best works of André Chénier, as the most perfect poem of the entire collection:

Toujours je la connus pensive et sérieuse;
Enfant, dans les ébats de l'enfance joyeuse
Elle se mêlait peu, parlait déjà raison;
Et quand ses jeunes soeurs couraient sur le gazon,
Elle était la première à leur rappeler l'heure,
A dire qu'il fallait regagner la demeure;
Qu'elle avait de la cloche entendu le signal;
Qu'il était défendu d'approcher du canal,
De troubler dans le bois la biche familière,
De passer en jouant trop près de la volière:
Et ses soeurs l'écoutaient. Bientôt elle eut quinze ans,
Et sa raison brilla d'atraits plus séduisants:
Sein voilé, front serein où le calme repose,
Sous de beaux cheveux bruns une figure rose,
Une bouche discrète au sourire prudent,
Un parler sobre et froid, et qui plaît cependant;
Une voix douce et ferme, et qui jamais ne tremble,
Et deux longs sourcils noirs qui se fondent ensemble.
Le devoir l'animait d'une grande ferveur;
Elle avait l'air posé, réfléchi, non rêveur:
Elle ne rêvait pas comme la jeune fille,
Qui de ses doigts distraits laisse tomber l'aiguille,

Et du bal de la veille au bal du lendemain
Pense au bel inconnu qui lui pressa la main.
Le coude à la fenêtre, oubliant son ouvrage,
Jamais on ne la vit suivre à travers l'ombrage
Le vol interrompu des nuages du soir,
Puis cacher tout d'un coup son front dans son mouchoir.
Mas elle se disait qu'un avenir prospère
Avait changé soudain par la mort de son père ;
Qu'elle était fille aînée, et que c'était raison
De prendre part active aux soins de la maison.
Ce coeur jeune et sévère ignorait la puissance
Des ennuis dont soupire et s'émeut l'innocence.
Il réprima toujours les attendrissements
Qui naissent sans savoir, et les troubles charmants,
Et les désirs obscurs, et ces vagues délices,
De l'amour dans les coeurs naturelles complices.
Maîtresse d'elle-même aux instants les plus doux,
En embrassant sa mère elle lui disait *vous,*
Les galantes fadeurs, les propos pleins de zèle
Des jeunes gens oisifs étaient perdus chez elle ;
Mais qu'un coeur éprouvé lui contât un chagrin,
A l'instant se voilait son visage serein :
Elle savait parler de maux, de vie amère,
Et donnait des conseils comme une jeune mère.
Aujourd'hui la voilà mère, épouse à son tour ;
Mais c'est chez elle encor raison plutôt qu'amour.
Son paisible bonheur de respect se tempère ;
Son époux déjà mûr serait pour elle un père ;
Elle n'a pas connu l'oubli du premier mois,
Et la lune de miel qui ne luit qu'une fois,
Et son front et ses yeux ont gardé le mystère
De ces chastes secrets qu'une femme doit taire.
Heureuse comme avant, à son nouveau devoir
Elle a réglé sa vie . . . Il est beau de la voir,
Libre de son ménage, un soir de la semaine,
Sans toilette, en été, qui sort et se promène
Et s'asseoit à l'abri du soleil étouffant,
Vers six heures, sur l'herbe, avec sa belle enfant.
Ainsi passent ses jours depuis le premier âge,

Comme des flots sans nom sous un ciel sans orage.
D'un cours lent, uniforme et pourtant solennel;
Car ils savent, qu'ils vont au rivage éternel.
Et moi qui vois couler cette humble destinée
Au penchant du devoir doucement entraînée,
Ces jours purs, transparents, calmes, silencieux,
Qui consolent du bruit et reposent les yeux,
Sans le vouloir, hélas! je retombe en tristesse;
Je songe à mes longs jours passés avec vitesse.
Turbulents, sans bonheur, perdus pour le devoir,
Et je pense, ô mon Dieu! qu'il sera bientôt soir!

The public and the critics were grieving over the premature demise of a talent who promised so much when they suddenly learned that the deceased was alive and, praise God, healthy. Sainte-Beuve, already well-known for the *History of French Literature in the XVIth Century*[2] and a scholarly edition of Ronsard, got the idea of printing his first poetic attempts under the fictitious name J. Delorme, probably wary of the strictures and severity of moral censorship. With its jolly outcome such a sad mystification ought to have been detrimental to the success of his poems; however, the new school ecstatically acknowledged and appropriated the new fellow as one of its own.

J. Delorme's opinions concerning French prosody are expounded in his *Thoughts*. The critics praised the accuracy, erudition, and novelty of these remarks. It seems to us that Delorme attributes too much importance to the innovations of the so-called *romantic* school of French writers, who themselves place too great an importance on the form of a line of verse, on the caesura, on the rhyme, on the use of a few archaic words, a few archaic idioms, etc. All this is all right, but it is too reminiscent of the rattles and diapers of infancy. There is no doubt that French prosody is the most capricious and, I dare say, groundless. How, for example, do you justify the exclusions of the *hiatus* which is so unbearable to French ears in a combination of two words: (as: *a été, où aller*) and which they themselves seek for harmony in proper names: *Zaire, Aglaë, Eléonore*. Let us note in passing that the French are indebted to the Latin *elisium* for the law about the *hiatus*. Because of the characteristics of Latin prosody a word which ends with a vowel loses it before another vowel.

Boileau replaced this rule with the law of the hiatus:

> Gardez qu'une voyelle à courir trop hâtée.
> Ne soit en son chemin par une autre hèutée.[3]

Secondly: how can one eternally rhyme for the eye and not for the ear? Why must rhymes agree in number (singular or plural) when the pronunciation in both cases is identical? However, the innovators still haven't touched all this; but their efforts are hardly fortunate.

Last year Sainte-Beuve issued another volume of poems with the title *Les Consolations*. In these Delorme appears reformed by the advice of friends, sedate and moral men. No longer does he desperately reject the comforts of religion, but just quietly doubts; he no longer visits Rosa, but he admits to occasional wanton lust. His style has calmed down too. In a word, taste and morality apparently satisfy him. One may even hope that in his third volume Delorme will be a perfectly respectable gentleman and as pious as Lamartine.

Unfortunately, we must admit that while rejoicing in the change in the man, we are sorry about the poet. Poor Delorme possessed an extremely important ability which almost none of the French poets of the modern generation achieve, a quality without which there is no true poetry, i.e. *sincere inspiration*. Nowadays the French poet has said to himself systematically: *soyons réligieux, soyons politiques,* or some even: *soyons extravagants,* and coldness of design, constraint, and compulsion are reflected in all of his works; we never see the movement of free momentary emotion, in a word—there is no true inspiration. God preserve us from being advocates of immorality in poetry (we do not understand this word in the childish sense in which some of our journalists use it)! Poetry, which by its higher and free nature should not have any goal other than itself, even less should demean itself by using the power of words to shake the eternal truths on which human happiness and greatness are founded, or transform its divine nectar into an inflammatory aphrodisiac compound. But it is not immorality to describe human weaknesses, errors, and passions, just as anatomy is not murder; and we do not see immorality in the elegies of the unfortunate Delorme, in confessions which rend the heart, in a strained description of his passions and faithlessness, in his complaints about fate and about himself.

[1831, *The Literary Gazette*]

### N O T E S

1. *Delorme was an invention of Sainte-Beuve.*
2. Tableau de la poésie française au XVIème siècle *(1828)*.
3. *From his* Art Poétique.

# THE TRIUMPH OF FRIENDSHIP, OR, ALEXANDER ANFIMOVICH ORLOV JUSTIFIED

*In arenam cum aequalibus descend.*
Cic.

**Amid the polemic which has been tearing our poor literature** apart, for more than ten years N. N. Grech and F. V. Bulgarin[1] have presented a consolatory example of accord based on mutual respect, a similarity of souls and of civil and literary occupations. This instructive union has been betokened by respected monuments. Faddey Venediktovich mostly acknowledged himself a pupil of Nikolai Ivanovich; N. I. hurriedly proclaimed Faddey Venediktovich "his clever comrade." F. V. dedicated his *Dimitri the Pretender* to Nikolai Ivanovich; N. I. dedicated his *Trip to Germany* to Faddey Venediktovich. F. V. wrote a laudatory foreword to Nikolai Ivanovich's *Grammar;** in *The Northern Bee* (published by Messrs. Grech and Bulgarin) N. I. published a laudatory announcement of *Ivan Vyzhigin*. Truly touching unanimity! —Now, Nikolai Ivanovich, considering Faddey Venediktovich insulted in an essay[2] printed in No. 9 of *The Telescope,* has interceded for his comrade with his characteristic candor and fervency. He printed an essay in *The Son of the Fatherland* (No. 27) which, of course, will make the impertinent opponents of Faddey Venediktovich be silent; for Nikolai Ivanovich proved irrefutably:

(1) That M. I. Golenishchev-Kutuzov was made a prince in June of 1812 (p. 64).

(2) That not the battle, but the battle-plan is the secret of the commander-in-chief (p. 65).

(3) That the priest walks straight toward the advancing enemy with a cross and holy water (p. 65).

(4) That the secretary walks out of the house in a worn-out civil-service uniform, in a three-cornered hat, with a sword, in worn-out white underwear (p. 65).

(5) That the proverb, *Vox populi—vox dei,* is a Latin proverb, and that it is the true reason for the French Revolution (p. 65).

(6) That *Ivan Vyzhigin* is not a model work, but, "relatively," a pleasant and useful thing (p. 62).

(7) That Faddey Venediktovich lives on his estate near Dorpat and has asked him (Nikolai Ivanovich) not to send him nonsense (p. 68).

And that therefore: "F. V. Bulgarin brings honor to his countrymen with his talents and works"—which was what should have been proved.

* See Grech's *Grammar*, published by Grech.

There is nothing to say against this; we are the first to loudly approve of Nikolai Ivanovich for his frank and crushing objections—which do as much honor to his logic as to the fervency of his sentiments.

But friendship (that sacred feeling) drew the fiery soul of Nikolai Ivanovich too far, and the lines which follow were ripped from his pen:

"There (in No. 9 of *The Telescope*) they took two idiotic little books published in Moscow (yes, in Moscow), written by a certain A. Orlov."

Oh, Nikolai Ivanovich, Nikolai Ivanovich! What example are you setting for young writers? What expressions are you using in an essay which begins with these stern words: *"The cynicism, ignorance, and unscrupulousness of our reviewers has long been complained about—and justly so."* Where has your moderation and knowledge of decorum gone to, your well-known scrupulousness? Re-read, Nikolai Ivanovich, re-read these few lines and you yourself, with regret, will admit your imprudence!

*"Two idiotic little books!"—"a certain A. Orlov!"* I leave it to the respected public—what critic, what journalist would decide to use these unpleasant expressions when speaking about the works of a living author? For, glory to God, my respected friend Alexander Anfimovich Orlov is alive! In spite of the envy and malice of the journalists, he is alive; to the joy of booksellers and the comfort of his multitudinous readers, he is alive!

*"Two idiotic little books!"* The works of Alexander Anfimovich, who shares with Faddey Venediktovich the love of the Russian public, are called *"idiotic little books"*! Unheard-of, astounding audacity—offensive not to my friend (for he is alive on his estate near Sokolniki, and he asked me not to send all kinds of nonsense to him), but offensive to the entire reading public.*

* See the critique of *Morning-Star* in *The Son of the Fatherland*.

*"Idiotic little books!"* But how will you prove this idiocy? Do you know, Nikolai Ivanovich, that more than 5,000 copies of these "idiotic little books" have been sold and are in the hands of the reading public, that Mr. Orlov's *Vyzhigins* enjoy the favor of the public equally as much as Bulgarin's *Vyzhigins*, and that the educated class of readers, which disdains both the former and the latter, cannot and should not judge books which it doesn't read?

Reluctantly, I continue my critique.

*"Two idiotic* (idiotic!) *little books published in Moscow* (yes, in Moscow). . . ."

"In Moscow, yes, in Moscow!" What is reprehensible about this? Why this sally against the first capital city? This isn't the first time we have noticed the strange hatred for Moscow in the publishers of *The Son of the Fatherland* and *The Northern Bee.* It is painful for the Russian heart to hear such remarks about mother Moscow, white-stoned Moscow, Moscow which suffered from the Poles in 1612 and from all sorts of rabble in 1812.

To this day Moscow is the center of our enlightenment. For the most part, really Russian writers have been born and educated in Moscow, not the upstarts, the renegades for whom *ubi bene, ibi patria,* for whom it makes no difference whether they run along under the French eagle or revile everything Russian in Russian—as long as they are sated.

What did Petersburg literature have to be so proud about? Mr. Bulgarin? I agree that this great writer, respected equally as much for his gifts as for his character, has earned immortal glory; but the works of Mr. Orlov put the Moscow writer if not higher, at least on a level with his Petersburg rival. In spite of the disagreement which reigns between Faddey Venediktovich and Alexander Anfimovich, in spite of the just indignation aroused in me by the incautious lines in *The Son of the Fatherland*, we will try to compare these two radiant suns of our literature.[3]

Faddey Venediktovich surpasses Alexander Anfimovich in captivating refinement of expression; Alexander Anfimovich is superior to Faddey Venediktovich in liveliness and wittiness of narration.

Faddey Venediktovich's novels are more carefully thought out; they show more patience* in the author (and demand even more patience from the reader); Alexander Anfimovich's tales are shorter, but more intricate and engaging.

Faddey Venediktovich is more a philosopher; Alexander Anfimovich is more a poet.

Faddey Venediktovich is a genius, for he invented the name *Vyzhigin* and by this bold innovation enlivened the banal imitations of *Sovestdral*[4] and *The English Milord*;[5] Alexander Anfimovich employed Mr. Bulgarin's invention artfully and drew infinitely varied effects from it!

Faddey Vendiktovich, it seems to us, is somewhat monotonous; for all of his works are nothing more than *Vyzhigin* with different names: *Ivan Vyzhigin, Peter Vyzhigin, Dimitri the Pretender, or, Vyzhigin in the XVIIth Century*, his own memoirs and moralistic articles—everything looks like the same subject. Alexander Anfimovich is astoundingly varied! Besides the countless number of *Vyzhigins*, how many flowers he has scattered on the field of literature! *The Plague's Meeting with Cholera, The Falcon Would Be a Falcon, but the Hen Ate Him, or, The Runaway Wife; Living Fainting Spells; The Burial of the Merchant*, and so forth and so on.[6]

However, dispassion demands that we indicate the area in which Faddey Venediktovich is unquestionably superior to his fortunate rival; I have in mind the moral aim of his works. Indeed, dear readers, what can be more moral than Mr. Bulgarin's works? From them we learn: how unpraiseworthy it is to lie, to steal, to give oneself up to drunkenness, gambling, and such like. Mr. Bulgarin punishes the characters with various diverting names; his murderer is named Knivev, his bribetaker—

---

* "Genius is patience in the highest degree," said the famous Buffon.

Bribetakev, the fool—Fooleyev, etc. Only historical accuracy prevented him from calling Boris Godunov "Earslapper," Dimitri the Pretender "Incarceratov," and Marina Mniszek "Princess Whorova"—but then these characters are presented rather palely.

In this respect Mr. Orlov definitely yields to Mr. Bulgarin. However, the most fiery of Faddey Venediktovich's appreciators admit a certain boredom in him, which is offset by instructiveness; and the most zealous of Alexander Anfimovich's admirers occasionally condemn his imprudence, forgivable, however, as bursts of genius.

For all that, Alexander Anfimovich has less fame than Faddey Venediktovich. What is the reason for this apparent inequality?

Dexterity, dear readers, the dexterity of Faddey Venediktovich, the clever comrade of Nikolai Ivanovich! *Ivan Vyzhigin* still existed only in the imagination of the respected author when *The Northern Archive, The Northern Bee,* and *The Son of the Fatherland* commented on it with the greatest praise. In his *Journey,* which aroused general interest in Paris, Anselot[7] proclaimed this as yet nonexistent *Ivan Vyzhigin* the best of the Russian novels. Finally *Ivan Vyzhigin* appeared; and *The Son of the Fatherland, The Northern Archive,* and *The Northern Bee* praised it to the skies. Everyone rushed to read it; many read it to the end, and meanwhile its praises did not cease in every number of *The Northern Archive, The Son of the Fatherland,* and *The Northern Bee.* These hard-working journals invited purchasers in caressing tones; they encouraged, urged lazy readers on; they threatened revenge on foes who hadn't read *Ivan Vyzhigin* just because of base envy.

However, what means of assistance did Alexander Anfimovich Orlov employ?

None, dear readers!

He did not give any dinners for foreign writers[8] who do not know Russian, in order to get a little place in their travel notes in return for his bread-salt.

He did not praise himself in the journals which he himself published.

He did not attract subscribers and buyers with debasing flattery and extravagant promises.

He did not engage in charlatanism with newspaper advertisements written in the style of posters for dog-and-puppet comedies.

He did not answer a single critic; he did not call his opponents fools, scoundrels, drunkards, oysters, and so forth.

But did he thus disarm his numerous enemies? Not a bit. This is how his colleagues commented on him:

> The author of the above-mentioned works is fiercely storming our poor Russian literature and wants to destroy the Russian Parnassus not with bombs, but with incendiary shells, with the help of obliging publishers who pay generously for every manuscript of this celebrated creator —twenty rubles apiece in current money, as booksellers who know their business assured us. The author is a man *from the learned class,* as is apparent from the Latin sentences with which his works are speckled; and their essence proves that he, as is said in *The Minor,* "fearing the abyss of erudition, turned around and went backward." The celebrated popular work, *The Mice Bury the Cat, or, Fairy Tale with Characters,* is an *Iliad* in comparison with the works of Mr. Orlov, and *Bova Korolevich* is a hero to whom the respected author has not yet risen. . . . Derzhavin is our *Alpha* and Mr. Orlov our *Omega* in literature, that is, the lost link in the chain of literary beings; and therefore *deserves attention, like everything unusual. . . .* His language, exposition, and opening intrigues can be compared only to the repulsive pictures with which these offspring of tastelessness are filled, and to the boldness of the author. Such works would never have seen light in Petersburg, and not one of the Petersburg street-vendors of books (to say nothing of the booksellers) would have undertaken to publish them. By what right did Mr. Orlov

* An important admission! Please listen!

get the idea of calling his oafs, the rascally steppe-dwellers, Ignat and Sidor, children of Ivan Vizhigin, and at the same time the author of Vyzhigin was publishing another novel with the same title too? . . . Never have such disgusting pictures appeared in the Russian language. Long live bookprinting in Moscow! (*The Northern Bee*, 1821, No. 46)

What a malicious and unjust criticism. We have already noted the unseemliness of the attacks on Moscow, but what is the respected Alexander Anfimovich accused of here? Of being paid twenty rubles for each of his works by the booksellers? So what? It is customary for the unselfish heart of my friend to think that in getting twenty rubles he has given someone else two thousand pleasures*; while a certain Petersburg writer made a hasty bookseller gasp when he took 30,000 for his manuscript!!!

It is considered a sin that he knows Latin. Of course it has been proved that Faddey Venediktovich (who published Horace with someone else's notes) does not know Latin, but can it be that he is obliged to this lack of knowledge for his immortal fame?[9]

They assured us that Mr. Orlov is *from the learned class*. Of course, it has been proved that Mr. Bulgarin is not learned at all; but again I repeat: can it be that ignorance is such an enviable merit?

That's not enough. They threateningly demand an answer from my friend: how did he dare appropriate for his characters a name sanctified by Faddey Venediktovich himself? But didn't A. S. Pushkin dare to introduce all of the characters of Bulgarin's novel in his *Boris Godunov*, and even to use many places in his tragedy (written, they say, five years earlier and well-known to the public in manuscript)?

I boldly appeal to the conscience of the publishers of *The Northern Bee* themselves: are these criticisms just? Is Alexander Anfimovich Orlov guilty?

* An historical truth!

But even more boldly I appeal to the respected Nikolai Ivanovich: doesn't he feel profound regret for having vainly offended a man with such outstanding gifts, *"who has no relations with him, who doesn't know him at all, and who hasn't written anything bad about him."*\*

FEOFILAKT KOSICHKIN[10]

[1831, *The Moscow Telegraph*]

# NOTES

1. *Faddey Bulgarin, or Tadeusz Bulharyn (1789–1859)—a prolific journalist, editor of the newspaper* The Northern Bee, *secret agent of the notorious Third Section (he specialized in denunciations of literary people—including Pushkin), former soldier in the French army, tireless author of sermonistic and chauvinistic novels. Along with Nikolai Grech (1787–1867) he was one of the most reactionary writers of the day. They were disliked intensely by Pushkin, Gogol, Vyazemsky, and most of the good writers of the period.*
2. *A withering essay by Nadezhdin. He attacked Bulgarin's* Vyzhigin *as well as three brochures by Orlov: "The Khlinov Steppe-dwellers Ignat and Sidor, or the Children of Ivan Vyzhigin" (1831), "The Khlinov Marriages of Ignat and Sidor, Children of Ivan Vyzhigin" (1831), and, mercifully, "The Death of Ivan Vyzhigin" (1831).*
3. *Gogol wrote an amusing variation on Pushkin's parody of polarities. See Gogol's letter to Pushkin of August 21, 1831.*
4. *"Sovest' "—"conscience," drat'—"to rip." From a chapbook tale: "The Adventures of Sovestdral of the Big Nose, the Resurrected Jester, and Great Rascal in Amatory Activities" (translated from the Polish, 1781).*
5. *Another chapbook tale: "The Story of the Adventures of the English Milord George and the Brandenburg Marquise Frederica Louisa, with the addition of One Story of the Former Turkish Vizir Martsimiris and the Sardinian Queen Teresa" (M. 1782).*

\* *The Son of the Fatherland, No. 27, p. 60.*

6. *Titles of Orlov's novels.*

7. *Jacques Ancelot.*

8. *Bulgarin and Grech organized a dinner for Ancelot in 1826, after which he praised Bulgarin's novels and Grech's* Grammar *in his* Six mois en Russie *(1827).*

9. *Bulgarin published Horace's* Odes *with the commentaries of Ezhevsky and other Latinists—without giving them credit.*

10. *One of Pushkin's polemical pen-names. This attack on Bulgarin was followed up by another entitled "A Few Words about Mr. Bulgarin's Little Finger Etc." See J. Thomas Shaw, "The Problem of the* Persona *in Journalism: Puškin's Feofilakt Kosičkin,"* American Contributions to the Fifth International Congress of Slavists (*The Hague, 1963*), II, 301–27.

# A LETTER TO THE EDITOR OF *LITERARY SUPPLEMENT TO THE RUSSIAN INVALID*

**I have just read** *Evenings near Dikanka.*[1] **It amazed me. Here is** real gaiety—honest, unconstrained, without mincing, without primness. And in places what poetry! What sensitivity! All this is so unusual in our present-day literature that I still haven't recovered. It was told that when the publisher went to the shop where *Evenings* were being printed, the typesetters began to chortle and snort, covering their mouths with their hands. The foreman explained their gaiety, confessing to him that the typesetters were dying of laughter while setting his book. Molière and Fielding would probably have been glad to make their typesetters laugh. I congratulate the public on a truly gay book, and I sincerely wish the author future success. For God's sake, take his side if the journalists, as is their custom, attack the "indecency" of his expressions, the "bad tone" etc. It's time, it's time to make fun of *les précieuses ridicules* of our literature, people who incessantly talk about the fair feminine readers (whom they have never had), about high society (where they are not invited)—and all this in the style of Professor Tredyakovsky's valet.

[1831, *Literary Supplement to the Russian Invalid*]

### N O T E

1. *Gogol's first collection of tales was published in 1831. Pushkin's information about the typesetters came from a letter Gogol wrote to Pushkin, August 21, 1831. They had first met three months earlier.*

# ON VICTOR HUGO

**Everyone knows that the French are the most antipoetic people.** Their best writers, the most famous representatives of this witty and practical people—Montaigne, Voltaire, Montesquieu, La Harpe, and Rousseau himself—have demonstrated how alien and incomprehensible esthetic feeling is to them.

If we turn our attention to the findings of their critics which circulate among the people and are accepted as literary axioms, we will be amazed at their insignificance and inaccuracy. In France Corneille and Voltaire are considered equals of Racine as writers of tragedy; to this day J. B. Rousseau has kept the title "great." The insufferable Béranger[1] is now considered their foremost lyric poet—a scribbler of strained and affected little songs which contain nothing passionate or inspired and which are far behind the charming light works of Colnet in gaiety and wit. I don't know whether they have finally admitted the lean and flaccid monotony of their Lamartine, but about ten years ago they were unceremoniously setting him on a level with Byron and Shakespeare. They equate Count de Vigny's mediocre *Cinq Mars*[2] with the great creations of Walter Scott. It goes without saying that their attacks are as unjustified as their love. Among the young talents of the present time, Sainte-Beuve is least well-known, but he is very probably the most remarkable.

Of course his poems are very original, and what is more important, filled with true inspiration. In the *Literary Gazette* they were mentioned with praise which seemed exaggerated. Nowadays V. Hugo, a poet and a man with true talent, has undertaken to justify the opinion of the Petersburg journal: under the title *Les Feuilles d'automne* he has published a volume of poems apparently written in imitation of Sainte-Beuve's book *Les Consolations*.

[1832, unpublished]

## N O T E S

1. *Pierre-Jean de Béranger (1780–1857)—in his day an extremely popular poet.*
2. *See below, pp. 216–219.*

# THE POETIC WORKS AND TRANSLATIONS OF PAVEL KATENIN

**The other day** *The Poetic Works and Translations of Pavel Katenin* were published.[1]

In the beginning of an extremely remarkable preface, the publisher (Mr. Baktin) mentioned that almost from the time he entered his literary career P. A. Katenin has been met by the most inaccurate and the most immoderate criticisms.

It seems to us that Mr. Katenin (just as all of our writers in general) could complain about the silence of criticism rather than its severity or prejudiced captiousness. Real criticism does not exist in our country: it would be unjust to demand it from us. Our literature barely exists; and "you can't judge nothing," says the irrefutable proverb. If the public can be satisfied with what we call criticism, it proves only that we still have no need of Schlegels or even La Harpes.

As for the unjust coldness the public has shown for Mr. Katenin's works, it does him honor in all respects: first, it proves the poet's abhorrence of the trivial devices for gaining success; and second, his originality. He has never tried to please the public's reigning taste; on the contrary, he has always gone along his own road, creating for himself what and how he pleased. He extended his proud independence even to abandoning one offshoot of poetry as soon as it becomes fashionable; and he moved away to where he was accompanied neither by the prejudice of the crowd nor the models of some writer who drew others along after him. Thus having been one of the first apostles of romanticism and the first to introduce language and subjects from the commonfolk into the sphere of elevated poetry, he was the first to renounce romanticism and turn to classical idols when the reading public began to like the novelty of the literary reform.

The first noteworthy work of Mr. Katenin was a translation of Bürger's famous *Lenore*. It was already well-known here from the inaccurate and charming imitation of Zhukovsky, who made of it the same thing Byron made of *Faust* in his *Manfred:* he weakened the spirit and form of his model. Katenin perceived this and got the idea of showing us *Lenore* in the energetic beauty of its original creation; he wrote *Olga*. But this simplicity and even crudity of expression, this "scum" which replaced the "ethereal chain of shadows," this gallows in place of rural scenes illumined by the summer moon, struck the unaccustomed readers unpleasantly, and Gnedich undertook to state their opinions in an essay the unjustness of which was exposed by Griboedov.[2] After *Olga* appeared *The Murderer*, perhaps the best of Katenin's ballads. The impression it produced was even worse—in a fit of madness a murderer abusively called the moon (the witness of his malefaction) "bald-headed"! Readers brought up on Florian[3] and Parny burst out laughing and considered the ballad beneath any criticism.

Such were Katenin's first reverses; they had influence on his subsequent works. In the theater he had decisive successes. From time to time his poems appeared in journals and almanacs, and they finally started to be given justice—although stingily and reluctantly. Standing out among these are *Mstislav Mstislavich*, a poem full of fire and movement, and *An Old Tale*, in which there is so much ingenuousness and true poetry.

In the book which has now been published enlightened readers will notice an *idyll*—where he perceives bucolic nature with such charming faithfulness, not Gesner's[4] prim and affected nature, but the ancient, broad, free nature—a melancholy *elegy*, a masterful translation of three cantos from the *Inferno*, and a collection of romances about El Cid, that folk chronicle which is so interesting and poetic. Connoisseurs will render justice to the erudite refinement and sonority of the hexameter and in general to the mechanism of Mr. Katenin's verse, something too much ignored by our best poets.

[1833, *Literary Supplement to The Russian Invalid*]

## N O T E S

1. *Pavel Alexandrovich Katenin (1792–1853)—poet, translator (Corneille, Racine), dramatist—generally classified as an "archaist."*
2. *Zhukovsky's and Katenin's adaptations of Bürger gave rise to a polemic in which Gnedich attacked Katenin for coarseness and Griboedov defended him for realism and accuracy.*

3. *Jean-Pierre Florian (1755–94). His poetry is flowery and polite.*
4. *Salomon Gesner (1730–88)—poet and painter, contemporary of Kleist and Wieland.*

# ON THE INSIGNIFICANCE OF RUSSIAN LITERATURE

**If[1] Russian literature offers few works which merit the** observation of literary criticism, just by itself (like every other phenomenon in the history of humanity) it should attract the attention of conscientious studiers of truth.

Russia long remained alien to Europe. Accepting the light of Christianity from Byzantium, she participated in neither the political upheavals nor the intellectual activity of the Roman Catholic world. The great epoch of the Renaissance had no influence on her; chivalry did not animate her ancestors with pure raptures, and the beneficial shock produced by the crusades was not felt in the regions of the frozen north. . . . A high destiny had been preordained for Russia. . . . Her boundless plains swallowed up the power of the Mongols; the barbarians did not dare to leave enslaved Rus at their rear, and they returned to the steppes of their East. Developing enlightenment was saved by a mutilated and expiring Russia. . . .*

For two dark centuries only the clergy, spared because of the amazing perspicacity of the Tartars, preserved the pale sparks of Byzantine learning. In the silence of monasteries, monks kept their uninterrupted chronicles. In their epistles the bishops spoke with princes and boyars, comforting their hearts in onerous times of temptation and hopelessness. But the inner life of the enslaved people did not develop. The Tartars did not

---

* And not Poland, as was asserted by the European journals not long ago; but in its relation to Russia, Europe has always been as ignorant as it is ungrateful.

resemble the Moors. Having conquered Russia, they did not give it algebra or Aristotle. The throwing off of the yoke, the quarrels of the great principalities with their appanages, absolutism along with the freedoms of the cities, autocracy along with the boyars, and conquests along with the independence of nationalities were not favorable to the free development of enlightenment. Europe was flooded with an incredible multitude of poems, legends, satires, romances, mystères, etc., but our ancient archives and libraries offer almost no food for the curiosity of researchers except chronicles. The half-expunged characteristics of our nationality were preserved by a few tales and songs which were constantly revised by oral tradition, and *The Song of Igor's Campaign* rises up as a solitary monument in the desert of our ancient literature.

But in the epoch of storms and upheavals, the Tsars and boyars were agreed on one thing: the necessity of moving Russia toward Europe. Thus the relations of Ivan Vasilevich with England, Godunov's correspondence with Denmark, the conditions presented to the Polish Grand Duke by the XVIIth-century aristocracy, the embassies of Alexei Mikhailovich. . . . Finally Peter appeared. . . .

Russia entered Europe like a ship launched with the pounding of an ax and the thunder of cannons. But the wars undertaken by Peter the Great were beneficial and fruitful. The success of the national reform was the result of the Battle of Poltava, and European enlightenment moored at the shores of the conquered Neva.

Much that Peter began, he didn't manage to complete. He died during maturity, in the midst of all his creative activity. He cast a preoccupied but penetrating glance at literature. He promoted Feofan, approved of Kopievich, didn't like Tatishchev because of his frivolity and free-thinking, foresaw an "eternal toiler" in the poor schoolboy Tredyakovsky. Seeds were sown. The son of the Moldavian *hospodar*[2] was educated on his campaigns; and the son of a fisherman from Kholmogorsk,[3] having run away from the White Sea, knocked at the gates of the Zaikonospassk school: a new literature, the fruit of a newly-educated society, was soon to be born.

French literature dominated Europe at the beginning of the eighteenth century. It was to have a long and decisive influence on Russia. First of all we must study this.

Examining the numberless multitude of shallow lyrics, ballades, rondos, virelais, and sonnets, allegorical and satirical poems, chivalric novels, folk-tales, fabliaux, mystères, etc., with which France was flooded in the beginning of the seventeenth century, it is impossible not to admit the fruitless insignificance of this sham superabundance. The tired researcher is rarely rewarded by a difficulty artfully overcome, a felicitously chosen repetition, lightness of phrase, an ingenuous joke, a sincere maxim.

Romantic poetry had flourished luxuriantly and magnificently all over Europe: Germany had long had its *Niebelungen;* Italy its tripartite poem; Portugal—*The Lusiad;*[4] Spain—Lope de Vega, Calderón, and Cervantes; England—Shakespeare; and among the French—Villon sang taverns and gallows in his coarse couplets and was considered the foremost national poet! His heir, Marot, lived at the same time as Ariosto and Camoëns,

Rima des triolets, fit fleurir la ballade.[5]

Prose already had a decisive dominance. The sceptic Montaigne and the cynic Rabelais were contemporaries of Tasso.

Men gifted with talent, struck by the insignificance and—one must say—the *baseness* of French versification, decided that barrenness of the language was to blame for this and started trying to re-create it on the model of ancient Greek. A new school was formed whose opinions, goal, and efforts are reminiscent of the school of our Slavist-Russians, among whom there were also men with talent. But the labors of Ronsard, Jodelle,[6] and Du Bellay[7] remained vain. Language rejected a direction alien to it, and again went along its own road.

Finally there came Malherbe—who was evaluated by a great critic with such brilliant precision and such severe justness:

Enfin Malherbe[8] vint et le premier en France
Fit sentir dans les vers une juste cadence,
D'un mot mis en sa place enseigna le pouvoir
Et réduisit la Muse aux règles du devoir.
Par ce sage écrivain la langue réparée
N'offrit plus rien de rude à l'oreille épurée.
Les stances avec grâce appirent à tomber
Et le vers sur le vers n'osa plus enjamber.[9]

But nowadays Malherbe is forgotten like Ronsard, these two talents who exhausted their powers in a struggle with the mechanism and improvement of the line of verse. Such is the fate which awaits writers who worry more about the external forms of a word than about the thought, its true life which does not depend on usage!

\* \* \*

By what miracle did the group of truly great writers who covered the end of the XVIIth century with such glitter appear amid this pitiful insignificance, lack of true criticism, and shakiness of opinion, amid the general fall of taste? Was it the political generosity of Cardinal Richelieu or the vainglorious patronage of Louis XIV that were the reasons for this? Or does fate predestine for each nation an epoch when a constellation of geniuses suddenly appears, glitters, and disappears? . . . Whatever the case, after a crowd of untalented, mediocre, or unfortunate versifiers who close the period of old French poetry, immediately Corneille, Boileau, Racine, Molière and La Fontaine, Pascal, Bossuet, and Fénelon step forward. And their rule over the intellectual life of the enlightened world is much more easily explainable than their unexpected advent.

Among other European peoples poetry existed before the appearance of the immortal geniuses who gifted humanity with their great creations. These geniuses went along a road which had already been broken. But among the French the elevated minds of the seventeenth century found national poetry in shrouds, scorned its weakness, and turned to the models of classical antiquity. Boileau, a poet gifted with mighty talent and an acute mind, promulgated his codex, and literature submitted to it. Old Corneille alone remained a representative of the romantic tragedy which he had so gloriously introduced on the French stage.

In spite of its manifest triviality, Richelieu felt the importance of literature. The great man who had humbled feudalism in France wanted to tie up literature as well. The writers (in France a poor, insolent, and scornful class) were invited to the court and given pensions like the gentry. Louis XIV followed the cardinal's system. Soon literature was concentrated around his throne. All the writers had their duties. Corneille and Racine entertained the king with tragedies made to order, the historiographer Boileau sang his victories and designated to him the writers worthy of his attention, at court the valet Molière laughed at the courtiers. The Academy set as the first rule of its code: praise of the great king. There were exceptions: a poor noble (in spite of the dominating devoutness) printed his jolly tales about nuns in Holland, and a dulcet-tongued bishop[10] placed a caustic satire on the glorified reign in a book filled with bold philosophy. . . . For that La Fontaine died without a pension, and Fénelon in his diocese, removed from the court for mystical·heresy.

Hence the courteous, delicate literature, glittering, aristocratic, somewhat finical—but because of this very thing comprehensible to all the courts of Europe, for the higher society, as a modern writer has accurately remarked, forms one family all over Europe.

Meanwhile the great age was passing. Louis XIV died, having outlived his glory and the generation of his contemporaries. New ideas, a new direction were echoed in minds craving novelty. The spirit of examination and repudiation was beginning to appear in France. Ignoring the blossoms of literature and noble games of the imagination, minds were preparing for the fateful predestiny of the XVIIIth century. . . .

Nothing could be more contrary to poetry than the philosophy to which the XVIIIth century gave its name. It was directed against the dominating religion—the eternal source of poetry for all peoples—and its favorite weapon was cold and sharp irony, rabid and vulgar mockery. Voltaire, the giant of the epoch, had mastered poetry too—as an important branch of the intellectual activity of man. He wrote an epic with the intention of blackening Catholicism. For 60 years he filled the theaters with tragedies in which (without worrying about either the verisimilitude of the characters or the naturalness of his devices) he made his personages, apropos and inapropos, express the rules of his philosophy. He flooded Paris with charming trifles in which philosophy spoke in a joking and easily understandable language which differed from prose only in rhyme and meter; and this lightness seemed the summit of poetry; finally he too, for once in his life, becomes a poet—when with all lack of restraint, all his destructive genius poured out into a cynical poem where all the elevated feelings precious to humanity were brought as sacrifice to the demon of laughter and irony, Greek antiquity was ridiculed, and the sacredness of both testaments blasphemed.

Voltaire's influence was incredible. The traces of the great age (as the French called the age of Louis XIV) disappear. Enervated poetry turns into trivial toys of wit; the novel becomes a boring sermon or a gallery of seductive pictures.

All elevated minds follow Voltaire. The pensive Rousseau proclaims himself his pupil; the ardent Diderot is the most zealous of his apostles. In the persons of Hume, Gibbon, and Walpole, England greets the Encyclopedia. Europe makes pilgrimages to Ferney. Catherine enters into a friendly correspondence with him. Frederick quarrels and makes peace with him. Society is submissive to him. Finally Voltaire dies in Paris giving his blessing to Franklin's son and greeting the New World with words theretofore unheard of!

The death of Voltaire does not stop the deluge. The ministers of Louis XVI step down into the arena with the writers. Beaumarchais drags onto the stage, strips bare, and flails everything that is still considered sancrosanct. The old queen laughs and applauds.

Old society was ripe for a great destruction. Everything is still calm, but already the voice of young Mirabeau, like a distant storm, rumbles remotely from the depths of the dungeons in which he knocks about. . . .

Stunned, enchanted by the glory of French writers, Europe worships them with servile attention. From the height of their chairs, German professors proclaim the rules of French criticism. England follows France in the field of philosophy; Richardson, Fielding, and Sterne maintain the glory of the prose novel. In the fatherland of Shakespeare and Milton, poetry becomes dry and insignificant, as in France; Italy renounces Dante's genius, Metastasio[11] imitates Racine.

Let's turn to Russia. . . .

[1834, unpublished]

# N O T E S

1. *This is Pushkin's outline of "On the Insignificance of Russian Literature":*

1) *A quick outline of French literature in the 17th century.*

2) *18th century.*

3) *The beginning of Russian literature. In Paris Kantemir ponders his satires, translates Horace. Dies at 28. Captivated by the harmony of rhyme, Lomonosov writes an ode filled with life in his earliest youth etc., and turns to the exact sciences* dégoûté *by Sumarokov's fame. Sumarokov. At this time Tredyakovsky is the only one who understands his business. Meanwhile the 18th century* allait son train.

4) *Catherine—pupil of the 18th century. She alone gives a push to her age. She pleases the philosophers. The* nakaz. *Literature refuses to follow her exactly as the people had (the members of the commission, the deputies). Derzhavin, Bogdanovich, Dmitriev, Karamzin, Cath., Fonvizin, and Radishchev.*

*The age of Alexander. Karamzin secludes himself to write his* History. *Dmitriev—a minister. General insignificance.* Meanwhile French literature gone shallow *envahit tout.*

*Voltaire and the giants do not have a single follower in Russia; but untalented pygmies, mushrooms grown up at the roots of oaks— Dorat, Florian, Marmontel, Guichard, Mme. Genlis—take over Russian literature. Sterne is alien to us, with the exception of Karamzin. Parny and the influence of sensual poetry on Batyushkov, Vyazemsky, Davydov, Pushkin, and Baratynsky. Zhukovsky and 1812 overcomes the German influence.*

The present influence of French criticism and young literature. Exceptions.

2. *Antioch Kantemir (1708–44)—one of Russia's first professional writers, author of ponderous neoclassical satires in syllabic verse.*

3. *Lomonosov was the son of a fisherman. He studied at the Slavo-Greco-Latin Academy of the Zaikonosspassk Monastery in Moscow.*

4. Os Lusíadas—*the Portuguese national epic, written by Luis de Camoëns (1524–80), published in 1572. It deals with heroic Portuguese (Lusians) of all ages, but especially with the adventures of Vasco da Gama.*

5. *From Boileau's* Art Poétique.

6. *Etienne Jodelle (1532–73)—lyric and dramatic poet.*

7. *Joachim Du Bellay (1522–60)—member of the Pléiade, pioneer classicist and sonneteer.*

8. *François de Malherbe (1555–1628)—poet of propriety and prudence—defined in the narrowest sense.*

9. *From* Art Poétique.

10. *François de Salignac de la Mothe-Fénelon (1651–1715) in* Les Adventures de Télémaque *(1699).*

11. *Pietro Antonio Domenico Bonaventura Trapassi Metastasio (1698–1782)—Italian poet and dramatist.*

# THE MEMOIRS OF CHUXIN, A WORK BY FADDEY BULGARIN

**In the preface to one of his works, Mr. Bulgarin informs the** public that there are people who do not acknowledge that there is any talent in him. This apparently surprises him very much. He even expressed his surprise with a punctuation mark (!).

For our part, we know people who acknowledge talent in Mr. Bulgarin, but we are not surprised by this.

Mr. Bulgarin's new novel does not yield at all to his earlier ones.

[1835, unpublished]

# ZAGOSKIN'S COMEDY, *THE DISSATISFIED*

**The Moscow journals pronounced a severe sentence on Mr.** Zagoskin's new comedy. They find it banal and boring.[1] *The Dissatisfied* is in fact a boring, sluggish play—written in rather light verse. The characters brought on the stage are not amusing and not natural. There is not a single comic situation, and the banal and stilted dialogue does not make one forget the absence of action.

Mr. Zagoskin has earned the public's favor with his novels. In them there is life, imagination, and interest, and even gaiety, that priceless quality, virtually the rarest of gifts. We have cursorily mentioned the failure of the author of *Roslavlev* here so as not to return again to a subject which is unpleasant for us.

[1836, unpublished]

# N O T E

1. *M. N. Zagoskin (1789–1852)—His play, produced in Moscow and Petersburg in 1835, got bad reviews from Belinsky and others. Zagoskin had more success with historical novels such as* Roslavlev *(1831) and* Yury Miloslavsky.

# *WASTOLA,* OR *DESIRES,* A TALE IN VERSE BY WIELAND, PUBLISHED BY A. PUSHKIN

In[1] one of our journals it was intimated that the publisher of *Wastola* wanted to appropriate someone else's work by placing his own name on the book he had published. An unjust accusation: it has not yet been forbidden to publish others' works with the agreement or at the request of the author. This is called *publishing;* the word is clear—at least no other has yet been invented.

In the same journal it was said that *Wastola* was translated by some poor writer, that A. S. P. only gave him his name for hire, and that he would have done better to give him a thousand rubles out of his pocket.

The translator of Wieland's poem, a citizen and writer of merit, the respected father of a family, could not have anticipated such a cruel attack. He is a poor, but honorable and noble man. He could have commissioned someone else with the pleasant task of publishing his poem, but of course he would not have accepted charity from anyone.

After such an explanation we cannot decide to name the actual translator here. We regret that a sincere desire to accommodate him could have given rise to such offensive insinuations.

[1836, *The Contemporary*]

## N O T E

1. *Christoph Martin Wieland (1733–1813)—German writer of romances and ironic tales, translator of Shakespeare. His epic* Oberon *was translated into English by John Quincy Adams. Wieland's three-part tale* Pervonte, oder die Wünsche *(1778) was translated into Russian by E. P. Lyutsenko, a former teacher at the Lycée. Here Pushkin answers an attack by Senkovsky in* The Library for Reading *(No. 2, 1836).*

# EVENINGS ON A FARM
# NEAR DIKANKA

(Stories published by the bee-keeper, Red Panko.
Second edition)

**Our readers of course remember the impression produced on** them by the appearance of *Evenings on a Farm:* everyone was made happy by this vivid description of a singing and dancing nationality, these fresh pictures of Ukrainian nature, the humor, at once ingenuous and sly. How amazed we were—a Russian book that made us laugh, we who had not laughed since the time of Fonvizin! We were so thankful to the young author that we willingly forgave him the unevenness and incorrectness in his style, the disconnectedness and improbability of a few of his stories—leaving these shortcomings for the critics to profit by. The author justified this good-will. Since then he has constantly been developing and improving. He published *Arabesques*,[1] which includes his "Nevsky Avenue," the most complete[2] of his works. Right after that *Mirgorod*[3] appeared—wherein everyone avidly read "Old-World Landowners," that joking, touching idyll which makes you laugh through tears of sorrow and sincere emotion, and "Taras Bulba," the beginning of which is worthy of Walter Scott. Mr. Gogol is still going forward. We hope and desire to have frequent occasion to speak about him in our journal.*

[1836, *The Contemporary*]

## N O T E S

1. *A collection of short stories and essays.*
2. *Polnyj—complete, full, solid.*
3. *The collection contains "Viy" and "The Tale of the Two Ivans" in addition to the stories Pushkin mentions.*
4. The Inspector General *was presented on April 19, 1836.*

# ALEXANDER RADISHCHEV

Il ne faut pas qu'un honnête
homme mérite d'être pendu.

(Karamzin's words in 1819)

**At the end of the first decade of Catherine II's reign several** young men, scarcely more than boys, were sent, at her command, to the University of Leipzig under the supervision of one tutor and accompanied by a confessor. Their studies did them no good. The supervisor thought only of his own profit; the confessor, a good-hearted but uneducated monk, had no influence on their minds or morality. The young men became pranksters and free-thinkers. They returned to Russia, where the civil-service and family cares replaced Gellert's[1] lectures and student pranks. Most of them disappeared leaving no trace

* In a few days his comedy *The Inspector General* will be presented at the theater here.[4]

behind them. Two became well-known: one revealed his absolute incapacity and unfortunate mediocrity in a prominent post;[2]
the other became famous in quite a different way.

Alexander Radishchev was born around 1750.[3] He studied
first in the Corps of Pages, and he attracted the attention of the
headmasters as a young man of great promise. University life
did him little good. He did not even take the trouble to learn
Latin and German properly, in order at least to be able to understand his professors. Restless curiosity rather than thirst for
knowledge was the distinctive feature of his mind. He was
modest and pensive. The close tie with young Ushakov had a
deep and decisive influence on his entire life. Ushakov was a
little older than Radishchev, but he had the experience of a man
of the world. He had already served as secretary to Secret
Councilor Teplov, and a brilliant career was open to his ambition when out of love for learning he left the civil service and
went to Leipzig with the young students. A similarity of minds
and interests brought him close to Radishchev. Helvetius fell
into their hands.[4] They avidly studied the fundamentals of his
trivial and sterile metaphysics. Grimm, a traveling salesman of
French philosophy, found the Russian students in Leipzig reading the book *On Reason* and took Helvetius news which flat-
tered his vanity and delighted his whole fraternity.[5] It would
be incomprehensible to us now how the cold and dry Helvetius
could become the favorite of ardent and sensitive young men,
if, to our misfortune, we did not know how seductive new ideas
and rules which are rejected by law and traditions can be for
developing minds. We already know French philosophy of the
eighteenth century too well; all its aspects have been examined
and evaluated. What once passed as the secret teaching of hiero-
phants was later made public, preached on the city-squares, and
it lost forever the charm of mystery and novelty. Other ideas,
just as childish, other dreams, just as unrealizable, replaced the
ideas and dreams of Diderot's and Rousseau's pupils; and in
them the lightminded worshipper of idle talk again sees the
goal of humanity and the solution of the eternal enigma—not

imagining that in their turn these ideas will be replaced by others.

Radishchev wrote *The Life of F. V. Ushakov*. From this fragment it is apparent that Ushakov was by nature witty and eloquent, and that he had the gift of charisma. He died at twenty-one years of age as a consequence of an intemperate life; but even on his death-bed he managed to teach Radishchev a terrible lesson. Condemned to death by the physicians, he heard his sentence indifferently; soon his torments became unbearable and he demanded some poison from one of his comrades.* Radishchev opposed this, but from that time suicide became one of the favorite subjects of his meditations.

Returning to Petersburg, Radishchev entered the civil service, at the same time continuing his literary activity. He married. His financial position was quite adequate for him. In society he was respected as an "author." He was the protégé of Count Vorontsov. The Empress knew him personally and assigned him to her own chancellery. In the normal course of events Radishchev would have achieved one of the highest state ranks. But fate was preparing something else for him.

In Russia at that time there were men known by the name *Martinists*.[6] Even in our time we have met a few old men belonging to this semi-political, semi-religious society. A strange mixture of mystical piety and philosophical free-thinking, unselfish love of enlightenment, and a practical philanthropy distinguished them from the generation to which they belonged. People who found their own profit in perfidious slander tried to portray the Martinists as conspirators and attributed criminal political views to them. The Empress, who had long viewed the efforts of French philosophers as the games of artful battlers— and had approved them with her own sovereign applause—was disturbed to see their triumph and with suspicion she turned her attention to the Russian Martinists, whom she considered proponents of anarchy and adepts of the encyclopedists. One

* A. M. Kutuzov, to whom Radishchev dedicated *The Life of F. V. Ushakov*.

cannot deny that many of them were dissatisfied; but their ill-disposition was limited to a querulous censuring of the present, innocent hopes for the future, and ambitious toasts at Freemasons' dinners. Radishchev landed in their society. The mysteriousness of their talks enflamed his imagination. He wrote his *Journey from Petersburg to Moscow,* a satirical call to indignation, printed it in his private press and calmly put it up for sale.

If we mentally transport ourselves back to 1791, if we recall the political circumstances then, if we imagine the power of our government, our laws, which had not changed since the times of Peter I, their severity—at that time not yet softened by the twenty-five-year reign of Alexander, an autocrat who knew how to respect humanity—if we think what austere men still surrounded the throne of Catherine, Radishchev's crime will seem to us an insane act. A petty functionary, a man without any power, without any support, is so audacious as to take up arms against the system, against autocracy, against Catherine! And note: a conspirator places his hope on the united efforts of his comrades; in case of failure the member of a secret society is either ready to win mercy through recantation or, depending on the numerousness of his co-conspirators, expects impunity. But Radishchev is alone. He has neither comrades nor co-conspirators. In case of failure—and what success can he expect —he alone answers for everything, he alone is offered to the law as a sacrifice. We have never considered Radishchev a great man. His deed has always seemed criminal to us, unexcused by anything, and *Journey to Moscow* an extremely mediocre book; but for all that we cannot help but acknowledge him a criminal with extraordinary spirit, a political fanatic—deluded of course—but acting with amazing self-sacrifice and with a kind of chivalrous conscientiousness.

But perhaps Radishchev himself did not understand the full importance of his mad delusions. Otherwise how can one explain his unconcern and the strange idea of sending his book to all his acquaintants, among others Derzhavin, whom he placed in an embarrassing position? However that may be, his book, at first unnoticed—probably because the first pages are extremely boring and tedious—soon caused an uproar. It reached the Empress. Catherine was powerfully struck. For several days in a row she read these bitter, outrageous satires. "He's a Martinist," she said to Khrapovitsky (see his notes), "he's worse than Pugachov; he praises Franklin."[7]—A profoundly notable statement: the monarch who was striving for the unification of all the heterogeneous parts of the state could not see the colonies tearing away from the dominion of England and remain indifferent. Radishchev was brought to trial. The Senate condemned him to death (see the *Complete Collection of Laws*). The Empress lightened the sentence. The criminal was stripped of rank and nobility and sent to Siberia in chains.

In Ilimsk Radishchev devoted himself to peaceful literary endeavors. He wrote the greater part of his works there; many of them relate to the statistics of Siberia, to Chinese trade, etc. His correspondence with one of the prominent men of the time has been preserved, a man who was perhaps not entirely unconnected with the publication of *Journey*. Radishchev was a widower then. His sister-in-law went to him to share the exile's sequestration. In one of his poems he mentions this touching circumstance:

> I will sigh on the place
> Where Ermak, boarding a boat
> With his troops, set out
> For that terrible cold land,
> For the land where amid calamities,
> But on the bosom of ardent friendship,
> I was blissful, and where I left
> Half of a delicate soul.
>
> <div align="right"><i>Bova</i>, Introduction</div>

Ascending the throne, Emperor Pavel I summoned Radishchev out of exile, returned his rank and nobility to him, treated him graciously, and made him promise not to write anything against the spirit of the government. Radishchev kept his word. During the whole reign of Emperor Pavel I he didn't write a single line. He lived in Petersburg, away from business affairs, occupying himself with the education of his children. Humbled by experience and years, he even changed the way of thinking which had marked his stormy and bumptious youth. He harbored no malice for the past in his heart, and he was sincerely reconciled to the glorious memory of the great Empress.

We are not going to reproach Radishchev for weakness and inconstancy of character. Time changes a man in a spiritual as well as in a physical respect. With a sigh, or with a smile, the grown man repudiates the dreams which stirred the youth. There is always something strange and amusing about youthful-looking ideas, as there is about a youthful-looking face. Only a fool does not change, for time brings him no development, and experience does not exist for him. Could the sensitive and ardent Radishchev not shudder at the sight of what happened in France during the Terror? Could he hear without deep loathing his once favorite ideas preached from the heights of the guillotine, to the vile applause of the rabble? Once carried away by the leonine roar of Mirabeau, he no longer wanted to become an admirer of Robespierre, that sentimental tiger.

When he ascended the throne Emperor Alexander I remembered Radishchev, and forgiving him what could be attributed to the ardency of youth and the delusions of the age, he saw in the author of *A Journey* good intentions and aversion to many abuses. He made Radishchev a member of the Commission on new legislation and ordered him to summarize his ideas concerning some civil regulations. Carried away by a subject once close to his speculative studies, poor Radishchev recalled the old days and in the project presented to the authorities he gave himself up to his former dreams. Count Zavadovsky was surprised by the youth of his gray hairs and said to him, as a friendly reproach: "Eh, Alexander Nikolaevich, you've got a hankering to prate in the old way! Or wasn't Siberia enough for you?" Radishchev saw these words as a threat. Chagrined and frightened, he returned home, remembered the friend of his youth, the Leipzig student who once gave him the first idea of suicide, and . . . poisoned himself. The end which he had long foreseen and which he had prophesied for himself!

The works of Radishchev in verse and prose (except *Journey*) were published in 1807. The most extensive of his works is a philosophical discussion *On Man, On His Mortality and Immortality*. Its ratiocinations are banal and not enlivened by the style. Though he takes a stand against materialism, the pupil of Helvetius is still visible in him. He more willingly expounds than refutes the arguments for pure atheism. Noteworthy among the literary essays is his opinion of the *Telemachus* and Trediakovsky[8]—whom he liked because of the same feeling which made him abuse Lomonosov: aversion to generally accepted opinions. His best work in verse is "The Eighteenth Century," a lyric poem written in the ancient elegiac meter, where we find the following lines which, coming from his pen, are so remarkable:

The urn of time pours out the hours like drops; the drops gather into streams; the streams grow into rivers—and on a most distant shore the foaming waves pour out eternities into the sea, and there are neither limits nor shores there. No island rises there, the sounding-lead finds no bottom there; ages have flowed into it, their trace disappears in it; but, famous among the ages for its bloody stream, our century flows thence with sounds of thunder; and the ship bearing hope has finally been destroyed—the dock was close, but it has been engulfed by the maelstrom. The ferocious whirlpool has swallowed up happiness, and virtue and liberty—look, the terrible debris is still floating in the stream. No, you will not be forgotten, insane and strange century, you will be cursed forever, forever you will astonish all people. There is blood in your cradle—your lullaby is the thunder of battles. Oh, century soaked in blood, you are falling into the grave. But look, two cliffs have jutted up amid the bloody streams, Catherine and Peter, the offspring of eternity!—and Russia.

The first canto of *Bova* also has merit. The character of Bova is drawn originally; his conversation with Karga is amusing. It's too bad that in neither *Bova* nor *Alyosha Popovich*,[9] his other long poem—which for some reason is not included in the collection of his works—there is not a trace of nationalism, which is essential in works of this genre; but Radishchev meant to imitate Voltaire, because he was always imitating someone or other. In general Radishchev wrote better in verse than in prose. He had no model for the latter, but Lomonosov, Kheraskov, Derzhavin, and Kostrov[10] had already succeeded in developing our verse language.

*A Journey to Moscow*, the cause of his misfortune and fame, is, as we have already said, a very mediocre work, to say nothing of its barbaric style. The lamentations on the unhappy condition of the peasants, on oppression by powerful noblemen, and so forth are exaggerated and stale. The outbursts of fastidious and pompous sensibility are sometimes extremely ridiculous. We could substantiate our opinion with a multitude of quotations. But all the reader has to do to ascertain the truth of what we have said is to open the book at random.

All the French philosophy of his age is reflected in Radishchev: the scepticism of Voltaire, the philanthropy of Rousseau, the political cynicism of Diderot and Renale—but all in a contorted, ungainly form, as all objects are distortedly reflected in a distorting mirror. He is a true representative of semi-enlightenment. Ignorant disdain for everything in the past, weakminded amazement at his own age, blind prejudice for novelty, particularized and superficial bits of information—that is what we see in Radishchev. It is as if he were *trying* to irritate the supreme power with his bitter malediction; wouldn't it have been better to point out the good which that power was capable of doing? He asperses the power of serf-owners as manifest illegality; wouldn't it have been better to suggest to the government and intelligent land-owners ways for the step-by-step improvement of the condition of the serfs? He gets incensed at the censorship; wouldn't it have been better to discuss the rules by which a lawgiver should be guided, so that on one hand writers would not be oppressed and that thought—the holy gift of God—would not be the slave and victim of senseless and capricious rule, and so that on the other hand the writer would not use this divine tool for the achievement of a base or criminal goal? But all this would have simply been useful and wouldn't have been forbidden or created an uproar; for not only did the government itself not ignore writers and not oppress them—it even requested their participation, invited them to be active, listened to their opinions, took their advice; it felt the need for the assistance of enlightened and thinking men—without fearing their boldness or being offended by their sincerity. What goal did Radishchev have? What specifically did he desire? It is hardly likely that he himself could have answered these questions satisfactorily. His influence was inconsequential. Everyone read his book and forgot it, in spite of the fact that there were a few reasonable ideas in it, a few well-meant suggestions which had no need of being couched in abusive and pompous phrases and illegally printed on the presses of a secret press with an admixture of trivial and criminal prating. They would have done more real good if they had been proffered with great sincerity and goodwill, for there is no persuasiveness in aspersions; and there is no truth where there is no love.

3 April 1836, St. Petersburg
[unpublished][11]

## N O T E S

1. *Christian F. Gellert (1715–69)—Professor of poetry and ethics at the University of Leipzig. Author of folkish* Fabeln und Erzählungen, *novels, and an influential correspondence.*

2. *O. V. Kozodavlev, Minister of Internal Affairs, 1810–19.*

3. *Alexander N. Radishchev (1749–1802)—poet and prose writer whose* Journey from Petersburg to Moscow *(1790) contained materialistic statements, anti-monarchical sentiments, and attacks on*

*serfdom*—*for which he was exiled to Siberia. Although eventually pardoned, he committed suicide.*

*Pushkin wrote this essay for* The Contemporary, *but at the direction of S. S. Uvarov (the "Minister of National Enlightenment"), it was not passed by the censorship. Radishchev was still a touchy subject, so it is impossible to determine how much of this essay was written with one eye on the censorship.*

4. *Claude Adrian Helvétius (1715–71)—his* De l'Esprit *(1758) was condemned by the Sorbonne and burned by the hangman. Helvétius was an anti-clerical deist, an ethical utilitarian (who influenced Bentham and Mill), and he believed differences in men arise almost exclusively from education.*

5. *Friedrich Melchior, Baron von Grimm (1723–1807)—spent forty-two years in Parisian salons.*

6. *Martinism was a sort of mythical pantheism derived from Martinez Pasqualis and his disciple Saint Martin (c. 330–397). By a series of exercises and contacts with superior spirits one re-unites oneself with the divinity.*

7. *Benjamin Franklin.*

8. *Tredyakovsky translated Fénelon's* Télémaque *into Russian. The Utopian political content probably interested Radishchev.*

9. *Pushkin mistakenly attributes this poem by Radishchev's son to Radishchev himself.*

10. *Ermil I. Kostrov (1752–96)—son of a peasant, official poet of Moscow University, translator of Homer, Apuleius, Voltaire, and Ossian.*

11. *The essay was finished, but the censors refused to pass it.*

# S. P. SHEVYREV'S
# *THE HISTORY OF POETRY*

*The History of Poetry*[1] **is a comforting phenomenon, an** important book!

By its position—geographical, political, etc.—Russia is the judge, the court of Europe. *Nous sommes les grands jugeurs.* The dispassionateness and common sense of our judgments concerning what does not happen in our country are amazing—examples of this.

Our literary criticism is insignificant: why? Because common sense is not enough for that; love and learning are also required. A look at our critics—Merzlyakov, Shishkov, Dashkov, etc.[2]

In his introduction itself Shevyrev promises not to follow either the empirical system of French criticism nor the abstract philosophy of the Germans (pp. 6–11). He chooses a historical method of exposition—and to good purpose; in this way he lends learning the allurement of a story.

The critic proceeds to the history of Western literatures.

In Italy he sees Roman sensuality conquered by Christianity, acquiring the patronage of religion, resurrected in the arts, subjecting strict Catholicism to its sumptuous influence, and again ruling its native land.

He recognizes the same origin in Spain, but encounters the Moors and sees a Mohammedan tendency in it.

Leaving the sumptuous South, Shevyrev shifts to the northern peoples, the slaves of need, the stepchildren of nature.

In foggy England he sees Need developing Richness, industry, labor, study, literature without legends, etc., materialism.

In the holy German forests he discovers the same tendency to the abstraction, seclusion, feudal disunity, which even today dominate the political make-up of Germany, the systems of its thinkers, the courts of its little princes, and the faculties of its professors.

France, *the focus of Europe,* the representative of social life, a life at once egotistical and national. There science and poetry are not ends, but means. The people *(der Herr Omnis)* rules with all the repulsiveness of democracy. It has all the signs of ignorance: scorn for what is foreign, *une morgue pétulante et tranchante,* etc.

Russia's motto: *Suum cuique.*

[1836, unpublished]

## NOTES

1. *Shevyrev's history was published in 1835. Pushkin outlines the opening chapter.*
2. *A. F. Merzlyakov, A. S. Shishkov, D. V. Dashkov—bad writers and critics at the turn of the century.*


# M. E. LOBANOV'S OPINION ABOUT THE SPIRIT OF LITERATURE, FOREIGN A·ND OUR OWN

(Read by him on Jan. 18, 1836 in the Imperial Russian Academy)

**Mr. Lobanov[1] thought it wise to give his opinion an indefinite,** totally un-academical, form: it is a short essay rather like "notes from a journal," placed in *Literary Supplements to The Russian Invalid.* It may turn out that what is good in a journal will seem too lightweight when it is pronounced in the presence of the entire academy and then solemnly publicized. However that may be, Mr. Lobanov's opinion deserves, and even demands, the most attentive examination.

Love for reading and desire for education [thus begins Mr. Lobanov's essay] have greatly increased in our fatherland during the past few years. Printing presses have multiplied; the number of books has multiplied; journals are sold in a large quantity; book trade is expanding.

Finding this occurrence "pleasant for an observer of successes in our fatherland," Mr. Lobanov utters an unexpected accusation:

Dispassionate observers [says he] who bear in their hearts love for everything that tends to the good of the fatherland, going over in their memory everything that they have read lately, can say, not without shuddering: "There is in our modern literature a certain reverberation of immorality and absurdity which has been engendered by foreign writers."

Not entering into an explanation of what he means by the words "immorality" and "absurdity," Mr. Lobanov continues:

One people borrows from another people, and it is useful to borrow; good sense prescribes imitating what is beautiful. But what is there to borrow nowadays (I am speaking of pure literature) from the most recent foreign writers?

They often reveal absurd, vile, and monstrous phenomena; they spread pernicious and destructive thoughts —about which the reader has never had the slightest idea until now, and which forcibly place in his soul the germ of immorality and unfaith, and consequently, of future misdeeds or crimes.

Can it be the life and bloody deeds of robbers, executioners, and the people like them who are flooding literature nowadays in stories and novels, in verse and prose, and who nourish nothing but curiosity, are presented as models for imitation? Can it be the most repulsive spectacles which inspire not an instructive horror, but disgust which revolts the soul, serve humanity usefully? Can it be the infinite sphere of the noble, the instructive, the good, and the elevated has been exhausted, so that they turned to the absurd, the *repulgant* (?), the disgusting, and even the hateful?

In support of these accusations Mr. Lobanov cites the well-known opinion of the Edinburgh journalists on "the current state of French literature." In this case the vaults of the Academy resounded with the names of Jules Janin, Eugène Sue,[2] and others; these names were affixed to strange adjectives. . . . But what if (beyond any expectation) Mr. Lobanov's essay is translated and these gentlemen see their names printed in a report of the Imperial Russian Academy? Won't all the eloquence of our orator be lost in vain? Won't they be right to be proud of such unanticipated honor, unheard-of in the chronicles of European academies, where until now only the names of those living people who had raised eternal monuments with their talents, services, and works were pronounced? (The Academies have been silent about others.) The critical essay of the English Aristarch was printed in a journal; there it occupied a place proper to it and produced its effect. Our *Library*[3] translated it, and did well to. But that is where things should have stopped. There are heights from which satirical reproaches ought not fall; there are callings which place on you the obligation of moderation and decorum, independent of the surveillance of the censorship, *sponte sua, sine lege*.[4]

> For France [writes Mr. Lobanov], for peoples befogged by the most recent philosophy (which is ruinous for humanity), who have been hardened by the bloody events of revolutions, and who have fallen into a slough of spiritual and intellectual debauchery, the most repulsive spectacles— for example, the vilest plays, the most disgusting chaos of hateful shamelessness and incest of *Lucrezia Borgia*[5]—do not seem such to them; the most extremely destructive thoughts are not so infectious for them, for they have long since been accustomed to them and, so to speak, grew up with them in the horrors of revolutions.

I ask, can one utter such terrible anathema on an entire people? The people which produced Fénelon, Racine, Bossuet, Pascal, and Montesquieu—which nowadays takes pride in Chateaubriand and Ballanche,[6] a people which acknowledged Lamartine as the foremost of their poets, who opposed to Niebuhr[7] and Hallam[8] Barante,[9] both Thierrys[10] and Guizot,[11] a people which has such a strong religious tendency, which so solemnly renounces the pitiful sceptical ratiocinations of the last century—can it be this entire people should answer for the works of a few writers, for the most part young men, who misuse their talents, who have based their selfish calculations on the curiosity and nervous sensibility of the readers? For the satisfaction of the public, which always demands novelty and strong impressions, many writers turned to repulsive depictions, little concerned about the beautiful, about truth, about personal conviction. But moral feeling, like talent, is not given to everyone. One cannot demand a striving toward one goal from all writers. No law can say: write precisely about such-and-such subjects, and not about others. Thoughts, like actions, are divided into the *criminal* and *those for which one is not answerable.* Law does not interfere with the customs of a private person; it does not demand an accounting of his supper, of his walks and so forth; the law does not interfere with the subjects chosen by a writer either; it does not demand that he describe the mores of a Genevan pastor, and not the adventures of a robber or an executioner; that he laud marital happiness and not laugh at the adversities of marriage. To demand elegance or a moral goal from all works of art would be the same as demanding a viceless life and education from every citizen. The law reaches only crimes, leaving weaknesses and vices to the conscience of each person. Contrary to Mr. Lobanov's opinion, we do not think that present-day writers "presented robbers and executioners as models for imitation." Writing *Gil Blas* and *Les aventures de Guzman d'Alfarache,* LeSage, of course, did not have the intention of teaching lessons in robbery and rascalry. Schiller, probably, did not write his *Robbers* with the goal of summoning young people from the universities onto the high roads. Why suppose criminal intents in present-day writers when their works simply express a desire to interest and strike the imagination of the reader? The adventures of clever rascals, terrible histories of robbers, of corpses, etc., have always interested the curiosity not only of children, but of grown-up babies too; and since ancient times story-tellers and poets have made use of this predilection of our souls.

We do not suppose that the present-day, annoying, "hasty, incoherent French literature was the result of political disturbances."* French literature had its own revolution, apart from

---

* *The Contemporary,* No. 1. "On the Trend of Journal Literature."

the political upheaval which toppled the ancient monarchy of Louis XIV. In the darkest time of revolution, literature was producing cloying, sentimental, moralizing books. Literary monsters began to appear already in the last period of the short and pious Restoration *(Restauration)*. The source of this phenomenon must be sought in literature itself. Having long submitted to capricious codes which gave it overly restrictive forms, it went to the other extreme, and began to consider that forgetting all rules was a legitimate freedom. The trivial and false theory established by ancient rhetorics that *usefulness* is the condition and goal of *belles-lettres* was destroyed by itself. It was felt that the goal of art is the *ideal* and not *moralizing*. But French writers understood only one half of this unquestionable truth, and supposed that moral ugliness too can be the goal of poetry, i.e. an ideal! Previous novelists had been presenting human nature in a kind of finical pomposity; the reward of virtue and punishment of vice were inevitable conditions of their every fiction; present-day writers, on the contrary, love to present vice as triumphing everywhere and always, and they find only two strings in the human heart—egoism and vanity. Of course, such a superficial view of human nature reveals shallowness of thought and will soon be as ridiculous and tiresome as the preciosity and solemnity of the novels of Arnaud[12] and Mme. Cottin.[13] For the time being it is still new, and the public, i.e. the majority of readers, out of unfamiliarity, sees in present-day novelists the profoundest experts on human nature. But already "the literature of desperation" (as Goethe called it), "satanical literature" (as Southey says), the literature of shock, prisons, punch, blood, and cigars etc., this literature, long since condemned by the higher criticism, is beginning to fall even in the opinion of the public.

French literature, which from Kantemir's time[14] has had a direct or indirect influence on our burgeoning literature, had to reverberate in our epoch too. But now its influence was weak. It was confined only to translations and a few scattered imitations which had no great success. Our journals, which as everywhere rightly and wrongly direct public opinion, in general turned out to be opponents of the new romantic school. The original novels which have had the most success in our country belong to the moralistic and historical genre. LeSage and Walter Scott served as their models, and not Balzac and not Jules Janin. Poetry remained alien to the French influence; more and more it grows close to German poetry and proudly maintains its independence from the tastes and demands of the public.

Pausing on the spirit and trend of our literature [continues Mr. Lobanov], every enlightened person, every right-thinking Russian sees: in the theories of sciences—inconsistency, impenetrable darkness, and the chaos of unconnected thoughts; in literary pronouncements—total irresponsibility, dishonesty, brazenness, and even violence. Decorum, respect, common sense have been rejected, forgotten, destroyed. For many people Romanticism—a word that is still undefined, but a magic word—has become the aegis for total irresponsibility and literary extravagance. Criticism, the modest instructress and conscientious friend of literature, has turned into street-corner buffoonery nowadays, into literary piracy, into a way of making a living from the pocket of weak-mindedness by means of audacious and violent sallies—often even against men of the government, celebrated both for civil and literary services. Nothing is respected—neither rank, nor intelligence, nor talent, nor age. Lomonosov passed for a pedant. The greatest genius, who left as Russia's heritage an elevated song to God, a song of which there is no equal in any language of all the peoples of the universe, seems not to exist for our literature; he seems to be *untalenned* [Mr. Lobanov probably meant to say *untalented*], left without attention. The name of Karamzin, a profound sage, a conscientious writer, a man of pure heart, is abandoned to mockery. . . .

Of course, our criticism is still at a youthful stage. It rarely maintains the solemnity and decorum peculiar to it; perhaps its decisions are often inspired by calculation and not by conviction. Disrespect for names sanctified by fame (the first sign of ignorance and weak thinking) is unfortunately not only considered permissible among us, but even praiseworthy boldness. But here too Mr. Lobanov made unjust charges. Lomonosov's title of poet has been questioned (very superficially), but as far as I recall, no one has ever called him a "pedant"; on the contrary, nowadays it has become customary to praise him as a scientist, at the expense of the poet. The name of the great Derzhavin is always pronounced with a feeling of almost superstitious prejudice. The pure, elevated fame of Karamzin belongs to Russia, and not one writer with true talent, not one truly learned person, even from among his opponents, has refused him the reward of profound respect and gratitude.

We do not belong to the group of servile admirers of our century, but we must admit that sciences have made a step forward. The ratiocinations of the great European thinkers were not vain for us either. The theory of sciences was freed from empiricism, assumed a more general form, displayed more striving for unity. German philosophy, especially in Moscow, found many young, ardent, conscientious followers;[15] and although they spoke a language little comprehensible to the uninitiated, nevertheless their influence was salutary, and as time goes on it is becoming more perceptible.

I am not going to speak either about the dominant taste or about concepts and teachings about the Beautiful. The former is everywhere apparent, revealed in everything, and well-known to everyone; and the latter are either so inconsistent and perverse in the latest ephemeral and mutually destructive systems, or so confused in idle lucubrations, that they are impenetrable by common sense. Nowadays it is hardly believed that the Beautiful, given only a few changes in form, was and is the same for all ages and peoples; that the Homers, Dantes, Sophocles, Shakespeares, Schillers, Racines, and Derzhavins, in spite of the differences of their forms, genres, beliefs, and customs, all created the beautiful for all ages; that whether they are romantics or classicists, writers must satisfy the intellects, imaginations, and hearts of educated and enlightened people, and not just the senseless, stupidly jabbering crowd and silly buffoons. No, nowadays they preach that the human intellect has marched far ahead, that it can leave the ancients in peace, and even celebrated modern writers, that it doesn't need guides and models, that nowadays every writing person is an original genius—and under the banner of this false teaching, striking down the great writers of antiquity with the name of ponderous and tiresome classics (who have, however, captivated their countrymen for thousands of years and will always give many elevated pleasures to their readers), under the banner of this false teaching, modern writers are irresponsibly befuddling the minds of inexperienced youths and leading both morality and literature to total decline.

Leaving this Philippic without objection, I cannot help pausing on the conclusion drawn by Mr. Lobanov from everything he has said:

Because of the multitude of immoral books published nowadays, the censorship is presented with the insuperable task of penetrating all of the contrivances of those who write. It is not easy to destroy perversity of opinions in literature, and to rein audacity of language, if, moved by evil intentions, it proclaims what is absurd and even harmful. Who should participate in this difficult feat? Every conscientious Russian writer, every enlightened father of a family, and most of all the Academy, which was established for this very purpose. Moved by love for the sovereign and the fatherland, it has a right, on it lies the duty to unslackeningly reveal, strike down, and destroy evil, wherever it is met in the sphere of literature. "The Academy" (it is said in its Code, Chap. III, sec. 2, and in His Majesty's Report, sec. III), "as a society established for the observation of morality, chastity, and purity of language, must consider the analysis of books (or critical judgments) one of its main obligations." Thus, dear sirs, let each of my fellow members, in accord with its Code, present for examination and printing in the collections of this Academy analyses of works and judgments about the books and journals of our latest literature and, thus contributing to the common good, let each carry out the true office of this most highly established society.

But where is this multitude of immoral books we have? Who are these audacious, evil-intentioned writers who are contriving to overthrow the laws on which the well-being of society is based? And can our censorship be reproached for incaution and slackness? We know the opposite. Contrary to Mr. Lobanov's opinion, the censorship should not "penetrate all the contrivances" of those who write. "The censorship should pay special attention to the spirit of the book being examined, to the apparent aim and intention of the author, and in its judgments always take the obvious sense of a speech as its basis, not allowing itself a capricious interpretation of it toward the bad side." (Code on Censorship, Sec. 6.) Such was the highest will—which gave us literary property and legal freedom of thought! If on first glance this basic rule of our censorship can seem extreme falsehood, on the most attentive examination we will see that without it, it would be impossible to print a single line, for every word can be re-interpreted toward the harmful side. The "absurd," if it is simply absurd, and contains nothing contrary to faith, government, morality, or personal honor, is not subject to be destroyed by the censorship. Absurdity, like stupidity, is subject to the ridicule of society, and does not require action of the law. There are many books passed by the censorship which an enlightened father of a family will not give to his children; books are not all written for the same age. A few moralists assert than an eighteen-year-old girl cannot be allowed to read novels; it doesn't follow from this that the censorship should forbid all novels. The censorship is a beneficent institution, not an oppressive one; it is the faithful guardian of personal and governmental well-being, and not a bothersome nurse-maid following at the heels of mischievous children.

We conclude with a sincere desire that the Russian Academy, which has already done true good to our fine language and accomplished so many celebrated feats, will encourage and enliven the literature of our fatherland by rewarding worthy writers with its active support—and by punishing unworthy ones with the one tool that is proper to it: inattention.

[1836, *The Contemporary*]

## N O T E S

1. *Mikhail Lobanov (1787–1846)—a minor writer and translator. Belinsky's sarcastic review of his play* Boris Godunov *was one reason for his attack on recent criticism.*

2. *Jules Janin (1804–74) and Eugène Sue (1804–59)—writers of l'école frénétique who influenced writers as different as Gogol and Dostoevsky.*

3. The Library for Reading, *Senkovsky's journal.*

4. *A quotation from the first book of Ovid's* Metamorphoses.

5. *A play by Victor Hugo (1833).*

6. *Pierre Simon Ballanche (1776–1847)—publisher and editor, author of numerous works containing mystical ideas and a vaguely sentimental philosophy of history.*

7. *Barthold Georg Niebuhr (1776–1831)—Pushkin knew P. A. Golbéry's translation* Histoire Romaine *(Paris, 1830–35).*

8. *Henry Hallam (1777–1859)—Whig, historian. Pushkin probably read* The View of the State of Europe during the Middle Ages *(1818).*

9. *Guillaume Barante (1782–1866)—politician and historian. Author of* Histoire des ducs de Bourgogne *(1824).*

10. *Amédée Simon Thierry (1797–1873)—author of* Histoire des Gaulois *(Paris, 1835), and Jacques Nicolas Thierry (1795–1856), author of* Histoire de la conquête de l'Angleterre par les Normands *(1825).*

11. *François Pierre Guizot (1787–1874)—author of* Histoire de la civilisation en Europe *(1828).*

12. *François, abbé Arnaud (1721–84)—epigrammist, author of articles published as* Variétés littéraires.

13. *Sophie Cottin (1773–1807)—author of historical novels such as* Mathilde *(1807), whose hero is mentioned in* Eugene Onegin, *III, IX.*

14. *Antioch Kantemir (1708–44).*

15. *See notes to* Morning-Star.

# VOLTAIRE

(Correspondence inédite de Voltaire avec le président de Brosses, etc. Paris, 1836)

**Not long ago Voltaire's correspondence with de Brosses**[1] **was** published in Paris. It concerns a purchase of land made by Voltaire in 1758.

Every line of a great writer becomes precious to posterity. We examine autographs with curiosity, even if they are nothing but fragments from an account book or a note to a tailor about the postponement of a payment. We are involuntarily struck by the thought that the hand which traced these humble figures, these insignificant words, also wrote great works, the objects of our studies and raptures, in the same script and, perhaps, with the same pen. But I think only Voltaire could have compiled a book which makes you laugh on every page out of a business correspondence about the purchase of some land, and made transactions and deeds as interesting as witty pamphlets. Fate sent such an amusing buyer a no less amusing seller. President de Brosses is one of the most remarkable writers of the last century. He is well-known for many learned works* but we consider the letters written by him from Italy in 1739–40 and recently republished under the title *L'Italie il y a cent ans,* the best of his works. De Brosses revealed extraordinary talent in these

* *Histoire des navigations aux terres Australes; Traité de la formation mécanique des langues; Histoire de VII siècle de la République Romaine; Traité du culte des dieux fétiches; etc.*

friendly letters. His true erudition (never burdened by pedantry), profundity of thought, joking wit, and carelessly but vividly and boldly drawn portraits, place his book above anything else of the same type that has been written.

Driven out of Paris, forced to flee Berlin, Voltaire sought refuge on the shore of Lake Geneva. Fame did not save him from troubles. His own personal freedom was not secure; he was worried about his capital, which he had divided among various hands. The protection of the small bourgeois republic did not hearten him too much. In any case, he wanted to be reconciled with his native country and wished (he himself writes) to have one foot in a monarchy, the other in a republic— in order to step back and forth—according to the circumstances. The village of Tourny, which belonged to President de Brosses, attracted his attention. He knew the president as a carefree, extravagant man who always had need of money, and he entered negotiations with him in the following letter:[2]

> I read with greatest pleasure what you write about Australia, but allow me to make you a proposition regarding real estate. You are not such a person that Tourny could bring you profit. Chouet, your renter, intends to tear up his lease. Do you want to sell me your land for life? I am old and ailing. I know that this would be an unprofitable thing for me, but it will be useful for you and pleasant for me—and here are the conditions which it has occurred to me to submit for your examination.
>
> I agree to construct a nice little house from the materials of your very wretched castle. I expect to use 25,000 *livres* for that. I will pay you the other 25,000 *livres* in hard cash.
>
> All the improvements I make, all the livestock, all the agricultural implements which I add to the holdings, will belong to you. If I die without having constructed the house you will be left with 25,000 *livres* in your hands, and if you please you will finish constructing it. But I will try to live two more years, and then you will have a very respectable little house for nothing.

On top of that, I agree to live not longer than four or five years.

In exchange for these honorable propositions, I require having complete control of your movable and immovable property, its rights, forest, livestock, and even the priest, until the time when he buries me. If this amusing trade seems profitable to you, you can affirm it—not in jest— with one word. Life is too short; business should not be drawn out.

I'll add one more word. I improved my cranny, nick-named *les Délices;* I improved the house in Lausanne; both are now worth twice their former price—I'll do the same with your land too. In its present condition you'll never get rid of it.

In any case, I request you to keep all this secret, and have the honor to be, etc.

De Brosses was not slow with his answer; his letter, like Voltaire's, is full of wit and jollity.

If I were in your neighborhood [he writes] at the time when you settled so close to the city,* enraptured, like you, over the physical beauty of the shores of your lake, I would have the honor to whisper in your ear that the moral character of the inhabitants demanded that you settle in France, for two important reasons: (1) because one must live in one's own home, (2) because one must not live among alien people. You can't imagine how much this republic makes me love monarchy. . . . Then I would offer you my castle, if it were worthy of you; but my castle doesn't even have the honor of being a relic; it's simply *rags*. You've got the idea of returning its youth to it as to Memnon; I very much approve your proposition. You don't know, perhaps, that M. d'Argental had the same intention for you. —Let's get down to business.

Here de Brosses examines one by one all the conditions proposed by Voltaire; with some he agrees, others he rejects, re-

* In 1755 Voltaire bought *les Délices sur St. Jean* near Geneva.

vealing keen-wittedness and cleverness which Voltaire, it seems, did not expect from the President. This aroused his self-esteem; he began to be sly; the correspondence developed with more liveliness. Finally, the deed was executed on December 15.

These letters containing the negotiations of the bargainers and a few others written after the conclusion of the bargain make up the best part of Voltaire's correspondence with de Brosses. They both show off to each other; they constantly leave business questions for the most unexpected jokes, for the frankest judgments of contemporary events and people. Voltaire appears as Voltaire in these letters, i.e., the most amiable of interlocutors; de Brosses appears as the witty writer who so originally described Italy's government and customs, its artistic—and voluptuous—life.

But soon the accord between the new renter of the land and its former owner was interrupted. The war, like many other wars, began from unimportant causes. Voltaire was angered by some trees that were cut down; he quarrelled with the president —no less irritable than he. One has to see what Voltaire's anger is like! Already he looks on de Brosses as an enemy, as on Fréron,[3] as the grand inquisitor. He intends to ruin him: *qu'il tremble!* he exclaims in a fury, *"il s'agit de le déshonorer!"* He complains, he weeps, he gnashes his teeth . . . and the whole thing over 200 francs. On his side, de Brosses does not want to give in to the hot-tempered philosopher; in answer to his complaints he writes the celebrated old man a haughty letter, reproaches him for inborn impertinence, advises him to abstain from his pen in moments of insanity, in order not to blush when recovering his senses afterward, and he ends the letter with Juvenal's wish:

Mens sana in corpore sano.

Outsiders meddle in the neighbors' strife. Their mutual friend, M. Rufié, tries to appeal to Voltaire's conscience and writes him a caustic letter (which was probably dictated by de Brosses himself):

You fear being deceived [says M. Rufié], but this is the better of the two roles. . . . You have never had law-suits: they are devastating, even when we win them. . . . Remember La Fontaine's oyster and the fifth scene of the second act of *Les Fourberies de Scapin*.* Apart from the lawyers you should also be afraid of the literary rabble who will be happy to throw themselves upon you. . . .

Voltaire was the first to get tired and give in. He sulked about the stubborn president, and was the reason that de Brosses did not get into the Academy (which at that time meant a great deal). Besides that, Voltaire had the pleasure of outliving him: de Brosses, the younger of the two by fifteen years, died in 1777, a year before Voltaire.

In spite of the multitude of materials collected for a history of Voltaire (a whole library of them), he is still very little known as a business man, capitalist, and landowner. The currently published correspondence reveals a great deal. In his foreword the publisher writes:

One has to see how the pet of Europe, the interlocutor of Catherine the Great and Frederick II, busies himself with smallest of trifles to maintain his local reputation; one has to see how he drives into his county in a holiday coat, accompanied by both of his nieces (who are covered with jewelry), how he hears out the speech of his priest and how his new subjects greet him with a salute from cannons rented from the Geneva Republic. He's in eternal strife with all the local clergy. *Gabelle* (the tax on salt) finds in him a clever and active opponent. Then he starts speculating in salt. He has his own courtiers: he sends them as ambassadors to Switzerland. And all this upsets him; he is sincerely worried about everything with the irritability of passions exclusively peculiar to him. He showers now the clever arguments of a lawyer, now the objections of a prosecutor, now the sly ruses of a merchant, now the hyperbole of a poet, now bursts of true eloquence. Really,

---

* The scene in which Leander makes Scapin confess to all his swindles on his knees.

his letter to the president about a brawl in the tavern calls to mind his intercession for the Callas family.

In one of these letters we discovered some unknown verses by Voltaire. The light stamp of his inimitable talent is on them. They are written to a neighbor who had sent him some rose bushes:

> Vos rosiers sont dans mes jardins,
> Et leur fleurs vont bientôt paraître.
> Doux asile où je suis mon maître!
> Je renonce aux lauriers si vains,
> Qu'à Paris j'aimais trop peut-être.
> Je me suis trop piqué les mains
> Aux épines qu'ils ont fait naître.

We confess to the *rococo* of our old-fashioned taste—in these seven lines we find more *style*, more life, more thought, than in a half dozen of the long French poems written in the current taste where thought is replaced by mutilated expression, Voltaire's lucid language by the pompous language of Ronsard, his liveliness by unbearable monotony, and his wit by vulgar cynicism or flaccid melancholy.

In general Voltaire's correspondence with de Brosses presents us with the nice side of the creator of *Mérope* and *Candide* His pretensions, his weaknesses, his childish irritability—none of this harms him in our imagination. We willingly forgive him and are ready to follow all the impulses of his ardent soul and his touchy sensitivity. But no such feeling is born on reading the letters the publisher has appended to the end of the book which we are examining. These new letters were found in the papers of M. de la Touche, the former French ambassador to the court of Frederick II (in 1752).

At the time Voltaire had not made peace with the Northern Solomon,* his former pupil. Maupertuis, the president of the Berlin Academy, had quarrelled with Professor König. The king took the side of his president; Voltaire interceded for the pro-

* This is what Voltaire called Frederick II in his panegyrical epistles.

fessor. A work entitled "A Letter to the President" appeared without the name of its author. In it König was condemned and Voltaire nettled. Voltaire objected and published his caustic answer in the German journals. After a short time "A Letter to the Public" was reprinted in Berlin with a depiction of the crown, sceptre, and Prussian eagle on the title page. Only then did Voltaire guess whom he had so incautiously taken on, and he started to consider a sensible retreat. From these acts he saw that the king had obviously grown cool toward him, and he had a premonition of disfavor. "I am trying not to believe it," he wrote to d'Argentale[4] in Paris, "but I fear being like cuckholded husbands who attempt to convince themselves of the faithlessness of their wives." In spite of his dejection, nevertheless he could not resist nettling his opponents again. He wrote the most mordant of his satires *(La Diatribe du Dr. Akakia)* and printed it, having by deception gotten permission for this from the king himself.

The consequences are well-known. At the command of Frederick, the satire was burned by the hand of the executioner. Voltaire left Berlin, was detained in Frankfurt by the Prussian police, was under arrest for several days, and was forced to give up some poems of Frederick which had been printed for a few people and among which was a satirical poem against Louis XIV and his court.

This entire pitiful story does little honor to philosophy. During the course of his entire long life Voltaire never knew how to maintain his own dignity. In his youth imprisonment in the Bastille, exile, and persecution couldn't draw compassion and sympathy for his person—things which a suffering talent was almost never denied. The confidant of sovereigns, the idol of Europe, the foremost writer of his century, the guide of minds and contemporary opinion, Voltaire did not draw respect for his grey hair even in his old age; the laurels which covered it were spattered with mud. The slander which pursues a celebrity, but which is always destroyed in the face of truth, did not disappear for him—contrary to the general law—for it was always verisimilar. He had no self-esteem and didn't feel it essential to have the esteem of other people. What drew him to Berlin? Why should he exchange his independence for the capricious grace of a sovereign alien to him who had no right to compel him to do it? . . .

To the honor of Frederick II we will say that the king himself, contrary to his inborn tendency to mockery, would not have humiliated his old teacher, would not have put the jester's coat on the foremost of French writers, would not have betrayed him to the ridicule of the world had not Voltaire himself asked for such pitiful disgrace.

Until this time it has been supposed that in a burst of noble indignation Voltaire had on his own accord sent Frederick the gentleman-in-waiting's key and the Prussian medal, tokens of his inconstant grace; but now it is revealed that the king himself demanded them back. The role is changed: Frederick is indignant and threatens, Voltaire weeps and implores. . . .

What can be concluded from this? —That genius has its weaknesses which comfort mediocrity, but sadden noble hearts, reminding them of the imperfection of humanity. That the writer's real place is his learned study, and that, finally, independence and self-esteem alone can lift us above the trivialities of life and the storms of fate.

[1836, *The Contemporary*]

## N O T E S

1. *Charles de Brosses (1709–77)—cantankerous president of the Dijon parlement, bon vivant, the member of the Académie who vetoed Voltaire, author of* Lettres familières *(or,* L'Italie il y a cent ans).

2. *I have given a literal English translation of Pushkin's own Russian translation of the French originals. However, I did this with the French version at hand and tried to stay as close to this as possible while still preserving any changes or paraphrases Pushkin allowed*

*himself. For the French of Voltaire's proposal and de Brosses' answer see: T. Besterman (ed.),* Voltaire's Correspondence *(Geneva, 1958), Vol. XXXIV, p. 80, p. 87.*

3. *Eli Catrin Fréron (1719–76)—a critic, one of Voltaire's many bitter enemies.*

4. *Actually, the letter was sent to Mme. Marie Louise Denis.*

# THE JOURNEY OF V. L. P.

*The[1] Journey of N. N. to Paris,* **written three days before the** journey. In three parts. Moscow, Platon Beketov's typog. 1808, in 16°. The picture is of V. L. Pushkin and Talm.

This book has never been for sale. A few copies were distributed to friends of the author, from whom I had the luck to get mine (almost the last). I keep it as a monument of good will which is precious for me. . . .

"The Journey" is a gay, unmalicious joke at one of the author's friends; the late V. L. Pushkin was setting out for Paris and his infantile rapture gave rise to the composition of a small poem in which all of Vasily Lvovich is depicted with amazing accuracy. It is a model of playful lightness and a lively, unmalicious joke.

For those who love Catullus, Gresset, and Voltaire, for those who love poetry not only in its lyrical transports or in the dejected inspiration of an elegy, not only in the vast creations of the drama and epic, but also in the playfulness of a joke, and in the mind's amusements, inspired by pure gaiety. Sincerity is precious in a poet. It is pleasant for us to see the poet in all the states and changes of his lively and creative soul: in sadness and in joy, in flights of rapture and when the feelings are at rest, in Juvenalian indignation and in mild vexation at a boring neighbor. . . .

I revere the creation of *Faust*, but I love epigrams, too.

I'm sorry: I would give all that has been written in Russia in imitation of Byron for the following unreflective and unenraptured verses in which the poet makes his hero exclaim to his friends:

> Friends! Sisters! I'm off to Paris!
> I've begun to live, but not to breathe! etc.

There are people who acknowledge no poetry except that which is passionate and high-flown; there are people who find even Horace prosaic (calm, intelligent, thoughtful, isn't that right?). So be it. But it would be a pity if the charming odes which even our Derzhavin imitated did not exist.

[1836, unpublished]

### N O T E

1. *The title of a humorous poem by I. I. Dmitriev. Fifty copies of the work—aimed at Pushkin's jovial uncle (a poet in his own right)—were printed in 1808.*

## ON THE DUTIES OF MAN,
## A WORK BY SYLVIO PELLICO

In[1] a few days a new translation of the famous Sylvio Pellico's work, *Dei doveri degli uomini*, will be published.

It is a book whose every word has been interpreted, explicated, preached at all ends of the earth, applied to all possible circumstances of life and events in the world, from which it is impossible to repeat a single phrase which everyone does not know by heart, a phrase which wouldn't already be a "proverb of nations"; it no longer contains anything with which we are not familiar. But it is called a Gospel, and if we are bored with the world or aggrieved by despondency, such is the book's ever new charm that if we open it at random, we are unable to resist its sweet enthrallment, and our spirit is enveloped by its divine eloquence.

And it isn't in vain that, intending to say a few words about the book of a humble sufferer, we dared to mention the divine Gospel. Few were the elect (even among the original pastors of the church) whose works in their humility of spirit, dulcet eloquence, and child-like simplicity of heart would approach the preachings of the heavenly teacher.

In later times the unknown creator of the book *On the Imitation of Christ*, Fénelon, and Sylvio Pellico belong in the highest degree to the elect whom the angel of the Lord greeted with the name "men of good will."

Sylvio Pellico spent ten years in various dungeons and published his notes after he was set free. The surprise was universal: people expected complaints brimming with bitterness—they read warm and touching meditations filled with pure tranquillity, love and good-will.

Let us confess our unfounded suspicion. Reading these notes where no expression of impatience, reproach, or hate ever slips from under the pen of the unfortunate prisoner, we involuntarily supposed some hidden intention in this imperturbable benignity in everything and toward everything; this temperance seemed artful to us. And while enraptured by the writer, we rebuked the man for insincerity. The book *Dei doveri* made us ashamed, and then gave us the answer to the mystery of a beautiful soul, the mystery of a Christian man.

Having said what book Sylvio Pellico's work reminded us of, we cannot and should not add anything to our praise. We were surprised to read the following words about Sylvio Pellico's book in one of our journals, in an essay by a writer of true talent, a critic[2] who deserves the confidence of enlightened readers:

If the book *On Duties* had not been published immediately

after the book *On Life (My Prisons)*, we would have considered it a series of clichés, a dry, arbitrarily dogmatic lesson which we would have sat through without attention.

Can it be Sylvio Pellico has need of an excuse? Can it be his book—entirely filled with sincere warmth, inexpressible charm, harmonious eloquence—could seem *dry* and coldly dogmatic to anyone in any circumstance? Can it be that if it had been written in the quiet of Fivaida or a philosopher's library, and not in the sad seclusion of a dungeon, it would be unworthy of attracting the attention of a man gifted with a heart? We cannot believe this was what the author of *The History of Poetry* really had in mind.

One of the most common charges of the critics is: "That is no longer new, that has already been said." But everything has already been said, all ideas have been expressed, and repeated, in the course of the centuries—what follows from that? That the human spirit no longer produces anything new? No, we aren't going to slander it; the mind is as inexhaustible in the assimilation of ideas as language is inexhaustible in the combination of words. All words are in the dictionary; but the books which are constantly being published are not basically repetitions of the dictionary. Taken separately, *an idea*[3] can never offer anything new, but *ideas* can be varied to infinity.

As the best refutation of Mr. Shevyrev's opinion, I quote his own words:

> Read it [Pellico's book] with the same faith with which it was written, and you will step from the dark world of doubts, disturbance, and cleavage of the head from the heart into the radiant world of order and harmony. The task of life and happiness will seem simple to you. You will somehow collect yourself—scattered in bits of passions, habits, and whims—and in your soul you will perceive two feelings which, unfortunately, are very rare in this epoch: the feeling of satisfaction and the feeling of hope.

[1836, *The Contemporary*]

## N O T E S

1. *Silvio Pellico (1788–1854)—Italian dramatist. Arrested on the charge of carbonarism in 1820, he was condemned to death, then imprisoned. The simple and naive egotism of* Le Mie prigioni *established his fame.*

2. *S. P. Shevyrev was the author of the essay in* The Moscow Observer *(Part VI, 1836).*

3. Mysl'—*"thought" or "idea."*

# A LETTER TO THE PUBLISHER

**Georgy Konisky,[1] about whom an essay was printed in the** first number of *The Contemporary*, begins his priestly teachings with the following remarkable words:

> I decided that the first word I say to you, pious listeners, people of Christ, should be about myself. . . . My office, as you yourselves see, is a teaching one; and good and ingenuous teachers teach themselves first, before others; as it is the closest, they preach into their own ear beforehand, not into others'.

Taking the journalists' staff, intending to preach true criticism, you would have acted in an extremely praiseworthy way, dear sirs, if preliminarily you had set forth before the flock of your readers your thoughts about the office of the critic and journalist, and offered a sincere confession of weaknesses which you do not share with human nature in general and the journalist in particular. At least you can set a good example for your colleagues by placing in your journal a few sincere observations which occurred to me on reading through the first number of *The Contemporary*.

The essay "On the Trend of Journal Literature" justly attracted general attention. In it you wittily, cuttingly, and straightforwardly set forth very many just observations. But I confess that it does not correspond to what we expected from the trend that you were going to give to your criticism. Reading through this somewhat inconsistent essay carefully, the thing that I saw most clearly was great bitterness toward Mr. Senkovsky. In your opinion our entire literature revolves around *The Library for Reading*. All other periodical publications were examined only in relation to it. *The Northern Bee* and *The Son of the Fatherland* are presented as some kind of strange rear guard supporting *The Library*. *The Moscow Observer*, according to what you say, was established with the sole intention of battling against *The Library*. It even got a stern rebuke because its attacks were limited to only two little essays; either they should not have begun at all, you say, or once they began they should not have desisted. You praise *Literary Supplements*, *The Telescope*, and *Chat* for their position opposing *The Library*. I confess this amazed those who had been awaiting the appearance of your journal impatiently. Can it be, they said, that the aim of *The Contemporary* is to follow at the heels of *The Library*, attacking it from ambush and using an armed hand to get subscribers away from it? I hope that these fears are false, and that *The Contemporary* will choose a broader and more noble sphere of activity for itself. . . .

Your accusations with regard to Mr. Senkovsky are limited to the following points:

1. Mr. Senkovsky took exclusive control over the critical section of the journal published in the name of the bookseller Smirdin.

2. Mr. Senkovsky corrects essays which he receives for publication in *The Library*.

3. In his criticical judgments Mr. Senkovsky does not always observe a tone of seriousness and dispassionateness.

4. Mr. Senkovsky does not use the pronouns *sej* and *onyj*.[2]

5. Mr. Senkovsky has about five thousand subscribers.

The first two accusatory points relate to the domestic, so to speak, arrangements of the bookseller Smirdin[3] and do not concern the public. As for the serious tone of criticism, I don't understand how one can speak about some works of our national literature without joking. The public demands a report on everything which comes out. Can it be the journalist must observe the same tone in relation to all the books which he is analyzing? There is a difference between criticizing *The History of the Russian State* and the novels of Messrs. —— etc. A critic who always tries to be equally polite and serious, without doubt sins against propriety. In society you bump a neighbor with your elbow and you excuse yourself—all right; but if, wandering around the marketplace, you bump a shopkeeper you don't say to him: *mille pardons*. You say: why ˙go bumping around the marketplace? Why mention books which aren't worth any attention? But if the public demands it without fail, why not please it? *Cela vous coûte si peu, et leur fait tant de plaisir!* And allow me to inquire: What is the meaning of your critique of the almanac *My New Home*, which you so felicitously compared to a scrawny cat miaowing on the roof of an emptied house? A very amusing comparison, but I don't see anything serious in it. *Physician! Heal thyself!* I confess, some of the funny critiques which have dotted *The Library for Reading* pleased me unutterably, and I would have been very sorry if the critic had preferred to maintain a majestic silence.

Mr. Senkovsky's jokes about the innocent pronouns *sej, sija, sie, onyj, onaja, onoe* are nothing but jokes. The public, and even a few writers, were free to take them as the real thing. Can the written language be exactly like the spoken one? No, just as the spoken language can never be exactly like the written one. Not just the pronouns *sej* and *onyj*, but the participle in general and a multitude of essential words are usually avoided in conversation. We don't say, "a galloping-over-the-bridge carriage," "a sweeping-the-room servant"; we say, "which is galloping," "who is sweeping," etc., substituting a flaccid turn of phrase for the expressive brevity of the participle. But it does not follow from this that the participle should be expunged from the Russian language. The richer a language is in expressions and turns of phrase, the better it is for a clever writer. The written language is constantly animated by expressions born in conversation, but it should not renounce what it has invented in the course of centuries. Writing solely the spoken language means not knowing the language. But you unjustly compared the persecution of *sej* and *onyj* to the introduction of *i* and *v* into the orthography of Russian words, and disturbed the ashes of Tredyakovsky in vain, since he never started arguments with anyone about these letters. Desiring to reform our orthography, the learned professor acted on his own accord, without a previous example. I will note in passing that Mr. Kachenovsky's orthography is not a difficult novelty, but has long existed in our holy books. Every writer who has received a classical education is obliged to know its rules, even if he doesn't follow them.

As for the last point, i.e., the 5,000 subscribers, allow me to express the sincere wish that next year you can deserve precisely the same accusation.

Confess that your attacks on Mr. Senkovsky are not very well grounded. Many of his essays, which you passed over without notice, were worthy of occupying a place in the best European journals. As uninitiated people we must believe his information about the East. He publishes *The Library* with amazing dexterity and regularity, to which Messrs. the Russian journalists have not yet accustomed us. We humble provincials are grateful to him—for the variety of essays, for the thickness of the volumes, for the fresh European news, and even for the report on miscellaneous literature. We regret that many writers whom we respect and love have refused to participate in Mr. Smirdin's journal, and we hope that *The Contemporary* will make up for this shortcoming for us; but we desire that the two journals not try to hurt each other and that each act in its own way for the general good and for the pleasure of a zealous reading public.

Turning to *The Northern Bee,* you reproach it for having indiscriminately included all the news, advertisements, etc. which had been thrown its way. But how can it do otherwise? *The*

*Northern Bee* is a newspaper, and a newspaper's profit comes precisely from advertisements, news, etc., all of which is printed indiscriminately. English newspapers, which count as many as 15,000 subscribers, make up for the outlay for publication only by printing advertisements. It is not for advertisements that *The Northern Bee* should be rebuked, but for the inclusion of boring essays with the signature F. B.[4] which (in spite of your disdain for the taste of poor provincials) we have long since evaluated according to their merit. Be assured that it is extremely vexing for us when we see that Messrs. the journalists suppose they can interest us with moralistic issues filled with the most childish thoughts and banal little jokes—which *The Northern Bee* probably inherited from *The Industrious Bee*.[5]

What you say about *Supplements to The Invalid* is in general correct. The publisher has left ineffaceable marks in the polemical sphere, and still pursues this same thing with unquestionable success. We recall the *Chameleon*,[6] a series of articles which were classic in their genre. But allow me to point out to you that you praise Mr. Voeykov for precisely the same thing for which you abuse Mr. Senkovsky: for joking critiques of that which does not deserve to be criticized seriously.

I regret that you didn't mention Mr. Belinsky[7] when speaking about *The Telescope*. He shows talent which offers great hope. If to independence of opinion and his wit he unites more scholarship, more knowledge of books, more respect for tradition, more prudence—in a word, more maturity—we would have an extremely remarkable critic in him.

Speaking of the journalists' indifference to important literary events, you pointed out Walter Scott's death. But Walter Scott's death is not a literary event; enough has been said, relevantly and irrelevantly, among us about Walter Scott and his novels.

You say that lately the public's indifference to poetry and wish for novels, stories and so forth has been noticeable. But isn't poetry always the pleasure of a small number of the elect, while stories and novels are read by everyone everywhere? And where did you note this indifference? One can sooner reproach our poets for inactivity than the public for growing cool. A third edition of Derzhavin's works was brought out; it is said a fourth is being prepared. On the title page of Krylov's fables (published last year) is written: *the thirtieth thousand.* The new poets Kukolnik[8] and Benediktov[9] were greeted with rapture. Koltsov[10] attracted general and favorable attention. . . . Where is the indifference of the public to poetry here?

You reproach our journalists for not saying to us: what was Walter Scott? What is present-day French literature? What is our public? What are our writers?

Indeed, extremely interesting questions! We hope that in the future you will resolve them, and that in your criticism you will avoid the shortcomings you so sternly and so justly condemned in the essay which we are right to call the program of your journal.*

Tver
23 April 1836                                                        A. B.

#### N O T E S

1. *These are the circumstances in which Pushkin wrote this letter: Gogol had written an essay "On the Trend of Journal Literature" which appeared anonymously in the first issue of Pushkin's new journal,* The Contemporary. *Central to Gogol's essay was a violent attack on Senkovsky and his highly successful* The Library for Reading. *(In their literary views Gogol and Senkovsky were natural enemies, a tendency which was exacerbated by Senkovsky's sarcastic reviews of Gogol's works.) Pushkin did some editing of Gogol's MS, but left it substantially as it was. He printed it with misgivings —he did not want to doom his journal in the first issue (an all-out*

---

* Including Mr. A. B.'s letter here with pleasure, I find it essential to give my readers a few explanations. The essay "On the Trend of Journal Literature" was printed in my journal, but it does not follow from this that all the opinions expressed in it with such youthful liveliness and straightforwardness are completely in accord with my own. In any case, it is not and could not be the program of *The Contemporary.*

*battle with Senkovsky's Library and other journals could be dangerous, and in any case Pushkin thought his journal had more important aims). This letter, sent anonymously to avoid offending Gogol, was designed to offset the effect of Gogol's article and assure prospective subscribers that Gogol's attack was not programmatic.*

2. *The archaic pronouns* sej *and* onyj *("this" and "that") have passed out of use since Pushkin's time.*

3. *Alexander Smirdin was a highly successful and unscrupulous publisher.*

4. *Faddey Bulgarin.*

5. *The* Industrious Bee—*The first non-governmental Russian magazine, published for one year (1759) by Sumarokov.*

6. *Feuilletons published by A. F. Voeykov in* The Slav *in 1828.*

7. *Vissarion G. Belinsky (1811–48) was to become Russia's best-known critic. In the drafts of his essay Gogol wrote: "In Belinsky's criticisms (published in* The Telescope*) one can see taste—though it is still young, hasty, and immature. But it serves as a guarantee of future development, because it is based on feeling and sincere conviction. Nevertheless, there is much in his work that is in the spirit of earlier domestic criticism—which is altogether out of place and improper, especially for the public."*

8. *Nestor V. Kukolnik (1809–68)—a classmate of Gogol at the Nezhin* gymnasium, *minor poet and dramatist.*

9. *Vladimir G. Benediktov (1807–73)—a minor poet whose works were often parodied later.*

10. *Alexei V. Koltsov (1809–1842)—a lyric poet whose imitations of folk genres are still read. His first book of songs was published in 1835.*

# ON MILTON AND CHATEAUBRIAND'S TRANSLATION OF *PARADISE LOST*

**The[1] French have long ignored the literature of their neighbors.** Certain of their superiority to all mankind, they have valued famous foreign writers relative to the degree by which they diverged from French customs and rules established by French critics.

One cannot read a single preface to books translated and published in the last century without the inevitable statement: we intend to oblige the public and at the same time do a service to our author by excluding from his book passages which might offend the taste of the educated French reader. It is strange when you think who was excusing whom to whom this way! And that is what an unenlightened passion for nationalism leads to! . . . Finally the critics came to their senses. They began to suspect that M. Letourneur[2] might have judged Shakespeare mistakenly, and that he hadn't acted altogether with common sense in correcting *Hamlet, Romeo,* and *Lear* to suit his own taste. They began to demand more accuracy from translators, and less fastidiousness and solicitude for the public; they wished to see Dante, Shakespeare, and Cervantes in their own form, in their national dress, and with their own faults. Even the opinion established by the ages and accepted by all, that the translator should try to transmit the spirit and not the letter, found opponents and clever refutations.

Now (an unheard-of instance) the foremost of the French writers translates Milton "word for word" and declares that a sublinear translation would be the summit of his art, if only it were possible![3] Such humility in a French writer, the foremost master of his craft, was bound to greatly amaze the advocates of "corrective translations" and will probably have a great influence on literature.

Of all the great foreign writers, Milton has been the most unfortunate in France. We won't mention the pitiful prose translations in which he was innocently slandered; we won't mention Abbot Delille's verse translation which horribly corrected his crude errors and embellished him without mercy; but how have the writers of the modern romantic school depicted Milton himself in their tragedies and novels? What was made of him by M. Alfred de Vigny,[4] whom the French critics have unceremoniously placed on the same level as W. Scott? How was he portrayed by Victor Hugo, another favorite of the French public? Perhaps our readers have forgotten both *Cinq Mars* and *Cromwell*, and therefore cannot judge about the absurdities of Victor Hugo's inventions. Let us present both for the judgment of every intelligent and reasonable person.

We will begin with the tragedy—one of the most absurd works of a man who is, however, gifted with talent.[5] We aren't going to follow the stumbling gait of this boring and monstrous drama; we wish only to show our readers how it presents Milton —a poet still unknown, but a political writer already famous in Europe for his bitter and audacious eloquence.

In his palace Cromwell is speaking with Lord Rochester, disguised as a Methodist, and with four jesters. Milton is present too, with his guide (a rather unnecessary character, for Milton went blind only much later). The Protector says to Rochester:[6]

CROMWELL: . . . Since we are alone now I want to laugh: I present you my jesters. When we are in gay spirits they are very amusing. We all write poetry, even my old Milton.

MILTON (with vexation): Old Milton! Excuse me, my lord; I am nine years younger than you.

CROMWELL: As you wish.

MILTON: You were born in 99, and I in 1608.

CROMWELL: What a fresh memory!

MILTON (with animation): You might treat me more civilly; I am the son of a notary, a city alderman.

CROMWELL: Well, don't be angry—I know that you are a great theologian and even a good poet, though a bit below Withers and Donne.

MILTON (speaking *à parte*): A bit below! How cruel a word! But we will wait. They will see if Heaven has refused me these gifts. The future is my judge. It will understand my Eve falling into the night of Hell like a sweet dream; Adam, culpable and good, and the arch-angel ruling over an eternity, grand in his despair, profound in his dementia, arising from a lake of fire which he beats with his immense wing! For an ardent genius is working within me. *In silence* I meditate a strange design. I live in my thought and Milton is consoled by that. Yes, I want in my turn to create my own world between Hell, Earth, and Heaven.

LORD ROCHESTER *(à parte)*: What the deuce is he saying?

ONE OF THE JESTERS: Risible dreamer!

CROMWELL (shrugging his shoulders): Your *Iconoclast* is a very good book, but your devil, Leviathan . . . (laughing) is very bad. . . .

MILTON (through his teeth, indignantly): And Cromwell laughs at my Satan!

ROCHESTER (approaching Milton): Mr. Milton!

MILTON (not hearing him and turning to Cromwell): He says that from envy.

ROCHESTER (to Milton, who listens distractedly): Really, you don't understand poetry. You are intelligent, but you lack taste. Listen, the French are our masters in everything. Study Racan, read his pastoral poems. Let Aminte wander in your meadows with Tircis; let her lead a lamb behind her on a blue ribbon. But Eve, Adam, Hell, a lake of fire! Naked Satan with scorched wings! It would be another matter if you hid him in a fashionable suit, if you gave him an ample perruque, a helmet with gold trimming, a rose-colored jacket, a Florentine cape— like the gala dress in which I recently saw the Sun at the Opéra de France.

MILTON (astonished): What kind of twaddle is that?

ROCHESTER (biting his lips): Again I forgot myself. Sir, I was joking.

MILTON: A very stupid joke!

Further on Milton asserts that it is a trifle to rule a nation; it is more difficult to write Latin verses. A little while later Milton throws himself at Cromwell's feet, imploring him not to solicit the throne, to which the protector answers him: Mr. Milton, secretary of the state council, you are a poet, in your lyric transport you have forgotten who I am, etc.

In a scene which possesses neither historical accuracy nor

dramatical verisimilitude, in the senseless parody of the ceremonial observed at the coronation of English Kings, Milton and one of the court jesters play the main roles. Milton preaches the republic, the jester picks up the glove of a royal knight. . . .

That's the kind of pitiful madman, the kind of insignificant babbler Milton is shown as—shown by a man who probably didn't know himself what he was doing, offending the great shade of Milton! In the course of the entire tragedy Milton hears nothing but jeers and curses; it is also true that the whole time he doesn't utter a sensible word himself. He is an old jester whom everyone scorns and to whom no one pays any attention.

No, Mr. Hugo! Not such was John Milton, the friend and associate of Cromwell, the grim fanatic, the austere creator of *Eikonoklastes* and the book *Defensio populi!* The man who had written Cromwell his famous prophetic sonnet:

Cromwell, our chief of men!

would not have talked to him that way.

The man who "in evil days, the sacrifice of evil tongues," in poverty, in exile, and in blindness had preserved adamancy of spirit and dictated *Paradise Lost*, could not be the laughing-stock of the depraved Rochester and court jesters.

If M. Hugo, himself a poet (albeit a second-rate one), understood the poet Milton so poorly, then anyone can easily imagine for himself what the character of Cromwell, with whom he had absolutely no empathy, became under his pen. But that is off our subject. Let us shift from the crude, uneven Victor Hugo and his deformed drama to the finical, affected Count Vigny and his slick novel.

In his *Cinq Mars* Alfred de Vigny introduces Milton to us in the following circumstances:[7]

A group of courtiers and scholars gathers at the home of the famous Marion de Lorme, the mistress of Cardinal Richelieu. Scudéry is explaining his allegorical map of love to them. The guests are enraptured over the fortress of *Beauty* standing on the river of *Pride*, over the village of *Billet-Doux*, the harbor of

*Indifference,* etc., etc. Everyone showers pompous praise on M. Scudéry—except Molière, Corneille, and Descartes, who are all there too. Suddenly the hostess introduces to the group a young traveling Englishman, John Milton by name, and makes him read the guests excerpts from *Paradise Lost.* All right—but how will the Frenchmen understand his verses without knowing English? Very simple: the passages which he is going to read are translated into French, copied on special sheets of paper, and the copies distributed to the guests. Milton will declaim, and the guests follow him. But why should he go to the trouble if the verses have already been translated? It must be that Milton is a great declaimer, or are the sounds of the English language extremely curious? And why did Count de Vigny have to get into all these absurd incongruities? —He had to have Milton read his *Paradise Lost* in Parisian society and to have the French wits make fun of it and not understand the spirit of it (except, of course, Molière, Corneille, and Descartes), and the following effect-filled scene results from this.

The hostess took the sheets of paper and passed them to the guests:[8]

Everyone sat down and became silent. It took a while to persuade the young foreigner to begin the reading and leave the window, where he seemed to be talking to Corneille with great pleasure. Finally he walked up to the armchair standing by the table; it appeared he was in feeble health and, one could say, he fell into it rather than sat down. He put his elbows on the table and with his hand covered his large and expressive eyes, which were half-closed and red from vigils or tears. He recited his verses from memory; his incredulous listeners looked at him haughtily, or at least condescendingly; others nonchalantly looked through the translation of his verses.

His voice, at first hollow, gradually cleared itself; soon the poetic inspiration transported him out of himself, and his gaze lifted to heaven, became as sublime as the gaze of Raphael's evangelist, for light was still reflected in it. In his verses he told of Man's first disobedience, and invoked the

Holy Spirit that prefers before all temples the upright heart and pure, that knows all and from the first was present.

This beginning was received with profound silence, and the last idea with a slight murmur. He heard nothing; he saw everything through some kind of cloud—he was in a world of his own creation, and he continued.

He told[9] about the Spirit of Hell fastened to the penal fire in adamantine chains, how nine times the space that measures day and night to mortal men he lay vanquished, about the darkness visible of the eternal dungeon, the fiery gulf in which the fallen angels swam; his voice thundering, he began the speech of the Prince of Demons: "If thou beest he," said Satan, "if thou beest he who shone with transcendant brightness in the happy realms of light— but O how fallen! Come with me. . . . What though the heavenly field be lost? All is not lost. We have all preserved unconquerable will, and study of revenge, immortal hate, and courage never to submit or yield—and what is else not to be overcome?"

At this point, a lackey announced the arrival of MM. de Montrésor and d'Entraigues in a ringing voice. They bowed to everyone, talked a bit, moved all the arm-chairs around, and finally took their seats. The listeners used this opportunity to begin a multitude of private conversations; in these one heard only words of blame and reproaches for bad taste; several witty people, overly attached to the routine habits of the past, exclaimed that they didn't understand it, that it was above their intelligence (without thinking that they were telling the truth); this false humility resulted in compliments for them and abuse for the poet—a double advantage. Others even said that it was profanation of a holy thing.

The interrupted poet covered his face with his hands and put his elbows on the table so as not to hear all this din of politesse and criticisms. Only three men came up to him: some officer, Poquelin, and Corneille; the latter said in Milton's ear: "I advise you to change your tableaux; the one which you have depicted for us is too elevated for your listeners."

In spite of the fact that the passages designated for the reading have been translated, and that he is supposed to read them in order, Milton searches through his memory for something which in his opinion will have more effect on the listeners, without worrying about whether they will understand him or not. But as a result of some miracle (not explained by M. de Vigny), everyone understands him. Des Barreaux finds him cloying, Scudéry—boring and cold. Marion de Lorme is very touched by the description of Adam in his native state. Molière, Corneille, and Descartes shower compliments upon him, etc., etc.

Either we are quite mistaken, or Milton, when passing through Paris, would not display himself as a touring buffoon in the house of an indecent woman to amuse society by reading verses written in a language unknown to any of those present, while mincing and posing, now "closing his eyes," now "lifting them toward the ceiling." His conversations with de Thou, with Corneille and Descartes, would not be trivial and refined twaddle; and in society he would play a role proper for him, the modest role of a noble and well-educated young man.

After the preposterous fantasies of V. Hugo and Count de Vigny do you want to see a scene painted in a simple manner by another artist? Read in *Woodstock* the meeting of one of the characters with Milton in Cromwell's study. . . .[10]

Of course, a French novelist wouldn't be satisfied with such an insignificant and natural description. For him, Milton, busy with affairs of state, would certainly lose himself in poetical daydreams and would scribble a few lines from *Paradise Lost* in the margins of some report; Cromwell would notice it, berate his secretary, call him a rhymester and babbler, etc., and this would create a striking *effect*—one of which poor W. Scott didn't even think!

The translation published by Chateaubriand expiates to a certain extent the transgressions of the young French writers who have insulted the great Milton's spirit so innocently, but so cruelly. We have already said that Chateaubriand translated Milton word for word, as closely as French syntax would allow:

a difficult and thankless task which the majority of readers remain unaware of, which can be prized by two or three connoisseurs! But is the new translation successful? Chateaubriand found a merciless critic in Nisard. In an essay filled with keen and penetrating wit, Nisard violently attacked both the method of translation chosen by Chateaubriand and the translation itself.[11] There is no doubt that in trying to transmit Milton "word for word" Chateaubriand, nevertheless, could not adhere to accuracy of thought and expression in his rendering. A sublinear translation can never be accurate. Each language has its own idioms, its own fixed rhetorical figures, its own adopted expressions, which cannot be translated into another language in corresponding words. Let's take elementary sentences: *Comment vous portez vous. How do you do.* Try to translate them word for word into Russian.*

If Russian, which is so pliable and powerful in its idioms and resources, so imitative and compliant in its relations with other languages, is not capable of a sublinear translation, of word for word rendering, then how will French, which is so cautious in its habits, so predisposed to its own traditions, so hostile even to languages of its own family, survive such an experiment, especially in a struggle with the language of Milton, a poet who is at once refined and ingenuous, obscure, confused, expressive, capricious, and daring even to the point of senselessness?

\* \* \*

The translation of *Paradise Lost* is a commercial undertaking. Chateaubriand, the foremost of contemporary French writers, the teacher of an entire writing generation, a man who was once a first minister, several times an ambassador, has

---

* Apropos: not long ago (in *The Telescope*, I think) someone criticizing a translation apparently wanted to show off his knowledge of Italian and rebuked the translator for allowing the expression *battersi la guancia* —to beat oneself on the cheeks—in his translation. *Battersi la guancia* means "to repent"; translated otherwise it has no sense.

translated Milton *for a piece of bread* in his old age. No matter what the result of the work he has undertaken may be, the work itself and its aim do honor to the celebrated old man. One who (if he bargained a little with himself first) could easily have availed himself of the generosity of the new government, its power, honors, and wealth, preferred honorable poverty to these things.

Shunning the Chamber of Lords, where his eloquent voice had long echoed, Chateaubriand comes to the bookstore with a manuscript for sale, but with a conscience which is not. What will the critics say after this? Are they going to discomfort the noble toiler with a harsh evaluation and disparage his goods like miserly merchants? But Chateaubriand has no need of condescension: he has appended to his translation two volumes which are just as brilliant as all his previous works—and the critics can show as much severity as they please toward the shortcomings, because the unquestionable beauties, the pages worthy of the best times of the great writer, will save his book from the disdain of readers in spite of all its shortcomings.

The English critics severely condemned the *Study in English Literature*.[12] They found it too superficial, too insufficient; believing the title, they demanded from Chateaubriand scholarly criticism and a perfect knowledge of subjects with which they themselves were intimately familiar; but that isn't what should be sought in this brilliant survey. Chateaubriand's scholarly criticism is not solid, he is timid and not himself—he talks about writers whom he hasn't read, he judges them superficially and from hearsay, and in one way or another avoids the tiresome duty of a biographer; but frequently inspired pages fly from under his pen, he frequently forgets critical research and freely develops his ideas about great historical epochs, which he compares to those which he himself witnessed. In these passages, there is much honesty, much sincere eloquence, much ingenuousness (occasionally childish, but always engaging); these passages are unconcerned with English literature, but they create the real value of the *Study*.

Chateaubriand's book begins with a brisk and sweeping depiction of the middle ages which serves as an introduction to the *History of English Literature:*[13]

The social order, outside of political order, is composed of religion, intellectual activity, and material industry. In any nation at a time of catastrophes and great events the priest prays, the poet sings, the scholar meditates, the artist, sculptor, and architect create and build, the laborer works. Looking only at them we see the real world, the true immutable base of the human edifice, but which seems to be apart from political society. However, the priest in his prayer, the poet, scholar, and artist in their creations, the laborer in his work, reveal from time to time the epoch in which they live; they echo the blows of events which make their complaints, their sweat and gifts of inspiration flow more powerfully and abundantly. . . .

The middle ages offer a bizarre tableau which seems to be the product of a puissant but deranged imagination. In antiquity each nation issues, so to speak, from its own source; a kind of primitive spirit penetrates everything and is felt everywhere. Mores and civil institutions become homogeneous. The society of the middle ages was composed of the debris of a thousand other societies. Roman civilization and paganism left their traces on it; Christian religion brought it its beliefs and ceremonies; the Franks, the Burgundians, the Anglo-Saxons, the Danes, the Normans kept their customs and the character peculiar to their race. All kinds of property rights and laws were mixed together . . . all forms of liberty and slavery clashed, the monarchical liberty of the king, the aristocratic liberty of the noble, the individual liberty of the priest, the collective liberty of the communes, the privileged liberty of the towns, the magistrates, the guilds of craftsmen and merchants, the representative liberty of the nation, Roman slavery, the servitude of the barbarian tribes, serfdom. Hence the chaotic events, customs, one contradicting the other, joined only by the bonds of religion. It seems that different peoples without any mutual rapport agreed to live under a single master, around a single altar.

[1837, *The Contemporary*]

## N O T E S

1. *Chateaubriand's translation was published in Paris in 1836.*
2. *Pierre Le Tourneur (1736–88)—translator of Young's* Night Thoughts, Ossian, Clarissa Harlowe, *and eight volumes of Shakespeare (1776–82), until then almost unknown in France.*
3. *This is one of the epigraphs to Vladimir Nabokov's magnificent* Onegin.
4. *Alfred de Vigny (1797–1863). His novel* Cinq Mars *was published in 1826.*

*It should be noted that what Pushkin says about* Cinq Mars *and* Cromwell *does not mean he thought Vigny and Hugo were consciously ridiculing Milton in their works. He was aware that Vigny wanted French society to suffer in comparison to Milton. Pushkin's point is that the whole situation is artistically unnatural and absurd, as well as "morally" disrespectful.*

5. *In the drafts Pushkin wrote: "The play* Cromwell *was the first experiment of romanticism on the stage of the Parisian theater. Victor Hugo considered it necessary to destroy all at once all of the laws, all of the traditions of French drama that had reigned from behind the classical curtains: unity of place and time, the majestic monotony of style, the prosody of Racine and Boileau—he threw over everything. However, justice demands pointing out that V. Hugo did not touch the unity of action or the unity of interest (intérêt); there is no action in his play, and even less interest."*

6. *I have given literal translations of Pushkin's translation of Hugo and the translation (Ochkin, 1835) of Vigny he uses. But, again, I had the French originals at hand and stayed as close to a literal translation of them as possible without distorting the texts Pushkin used.*

*The passage from* Cromwell *is in Act III, Scene II.*

7. *See Chapter XX of* Cinq Mars.

8. *This passage involves translating into English Pushkin's (Ochkin's) Russian translation of Vigny and Vigny's French translation of Milton's English (to close this vicious circle). As usual I tried to render Pushkin's text accurately while staying close to Vigny and, in this case, using direct quotations from* Paradise Lost *wherever this does not violate Pushkin.*

9. Paradise Lost, Book I, lines 1–110.

10. *Pushkin left a space in the MS for a quotation from Scott's novel. But Milton is mentioned only briefly in* Woodstock; *he is not a character.*

11. *Désiré Nisard (1806–88) criticized the translation of* Paradise Lost *in "Du dernier ouvrage de M. de Chateaubriand" (Revue de Paris, September, 1836). He compares the elegant paraphrases Chateaubriand used in* Le Génie du Christianisme *to the literal translations from English literature, finding the former graceful and readable, while in the latter:*

> ... je ne vois qu'un mot à mot un peu commun, çà et là *sauvage* comme la traduction interlinéaire, où il n'y a guère à admirer que le dévouement de l'écrivain qui a pu appesantir et garrotter ainsi la plume d'or des fragments, briser le moule de sa phrase majestueuse, rompre sa prosodie, métamorphoser en un langage laborieusement bâtard un style merveilleux de grâce, de couleur et de nombre. Que j'aime bien mieux les inexactitudes de la première. . . .

*This polemic over exact versus inexact translation [see Marie-Jeanne Durry,* La Vieillesse de Chateaubriand *(Paris, 1833), II, 433–34] is very strongly reminiscent of the polemic caused by Nabokov's* Eugene Onegin. *Nisard played Edmund Wilson's role.*

12. Essai sur la littérature anglaise, et Considérations sur le génie des temps, des hommes et des révolutions *(Paris, 1836).*

13. *Translated from Russian with the help of the original, in* Chateaubriand, Oeuvres complètes *(Paris, 1855–61), XI, 492–93.*

# THE SONG OF IGOR'S CAMPAIGN

*The Song of Igor's Campaign* **was found in the library of A. Iv. Musin-Pushkin**[1] **and published in 1800. The manuscript burned up in 1812.** Experts who saw it say its calligraphy was in the style of the XVth century. The first editors appended to it a translation which is generally satisfactory, though several passages remained obscure or totally incomprehensible. After this, many people attempted to explain them. But though in investigations of this sort the last are the first (for the mistakes and discoveries of the predecessors open and clear the road for the successors), the first translation—in which truly erudite men took part—still remains the best. The other interpreters have eagerly vied in obscuring nebulous phrases with their own whimsical corrections and conjectures—based on nothing. For the most important explanations we are obliged to Karamzin, who, in passing, resolved several mysterious passages in his *History.*

Several writers[2] doubted the authenticity of the ancient monument of our literature and aroused heated objections. A successful forgery can lead the uninformed into error, but it cannot be concealed from the eyes of true experts. Walpole did not fall for the ruse when Chatterton[3] sent him the poem of the old monk Rowley. Johnson immediately exposed MacPherson.[4] But neither Karamzin, nor Ermolaev, nor A. X. Vostokov, nor Khodakovsky ever doubted the authenticity of *The Song of Igor's Campaign.*[5] The great critic Schlözer,[6] without seeing *The Song of Igor's Campaign,* doubted its authenticity; but when he had read it he declared firmly that he regarded it an authentic work and didn't even consider it necessary to cite evidence for it—the truth seemed so apparent to him!

There is no proof like the words of the creator of the song himself. The authenticity of the song is proved by the spirit of antiquity, which it is impossible to forge. Who of our eighteenth-century writers could have had enough talent for that? Karamzin? But Karamzin is not a poet. Derzhavin? But Derzhavin didn't even know the Russian language, let alone the language of *The Song of Igor's Campaign*. All of the others taken together didn't have as much poetry as there is in Yaroslavna's lament, in the description of the battle and escape. To whom would it have occurred to take the obscure campaign of an unknown prince as a subject? Who could have so artfully obscured several passages of his song with words subsequently discovered in old chronicles or found in other Slavic dialects, where they are still preserved in all their freshness of usage? This would presuppose a knowledge of *all* the Slavic dialects. Let's suppose he did command them, would such a mixture be natural? Homer, if he existed, was distorted by the singers.

Lomonosov did not live in the XIIth century. Lomonosov's odes are written in Russian with an admixture of some expressions he took out of the Bible which lay before him. But you will not find Polish, Serbian, Illyrian, Bulgarian, Bohemian, Moldavian, and the other Slavic dialects in Lomonosov. . . .[7]

[1836, unpublished]

# N O T E S

1. *Alexei I. Musin-Pushkin (1744–1817)—a collector of ancient manuscripts. The* Song *was in a MS he acquired in 1795.*
2. *Including Senkovsky and Kachenovsky.*
3. *Thomas Chatterton (1752–70) sent* The Ryse of Peyncteyne yn Englande, *wroten by T. Rowleie, 1469, for Mastre Canynge to Horace Walpole, who was at first fooled by the mystification. His friends Gray and Mason pronounced the poetry modern, and Walpole coldly dismissed Chatterton (most of whose poetry was published posthumously).*
4. *James Macpherson's* Fragments of Ancient Poetry *(1760), the Ossianic poems.*

5. *A. I. Ermolaev, A. Kh. Vostokov, Zorian Khodakovsky—Russian historians and antiquarians.*
    6. *August Ludwig von Schlözer (1735–1809)—historian and publicist. Catherine II made him a Professor of Russian History and member of the Russian Academy.* Author of Geschichte Russlands bis zur Erbauung Moskaus *(1769) and* Ubersetzung der russiche Nestorchronik *(1802–1809).*
    7. *I have not translated the last six pages of Pushkin's essay—those in which he discusses the textological and linguistic problems.*

# THE LAST OF JOAN OF ARC'S RELATIVES

**Last year (1836) in London a certain M. Dulys (Jean-François-Philippe Dulys) died**, a descendant of the brother of Joan of Arc, the famed maid of Orléans. M. Dulys moved to England at the beginning of the French Revolution; he was married to an Englishwoman, but he left no children. In his will he designated a relative of his wife as his heir—James Bailey, an Edinburgh bookseller. Found among his papers were authentic certificates of Kings Charles VII, Henry IV, and Louis XIII proving the nobility of the d'Arc Dulys family. All these certificates were sold at public auction for an extremely high price, as was a curious autograph: a letter from Voltaire to the father of the late M. Dulys.

Apparently Dulys père was a good nobleman who paid little heed to literature. Around 1767, however, it came to his attention that a certain M. de Voltaire had published some work about the heroine of Orléans. The book sold very dearly. However, M. Dulys decided to buy it, expecting to find a reliable history of his famous great-grandmother in it. He was astonished in a most unpleasant way when he received a small book in-18 printed in Holland and embellished with amazing little pictures. In the first heat of indignation he wrote Voltaire the following letter, a copy of which was also found among the papers of the deceased. (This letter, like Voltaire's answer, was printed in the journal *Morning Chronicle*.)

Dear Sir:
    I recently had occasion to acquire, for six gold louis, the history of the siege of Orléans in 1429 written by you. This work contains a superabundance not only of egregious errors inexcusable for a man who knows anything about the history of France, but also of absurd calumny regarding King Charles VII, Joan of Arc, called the maid of Orléans, Agnes Sorel, the La Trémouilles, La Gire, Baudricourt and other noble and celebrated personages. From enclosed copies of reliable certificates which are preserved in my castle (Tournebu, baillage de Chaumont en Tourraine), you will see clearly that Joan of Arc was the natural sister of Lucas d'Arc, seigneur du Feron, from whom I descend in direct line. And therefore I not only consider myself in the right, but I even make it my certain duty, to demand satisfaction from you for the insolent, malicious, and fraudulent statements which you permitted yourself to print about the above-mentioned maid. Therefore, I request you, dear sir, to let me know the place and time, and also the weapon you have chosen for immediate completion of this matter.

I have the honor, etc.

In spite of the amusing side of this matter, Voltaire did not take it as a joke. He was frightened by the uproar that this could cause—and perhaps by the sword of the touchy nobleman as well—and he immediately sent the following answer:

22 May, 1767

Dear Sir:
    The letter which you vouchsafed me found me in the bed which I have not left for about eight months now. It seems you did not know that I am a poor old man dispirited by illnesses and sorrows, and not one of the brave knights from whom you descend. I can assure you that I

took absolutely no part in the putting together of the stupid rhymed chronicle (*l'impertinente chronique rimée*) about which you deign to write me. Europe is flooded with printed stupidities which the public magnanimously ascribes to me. About forty years ago I had occasion to print a poem with the title *Henriade*. Enumerating in it the heroes who have covered France with glory, I took on myself the boldness of apostrophizing your celebrated relative (*votre illustre cousin*) with the following words:

> Et toi, brave Amazone,
> La honte des Anglais et le soutien du trône.

That is the only place in my works where the immortal heroine who saved France is mentioned. I regret that I did not devote my weak talent to glorifying God's wonders instead of laboring for the pleasure of a senseless and unthankful public.

> I have the honor to be,
> **Dear Sir,**
> Your most humble servant
>
> Voltaire, *gentilhomme de
> la chambre du roy.*

Apropos of the publication of this correspondence an English journalist makes the following comments:

> Joan of Arc's fate with regard to her fatherland is truly worthy of surprise. Of course, we must share with the French the shame of her trial and execution. But the barbarity of the English can still be excused by the prejudices of the age, by the bitterness of offended national pride, which honestly attributed the feats of the young sheperdess to the action of demonic power. The question arises how the cowardly ingratitude of the French can be excused. Not, of course, by fear of the devil, whom they haven't been afraid of since the days of yore. At least we did something for the memory of the famed maiden; our laureate devoted his first pure bursts of (not yet purchased) inspiration to her.[1] England gave shelter to the last of her family.

But how did France try to efface the bloody spot which stains the most melancholy page of her chronicle? True, Joan of Arc's family was granted nobility; but her heirs grovelled in oblivion. Not one d'Arc or Dulys is seen at the court of the French kings from Charles VII to Charles X. Modern history presents no more touching, more poetic subject than the life and death of the heroine of Orléans— what did Voltaire, that worthy representative of his people, make out of it? Once in his life he happened to be a true poet, and look what he uses his inspiration for! With satanic breath he blows on the sparks dying in the ashes of the martyr's pyre, and like a drunken savage[2] dances around his amusing fire. Like a Roman executioner, he adds profanation to the mortal torments of the maid. The laureate's poem, of course, does not match Voltaire's poem in power of invention, but Southey's work is the deed of an honorable man and the fruit of noble rapture. Let us note that Voltaire—surrounded in France by enemies and enviers, subject to the most acid censure at every step—found almost no accusers when his criminal poem appeared. His most embittered enemies were disarmed. Everyone received with rapture a book in which scorn for everything that is considered sacred for a man and citizen is carried to the last degree of cynicism. It occurred to no one to intercede for the honor of his fatherland, and the challenge of the good and honorable Dulys, if it had been made known then, would have aroused inexhaustible laughter not only in the philosophical drawing-rooms of Baron Holbach and Mme. Jeoffrin, but even in the ancient halls of the descendants of La Gire and La Trémouille. A sorry age! A sorry people![3]

[1837, *The Contemporary*]

# NOTES

1. *Robert Southey, made poet-laureate in 1813, published his long poem* Joan of Arc *in 1796.*
2. Un sauvage ivre—*to use the phrase Pushkin took from Voltaire*

*himself. In the* Dissertation sur la tragédie *he wrote of Hamlet: "On croirait que cet ouvrage est le fruit de l'imagination d'un sauvage ivre." See Note 15 to "Refutations of Criticisms."*
3. *This article was published after Pushkin's death. All of the documents and facts in it are his own inventions. This is only one of many mystifications in which Pushkin indulged.*

# NOTES AND APHORISMS

**Only a revolutionary mind like Mirabeau or Peter can love** Russia, as only a writer can love its language.

Everything must be created in this Russia and in this Russian language.

(1823)

\* \* \*

Making the bust of a famous man, Thorwaldsen[1] was amazed by the strange division of the face (a handsome one, incidentally)—scowling, menacing above, expressing a constant smile below. Torvaldsen didn't like that:

Questa è una bruta figura.

(1828)

\* \* \*

Literature exists in our country, but criticism still does not. In our country journalists use the name "romantic" as abuse, in the same way old ladies abuse rakes as Freemasons or Voltaireans—with no understanding either of Voltaire or of Freemasonry.

(1829)

\* \* \*

French critics have their own concept of romanticism. They attribute to it all works which bear the stamp of dejection or dreaminess. Some even call neologisms and grammatical errors romanticism. Thus André Chénier, a poet steeped in antiquity, whose shortcomings actually result from a desire to use the forms of Greek prosody in French, has landed among the romantic poets in their criticism.

(1830)

\*  \*  \*

The first unhappy sigher arouses the sensitivity of a woman, the rest are either barely noticed or serve only. . . . Thus in the beginning of a battle the first wounded man produces a painful impression and exhausts our compassion.

(1830)

\*  \*  \*

At the instant love disappears, our heart already cherishes its memory. Thus Byron's gladiator consents to die, but his imagination soars along the banks of his native Danube.[2]

(1830)

\*  \*  \*

Milton said: "A small number of readers is enough for me, if only they are worthy of understanding me."[3] This proud desire of the poet is repeated occasionally in our time, but with a small change. Some of our contemporaries overtly and underhandedly try to convince us that "a small number of readers is enough for them, if only there are many *buyers*."

(1830)

\*  \*  \*

In the newspaper *Le Furet*[4] is printed a communiqué from Peking that a certain mandarin ordered a certain journalist beaten with sticks. The publisher notes that that is shameful for the mandarin, but healthy for the journalist.

(1830)

\*  \*  \*

Translators are the post horses of enlightenment.

(1830)

\* \* \*

Envy is the sister of competition, consequently from a good family.

(1830)

\* \* \*

In our country it is for the most part journalists who occupy themselves with criticism, i.e. *entrepreneurs*, people who understand their business well, but not only not *critics*, but not even literary men.

In other countries writers write either for the crowd or for a small number.\* Among us the latter is impossible, one must write for one's own self.

(1833)

\* \* \*

D. used to say that the most complete satire on some literary societies would be a list of the members with a designation of what had been written by whom.

(1833)

\* \* \*

Grammar does not prescribe laws for language, but elucidates and states its customs.

(1833)

\* \* \*

Don't put off until supper that which you can eat at lunch.[5]

\* \* \*

---

\* Having lovingly studied a new work they pass judgment on it; and thus the work, not subject to the judgment of the public, receives the value and place in the public's opinion which belongs to it.

L'exactitude est la politesse des cuisiniers.[6]

\* \* \*

The stomach of an enlightened man possesses the best qualities of a kind heart: sensitivity and gratitude.

(1834)

\* \* \*

Ne pas admettre l'existence de Dieu c'est être plus absurde que ces peuples qui pensent du moins que le monde est posé sur un rhinocéros.

(1830)

\* \* \*

La libération de l'Europe viendra de la Russie, car c'est là seulement que le préjugé de l'Aristocratie n'existe absolument pas. Ailleurs ont croit à l'Aristocratie, les uns pour la dédaigner, les autres pour la haïr, les troisièmes pour en tirer profit, vanité etc. En Russie rien de tout cela. On n'y croit pas, voilà tout.

(1835)

# N O T E S

1. *Bertel Thorwaldsen (1768–1844)—a Danish sculptor. The famous man whose bust he sculpted was Alexander I.*
2. Childe Harold, *IX, CXL.*
3. *This was "reported" in* The Literary Gazette *(March 17, 1830).*
4. *A French language newspaper published in St. Petersburg. Pushkin's little note, printed in* The Literary Gazette *in 1830, was directed at the "Chinese anecdotes" published in Bulgarin's* Northern Bee.
5. *Pushkin had been reading Jacques Savary's (or Savary des Brulon's—1657–1716)* Physiology of Taste. *Pushkin began one other (not very polite) culinary aphorism: "Don't offer your guest that which you yourself. . . ."*
6. *A play on Louis XVIII's "L'exactitude est la politesse des rois."*

# TABLE-TALK

Once[1] Dennis Davydov[2] reported to Prince Bagration[3] in the advance guard and said: "The commander-in-chief ordered me to inform your excellency that the enemy is on our nose, and request you to retreat at once." Bagration answered: "The enemy is on our nose? On whose? if on yours, then he is close; but if on mine, we will still have time to finish dinner."

\* \* \*

One day Barkov[4] quarrelled with Sumarokov about which of them could write an ode faster. Sumarokov locked himself in his study, leaving Barkov in the living room. In a quarter of an hour Sumarokov emerges with an ode ready but no longer finds Barkov there. The servants report that he's left and ordered them to tell Alexander Petrovich that *what he had done was in the hat.*[5] Sumarokov guesses that there's some prank in this. And in fact, he sees his hat on the floor, and —— —— ——.[6]

\* \* \*

No one knew how to anger Sumarokov like Barkov. Sumarokov highly respected Barkov as a learned and witty critic, and always asked his opinions about his works. One day Barkov, who did not usually pamper him, arrived at Sumarokov's: "Sumarokov is a great man; Sumarokov is the first Russian poet!" he said to him. The overjoyed Sumarokov ordered him given vodka immediately, and that was all that Barkov wanted. He drank himself drunk. Leaving, he said to him: "Alexander Petrovich, I lied to you: *I* am the first Russian poet, second is Lomonosov, and you are only third.'" Sumarokov almost cut his throat.

\* \* \*

One day a young Negro who was accompanying Peter I on his walk stopped for a certain necessity and suddenly cried out in fright: "Sire! Sire! My intestine is crawling out of me." Peter walked up to him, and seeing what the matter was, said: "You're lying: that's not an intestine, but a tapeworm"—and pulled the tapeworm out with his own hands. The anecdote is not too clean, but it illustrates the customs of Peter.

\* \* \*

A certain retired warrant-officer, when he was still a child, was presented to Peter I among the gentry sent for the service. The sovereign pushed the hair off his forehead, glanced into his face, and said: "Well! This one's bad. However, enlist him in the navy. Maybe he'll get promoted as far as warrant-officer." The old man loved to tell this anecdote and always added: "Such was the prophecy—that I became a warrant-officer only when I was retired." (Heard from Prince A. N. Golytsyn)

\* \* \*

Everyone knows the words of Peter the Great when he was presented the twelve-year-old schoolbay Vasily Tredyakovsky: *eternal toiler!* What an eye! What precision of definition! What, in fact, was Tredyakovsky if not an eternal toiler?

\* \* \*

Peter I often said: "If you fear unhappiness, you will not see happiness."

\* \* \*

For a long time the sovereign had not promoted Boldyrev to general because of his card-playing. Once on some holiday in the palace, he went past him into church and said: "Boldyrev, I congratulate you." Boldyrev rejoiced; all those present thought the same thing he did and congratulated him. The sovereign, having left church and walking past Boldyrev, said to him: "I congratulate you; they say you won yesterday." Boldyrev was in desperation.

\* \* \*

Goethe had a great influence on Byron. Faust stirred the imagination of Childe Harold. Twice Byron tried to do battle with the giant of romantic poetry—and came out as lame as Jacob.[7]

\* \* \*

A certain lord, a well-known lazybones, parodied the well-known commandment for his son: "Never do yourself that which you can have done by someone else." N., a well-known egotist, added: "Never do for another that which you can do for yourself."

\* \* \*

At Krylov's over the divan where he usually sat hung a large painting in a heavy frame. Someone pointed out to him that the nail on which it hung was not firm and that the painting could some time tear loose and kill him. "No," answered Krylov, "in that case the corner of the frame will certainly describe an oblique line like so and just miss my head."

\* \* \*

Once Delvig invited Ryleev to visit the whores. "I'm married," answered Ryleev.—"So what," said Delvig, "do you mean you can't have dinner in a restaurant just because you have a kitchen at home?"

\* \* \*

Delvig didn't like mystical poetry. He used to say, "The closer to heaven, the colder it gets."

\* \* \*

Once Delvig challenged Bulgarin to a duel. Bulgarin refused

saying: "Tell Baron Delvig that in my time I've seen more blood than he has ink."

\* \* \*

I met Nadezhdin at Pogodin's. He seemed to me extremely plebeian, *vulgar*, boring, insolent and without any decorum. For example, he picked up a handkerchief I had dropped. His criticisms were written very stupidly, but with liveliness and occasionally even with eloquence. There were no ideas in them, but there was movement; the jokes were flat.

\* \* \*

Boudry, professor of French literature at the Tsarskoe Selo *lycée*, was Marat's brother.[8] Catherine II changed his name at his request, giving him the aristocratic particle *de*, which Boudry scrupulously preserved. He was from the Boudry family. He very much respected the memory of his brother, and one day in class, speaking of Robespierre, said to us as if it were nothing: *"C'est lui qui sous main travailla l'espirit de Charlotte Corday et fit de cette fille un second Ravaillac."* Incidentally, in spite of his birth, democratic ideas, greasy vest, and in general an exterior appearance reminiscent of a Jacobin, Boudry was a very agile courtier on his short little legs.

Boudry said that his brother was extraordinarily strong, in spite of his thinness and small stature. He also spoke a great deal about his good-naturedness, love for relatives, etc., etc. In his youth, in order to keep his brother away from depraved women, Marat took him to a hospital, where he showed him the horrors of venereal disease.

\* \* \*

The Jesuit Possevino,[9] so famous in our history, was one of the most zealous persecutors of Machiavellian memory. He collected in one book all the slander, all the attacks, which the works of the immortal Florentine had occasioned, and by this means stopped a new edition of them. Conringius, the scholar who published *Il principie* in 1660, proved that Possevino had never read Machiavelli and interpreted him from hearsay.

\* \* \*

By his nature man is more disposed to censure than to praise (says Machiavelli, that great expert on human nature).

Foolishness of censure is not as noticeable as foolish praise; a fool sees no merit in Shakespeare and this is attributed to the fastidiousness of his taste, eccentricity, etc. The same fool is ecstatic over Ducray-Duminil's[10] novel or Mr. Polevoi's *History*[11] and he is viewed with contempt, even though to a thinking man his foolishness was expressed more clearly in the first case.

\* \* \*

*Divide et impera* is a rule of state, not just of Machiavelli (I take this word in its general sense).

\* \* \*

The shape of Arabic numerals is made up from the following figure:

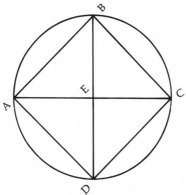

A

(1), ABDC (2), ABECD (3), ABD AE (4) etc.

D

Roman numerals are made up from the same model.

\* \* \*

Othello is not jealous by nature—on the contrary, he is trusting. Voltaire understood this, and developing Shakespeare's creation in his own imitation, he put the following verse into the lips of his Orosmane:

Je ne suis point jaloux. . . . Si je l'étais jamais! . . .[12]

\* \* \*

The characters created by Shakespeare are not, as in Molière, basically types of such and such a passion, such and such a vice, but living beings filled with many passions, many vices; circumstances develop their varied and many-sided personalities before the viewer. In Molière, the miser is miserly—and that's all; in Shakespeare, Shylock is miserly, acute, vindictive, philoprogenitive, witty. In Molière the hypocrite dangles after the wife of his benefactor—hypocritically; takes the estate into his care—hypocritically; asks for a glass of water—hypocritically. In Shakespeare the hypocrite passes sentence with vainglorious severity—but justly; he justifies his cruelty with the profound judgment of a statesman; he seduces innocence with powerful, convincing sophisms—not with a ridiculous mixture of piety and rakery. Angelo is a hypocrite because his public acts contradict his hidden passions![13] And what profundity there is in this character!

But perhaps nowhere is the many-sided genius of Shakespeare reflected with such variety as in Falstaff, whose vices, one connected to the other, form an amusing, ugly chain, like an ancient bacchanalia. Analyzing Falstaff's character, we see that its main feature is voluptuousness; probably from youth, coarse, cheap woman-chasing was his first interest, but he is already past fifty, he's gotten fat, grown decrepit; gluttony and wine have noticeably won out over Venus. Secondly, he is a coward, but spending his life with young scape-graces, constantly subjected to their mockery and pranks, he conceals his cowardice by means of evasive and mocking boldness. By habit and calculation he is boastful. Falstaff is not at all stupid—on the contrary. He even has some of the customs of a man who has occasionally seen good society. He has absolutely no principles. He's as weak as a woman. He needs strong Spanish wine (*the sack*), rich dinners, and money for his mistresses; in order to acquire them he is ready for anything—except manifest danger.

In my youth chance brought me together with a man in whom nature, it seemed, wishing to imitate Shakespeare, reproduced his great creation. —— was a second Falstaff: voluptuous, a coward, boastful, not stupid, amusing, without any principles, tearful, and fat. One circumstance lent him an original charm. He was married. Shakespeare didn't manage to marry off his bachelor. Falstaff died among his girl-friends, not having managed to be a horned spouse, nor the father of a family—how many scenes lost to the brush of Shakespeare!

Here is a touch from the domestic life of my respectable friend. One day in his absence his four-year-old son, the very image of his father, a little Falstaff III, kept repeating to himself: "How bwave papa is! How the soveweign loves papa!" The boy was overheard and they called to him: "Volodya, who told you that?"—"Papa" answered Volodya.

\* \* \*

One lady told me that if a man started talking to her about insignificant matters as if accommodating himself to the weakness of feminine understanding, in her eyes he immediately betrayed his ignorance of women. Really, isn't it ridiculous to consider women—who so often strike us with the rapidity of their understanding and subtlety of feeling and logic—inferior beings in comparison to us? This is especially strange in Russia, where Catherine II ruled, and where women are in general more enlightened, read and follow the course of European events more than we who, God knows why, are so proud.

\* \* \*

ON DUROV

Durov—the brother of the Durova who entered the military service in 1807—earned a St. George Cross and is publishing his memoirs now. In his way, the brother does not yield to the sister in eccentricity; I met him in the Caucasus in 1829, when I was returning from Erzerum. He was being treated for some exotic disease like catalepsy and he played cards from morning till night. Finally he lost everything, and I took him to Moscow in my carriage. Durov had a monomania: he absolutely had to have one hundred thousand rubles. He had thought up and re-thought all possible ways of getting it. Sometimes on the road at night he would wake me up with the question, "Alexander Sergeevich! Alexander Sergeevich! How do you think I could get one hundred thousand?" Once I told him that if I were in his place and the one hundred thousand was essential for my tranquillity and well-being, I would steal it. "I've thought of that," Durov answered me—"Well, what then?"—"Simple—you can't find one hundred thousand in every man's pocket, and I don't want to knife or rob a man for a trifle—I have a conscience."—"Well, steal a regimental payroll."—"I've thought of that."—"What?"—"It could be done in the summer when the regiment is in camp and the wagon with the payroll stands by the regimental commander's quarters. You could throw a long rope over the wagon tongue and hitch a horse to it from a distance and then gallop off on it; seeing the wagon galloping without horses the sentry would probably be afraid and not know what to do; two or three versts away you could break open the wagon and escape with the payroll. But there are a lot of obstacles in this too. Don't you know any other way?"—"Ask the sovereign for money."—"I've thought of that."—"Well?"—"I even asked."—"What? Without any right?"—"That's what I began with: your majesty! I have no right to ask you for what would make the happiness of my life; but, your majesty, there is no model for charity, and so forth."—"What did he answer?"—"That's surprising. You should turn to Rothschild."—"I've thought of that."—"Well, how did that plan go?"—"Well, do you see, one way of enticing Rothschild to give one hundred thousand was to write him such a weird and amusing request that afterward he would be happy to tell an anecdote which cost one hundred thousand. But so many difficulties! . . ." In a word, it was impossible to think up stupidities and absurdities that Durov hadn't already thought of. His last project was to wheedle the money out of the English by exciting their national pride and in hope of their love for eccentricities. He wanted to address the following speech to them: "Englishmen! I have bet 10,000 rubles that you wouldn't refuse to loan me 100,000. Englishmen! Save me from the loss which I risked in hope of your magnanimity which is known to the whole world." Durov asked me to try to arrange this through the English ambassador in Petersburg, and he didn't tell his project to me until he had taken my word of honor that I would not use it myself. He was always ready to bet on anything whatever. If a woman was being talked about—"Do you want to bet me," interrupted Durov, "that I can have her in three days?" If people were target-shooting with pistols, Durov would propose standing at 25 paces and bet 1,000 rubles that you couldn't hit him. His passion for women was also very remarkable. When he was mayor of Elabug he fell in love with a red-haired peasant woman who had been sentenced to the lash—at the very moment that she had already been tied to the post and as his duty he was present at her punishment. He whispered to the executioner to spare her and not to touch her white and plump charms—which order was carried out, after which Durov lived with the beautiful prisoner for several days. Not long ago I received a letter from him; he writes me: "My story is short: I got married, I still have no money." I answered him: "I am sorry that of the 100,000 ways of getting 100,000 rubles, apparently not one has yet succeeded for you."

*8 October 1835*

\* \* \*

Once early in the morning Count Rumyantsev[14] was walking around his camp. Some major was standing in front of his tent in a dressing gown and night cap, and in the morning darkness he did not recognize the approaching field marshal until he saw him face to face. The major wanted to hide, but Rumyantsev took him by the arm and, asking various questions, took him with him around the camp, which meanwhile was waking up. The poor major was in desperation. Strolling about in this manner, the field marshal returned to his headquarters, where his entire retinue was already awaiting him. Dying from shame, the major found himself among generals in full-dress uniform. Still not satisfied, Rumyantsev was cruel enough to treat him to tea and only then dismiss him without making any comment.

\* \* \*

One day Potemkin was told that a certain Count Morelli, an inhabitant of Florence, played the violin excellently. Potemkin wanted to hear him—he ordered that he be summoned. One of the adjutants set off as a courier to Italy, appeared before Count Morelli, informed him of his excellency's order, and proposed that he get in his carriage immediately and gallop to Russia. The noble virtuoso became furious and sent both Potemkin and the courier with his carriage to the devil. There was nothing to be done. But how could he appear before the Prince without having fulfilled his order? The resourceful adjutant found a violinist, a poor man not without talent, and easily persuaded him to call himself Count Morelli and go to Russia. He was brought and presented to Potemkin, who was satisfied with his playing. Afterward, he was accepted in the service under the name Count Morelli and served until he advanced to the rank of colonel.[16]

\* \* \*

Potemkin often had the chrondria. He would sit by himself for days in total inactivity, admitting no one to see him. Once when he was in a state like this many papers which demanded his immediate decision piled up, but no one dared to go into his room with a report. A young clerk named Petushkov, hearing this talk, volunteered to present the Prince with the papers which needed signatures. These were given to him gladly, and everyone waited to see what would happen. Petushkov walked straight into the private office with the papers. Potemkin was sitting in a bathrobe, barefoot, uncombed, and biting his nails pensively. Petushkov boldly explained to him why he had come and put the papers before him. Without saying anything Potemkin took a pen and signed them one after the other. Petushkov bowed and went out into the anteroom with a triumphant face: "He signed." Everyone rushed up to him and looked—indeed, all of the papers were signed. They congratulate Petushkov, "Good boy! What can one say!" But someone examines the signature more closely—and what does he see? On all of the papers, instead of Potemkin, was the signature: "Petushkov," "Petushkov," "Petushkov," . . .

\* \* \*

During the Ochakov campaign Prince Potemkin was in love with Countess ——.[17] When he had obtained a rendezvous and was alone with her in his headquarters, he suddenly yanked the bell, and cannons around the entire camp thundered. When he learned the reason for the salvo, Countess ——'s husband, a witty and immoral man, shrugged his shoulders and said, "What a cock-a-doodle-do."

## N O T E S

1. *Pushkin himself used this English title. He had probably read Hazlitt's* Table Talk *(1821). Pushkin wrote down these anecdotes and remarks at various times during the 1830's, but never finished putting them in order. Most of them deal with history; none was ever published. I have translated only about half of the pieces, concentrating on those of literary interest.*

2. *Dennis Davydov (1784–1839)—a military hero during 1812*

(*prototype of Denisov in* War and Peace) *and a poet (author of popular verses in a "hussar" style).*

3. *Peter I. Bagration (1765–1812)—a famous general.*

4. *Ivan S. Barkov (1732–68)—famed for filthy poetry which circulated in hand-written manuscripts then and now.*

5. Delo v shlyape—*the corresponding English idiom is "it's in the bag." Here it is used both literally (Barkov's "production" was in the hat) and figuratively.*

6. *I presume the reader can guess what Barkov had done in the hat. This, it seems to me, is the ultimate criticism of the neoclassical ode.*

7. *In* Manfred *and* The Deformed Transformed.

8. *David I. de Boudry (1756–1821), Marat's brother, went to Russia in 1784. He remained there the rest of his life, teaching at the Lycée from 1811 to 1821.*

9. *Antonio Possevino (1553–1611) went to Russia during the reign of Ivan the Terrible to try to unite the Roman Catholic and Orthodox churches. He attacked Machiavelli in* A Judgment of Four Writers *(1592). Pushkin read about this in a ten-volume edition of Machiavelli (Paris, 1823–26).*

10. *François Ducray-Duminil (1761–1819), author of novels such as* Victor ou l'Enfant de la forêt *and* Lolotte et Fanfan.

11. *Nikolai Polevoi,* The History of the Russian People *(Moscow, 1829).*

12. *From Voltaire's* Zaïre, *Act I, Scene V.*

13. *Angelo—in* Measure for Measure. *Pushkin did a free translation of this play (some scenes close to the text, some not). The changes he made are extremely interesting. Complaining of the critics' low opinion of it (when the poem was published in 1834), Pushkin said he had written nothing better.*

14. *Peter A. Rumyantsev—a Russian field marshal.*

15. *Grigory A. Potemkin (1739–91)—general, field marshal, political figure, "favorite" of Catherine the Great.*

16. *An Italian violinist named Rozatti did serve as colonel under Potemkin (using the name Count Morelli) during the Russo-Turkish War (1787–91).*

17. *Countess Ekaterina Dolgorukova (1769–1849)—wife of Lt. Gen. V. V. Dolgorukov, who took part in the taking of Ochakov (1788).*

# APPENDIX


## WORKS BY PUSHKIN'S CONTEMPORARIES

# On the Trend of our Poetry,
## Especially the Lyric, in the Past Decade

BY Wilhelm Küchelbecker

---

### Wilhelm Karlovich Küchelbecker (1797–1846)

Küchelbecker (or Kjuxel'beker) was one of Pushkin's classmates at the Lycée. His poetry was first published in 1815, beginning a career which was interrupted by Küchelbecker's arrest and exile for his part in the Decembrist uprising. He spent the last twenty years of his life in various fortresses and in Siberia. But Küchelbecker continued to write. His works include a great variety of short and long poems (often on classical subjects), novels, verse plays, and translations of Shakespeare.

His last literary activity before the Decembrist uprising was the publication of the almanac *Mnemosyne*. "On the Trend of Our Poetry" was published in the second of the four parts which appeared in 1824 and 1825. The essay shows Küchelbecker's preference for the "high" genres and style. Küchelbecker had been a member of Shishkov's Society of Lovers of the Russian Word, and he objected to the nicety and gallicisms of Karamzin's successors, saying they would turn the poetic language into *un petit jargon de coterie*. His attack on elegiac poetry in this essay gave rise to a spirited exchange of articles in the journals. Pushkin's reaction can be judged by the piece entitled "An Objection to Küchelbecker's Essay in *Mnemosyne*" (above, pp. 42–44).

The text used for the translation is in *Russkaja literatura XIX v.— Xrestomatija kritičeskix materialov*, Vypusk I, pp. 198–206.

Deciding to talk about the trend of our poetry during the last decade, I foresee that there are not many whom I will greatly please, and that I will arm many against me. And I, just as much as many people, could go into raptures over the incredible successes of our literature. But a flatterer is always contemptible. As a son of the Fatherland, I set it as my duty to boldly tell the truth.

From Lomonosov to the last transformation of our poetry by Zhukovsky and his followers, there has been in our country, almost without interruption, a generation of lyric poets whose names have remained the heritage of posterity, whose works Russia should be proud of.[1] Lomonosov, Petrov, Derzhavin, Dmitriev, Derzhavin's companion and friend Kapnist, to a certain extent Bobrov, Vostokov, and at the end of the penultimate decade a poet who deserves to occupy one of the first places of the Russian Parnassus, Prince Shixmatov, are the leaders of this mighty family; in our time they have almost no successors. Among us the elegy and epistle have supplanted the ode. Let us examine the qualities of these three genres and try to define the degree of their poetic merit.

Power, freedom, inspiration are the three essential conditions for any poetry. In general, lyric poetry is nothing other than the extraordinary, i.e. the powerful, free, and inspired expression of the emotions of the writer himself. From this it follows that the more it is elevated above mundane events, above the base language of the rabble who do not know inspiration, the more excellent it is. All of the requirements which this definition presupposes are fully satisfied only by the *ode*—and therefore without doubt the ode occupies the first place in lyric poetry or, better said, it alone totally deserves the name lyric poetry. But the other genres of versified expression of one's own emotions either subordinate these emotions to narration— as the hymn and even more so the ballad—and therefore they are a transition to epic poetry, or the insignificance of the subject itself lays chains on genius, smothers the fire of its inspiration. In the latter case these works are distinguished from prose only by the verse form, because just as much charm and euphony (the merits to which they are by necessity limited) can be found in rhetoric as in these genres. The ode soars, thunders, glitters; it enslaves the hearing and soul of the reader as it is carried away by elevated subjects, transmitting to the ages the great deeds of heroes and the Fatherland, soaring up to an all-high throne, and making prophecies to a reverential people. In addition, the poet is unselfish in the ode. He is not made joyful by the insignificant events of his own life, he does not lament them; he prophesies the truth and judgment of Providence, he rejoices in the greatness of his native land, he casts lightning bolts at foes, he blesses the pious man of truth, curses the miscreant.

In the elegy—the modern and the ancient—the poet speaks about himself, about *his own* griefs and pleasures. The elegy almost never grows wings, it doesn't rejoice; it *has* to be quiet, smooth, considered; it *has* to, I say, because anyone who is made too ecstatically joyful by his own good fortune is ridiculous; and unrestrained sadness is frenzy, not poetry. The lot of the elegy is moderation, mediocrity (Horace's *aurea mediocritas*)*:

> Son enthousiasme paisable
> N'a point ces tragiques fureurs;
> De sa veine féconde et pure
> Coulent avec nombre et mesure
> Des ruisseaux de lait et de miel,
> Et ce pusillanime Icare
> Trahi par l'aile de Pindare
> Ne retombe jamais du ciel!³

It is only interesting when, like a beggar, it manages to gain sympathy by tears or entreaties, or when the freshness, the playful variety of colors which it scatters on its subject makes one forget its insignificance for an instant. The last requirement is less or more satisfied by the elegies of the ancients and

---

* Voltaire said that all genres are good except the boring; he didn't say that all are equally good. But Boileau, the supreme, indisputable lawgiver in the eyes of the crowd of Russian and French Saint-Maurs and Aujers,² declared:

Un sonnet sans défaut vaut seul un long poème!

However, there are barbarians in whose eyes just the boldness of undertaking the creation of an epos outweighs all possible sonnets, triolets, charades, and perhaps, ballads. W. K.

Goethe's elegies, which he called Roman; but our Grays[4] have almost never been tempted by this radiant southern genre of poetry.*

Our epistle is the same elegy, only in the most disadvantageous garb possible; or else it is a satirical flourish such as the satires of the wits of prosaic memory, Horace, Boileau, and Pope, or it is simply a letter in verse. It's difficult not to be bored when Ivan and Sidor croon to us about their misfortunes; it's even more difficult not to fall asleep re-reading, as they occasionally tell each other in three hundred trimeters, that—glory to God!—they are in good health and that they are dreadfully sorry they haven't seen each other in such a long time! It's easier if at least the ardent writer instead of beginning:

> *Dear sir NN,*

exclaims:

> *. . . sensitive singer,*
> *You (and I) are destined for the crown*
> *of immortality!*

and then limits himself to the announcement that he is reading du Marsay,[5] studying the alphabet and logic, that he never writes either *semo* or *ovamo*[6] and he desires to be clear! It's easier on the spirit—I say—if he doesn't top that off by supplying us with a detailed description of his pantry or library or Schwabian geese or his friend's Russian ducks.

Now I ask: have we gained by replacing the ode with the elegy and epistle?

Zhukovsky was the first of us to start imitating the *modern* Germans, primarily Schiller. Contemporaneously with him, Batyushkov took two pygmies of French literature—Parny and Millevoye—as models. For a while Zhukovsky and Batyushkov became the leading figures among our poets, especially the school which nowadays is passed off as romantic.

---

\* Baron Delvig wrote several poems from which, *as far as I remember*, one could get a fairly accurate idea of the spirit of the ancient elegy. However, I don't know if they have been printed or not.

But what is romantic poetry?

It was born in Provence and it educated Dante, who gave it life, power, and boldness; he bravely threw off the yoke of slavish imitation of the Romans, who themselves were the only imitators of the Greeks, and he decided to do battle with them. Subsequently in Europe they began to call any free and national poetry "romantic." Does romantic poetry, in this sense, exist among the Germans?

Excepting Goethe, and he only in very few of his works, they were always, in every case, students of the French, Romans, Greeks, English, and finally the Italians and Spanish. What is the echo of their works? What is our romanticism?

Let us not, however, be unjust. Given the total ignorance of ancient languages which, to our shame, is a distinguishing feature of almost all Russian writers who have talent, a knowledge of German literature is indubitably not without use for us. Thus, for example, we are obliged to its influence that now we don't write just in Alexandrines and iambic and trochaic tetrameter.

By their study of nature, their power, their abundance and variety of emotions, tableaux, language, and ideas, by the nationalism of their works, the great poets of Greece, the East, Britain have ineffaceably chiseled their names into the rolls of immortality. Can it be we dare hope that on the road which we are now traveling we compare with them? No one (except our common translators) translates translators. An imitator does not know inspiration: he does not speak from the depth of his soul, he forces himself to retell other people's ideas and feelings. Power?—Where will we find it in our turbid, vague, effeminate, colorless works? Among us everything is *dream* and *vision*, everything is *imagined* and *seems* or *appears to be*, everything is just *as if, somehow, something or other, something*. Richness and variety?—Having read any elegy of Zhukovsky, Pushkin, or Baratynsky you know everything. We haven't had any feelings for a long time; the feeling of dejection has swallowed up all the others. We all lament to each other about our lost youth;

we chew and re-chew this melancholy to infinity and we incessantly flaunt our faint-heartedness in periodical publications. If this grief were not simply a rhetorical figure, someone—judging from our Childe Harolds—might think that in our Russia poets are born already old men. The tableaux are the same everywhere: The *moon* which, of course, is *dejected* and *pale*, cliffs and oak groves where they never existed, a forest beyond which the setting sun and dusk has been described a hundred times; sometimes long shadows and ghosts, something or other invisible, something or other unknown, banal allegories, colorless, tasteless personifications of *Labor, Sweet Bliss, Tranquillity, Gaiety, Sadness,* the *Laziness* of the writer and the *Boredom* of the reader, but, especially, *fog*: fogs over the waters, fogs over the pine grove, fogs over the fields, fog in the writer's head.

From the rich, powerful, Russian vocabulary they are trying to extract a small, fastidious, cloying, artificially meagre language adapted *for a few, un petit jargon de coterie*. They mercilessly purge it of all Slavic expressions and turns of speech, and they enrich it with *architraves, columns, barons, mournings,* Germanisms, Gallicisms, and barbarisms. Even in prose they try to replace participles and verbal adverbs with an infinity of pronouns and conjunctions. About ideas there's nothing to be said. The stamp of nationality distinguishes about 80 lines of Zhukovsky's *Svetlana* and *Epistle to Voeykov*, a few minor poems by Katenin, and two or three passages in Pushkin's *Ruslan and Ludmila.*

Freedom, invention, and novelty are the three main advantages of romantic poetry over the so-called classical poetry of the most recent Europeans. The fathers of this seemingly classical poetry were the Romans more than the Greeks. It abounds in versifiers—not *poets,* who are as rare as albinos in the physical world. In France this flaccid tribe dominated for a long time; the best, the true poets of that land, for example Racine, Corneille, Molière, in spite of their inner loathing, had to oblige them, subordinate themselves to their arbitrary rules, to dress in their ponderous *kaftans,* wear their huge powdered wigs, and not infrequently make sacrifices to the ugly idols which they called taste, Aristotle, and nature, bowing down, under these names, to nothing but finicality, decorum, and mediocrity. Then the worthless robbers of ancient treasures were able to vulgarize the best depictions, phrases, and ornaments of those treasures by means of frequent, cold repetition: the helmet and armor of Hercules crushed dwarfs who were not only not able to rush into battle and strike hearts and souls, but were deprived of life, movement, and breath beneath their weight. Aren't our repetitions the same thing: *youth* and *joy, dejection* and *voluptuousness,* and those nameless, anonymous, obsolete gripes which even in Byron himself *(Childe Harold),* I hope, are far from worthy of Homer's Achilles, or Ariosto's Orlando, or Tasso's Tancred, or the glorious Cervantes' knight of sad countenance, which are weak and underdrawn in Pushkin's "Prisoner" and elegies, which are unbearable, ridiculous under the pen of his *copyists.*—Let's be thankful to Zhukovsky for freeing us from the yoke of French literature and from the dominion of the laws of La Harpe's *Lycée* and Batteux's *Course*[7]; but let us not allow him or anyone else, even if he possessed ten times his talent, to place the chains of German or English sovereignty on us!

It is best to have a national literature. But isn't France obliged partly to Euripides and Sophocles for Racine? Working on the path of his great predecessors, a man with talent sometimes discovers spheres of new beauties and inspirations which had hidden from the eyes of these giants, his mentors. So if one is going to imitate, it isn't a bad idea to know which of these foreign writers is worth direct imitation. However, our live catalogers whose "looks," "critiques," and "discussions" one meets in the *The Son of the Fatherland, The Emulator of Enlightenment and Philanthropy, The Well-Intentioned,* and *The Messenger of Europe* usually place on the same level: Greek literature—and Latin; English—and German; the great Goethe—and Schiller (who did not mature); the giant among giants

Homer—and his pupil Virgil; the luxuriant, thunderous Pindar—
and the prosaic versifier Horace; Racine, a worthy heir of the
ancient tragedians—and Voltaire, who was alien to true poetry;
the vast Shakespeare—and the monotonous Byron! There was a
time when we blindly fell down before every Frenchman, Roman, or Greek sanctified by the pronouncement of La Harpe's
*Lycée*. Nowadays we venerate any German or Englishman as
soon as he is translated into French, for to this time the French
have not stopped being our legislators; we have dared to peek at
the works of their neighbors solely because *they* started to
read them.

With more thoroughgoing basic knowledge and greater love
of work on the part of our writers, Russia could, with its geographical position, assimilate all the treasures of the minds of
Europe and Asia. Pherdousi, Gafis, Saadi, and Dzhami await
Russian readers.[8]

But, I repeat, it is not enough to assimilate the treasures of
other nations: may a truly Russian poetry be created for the
glory of Russia, may Holy Russia be the foremost power of the
universe in the moral world as well as the political one! The
faith of our forefathers, national mores, chronicles, folk songs
and legends are the best, the purest, the surest sources for our
literature.

Let us hope that finally our writers, of whom a few young
ones are especially endowed with real talent, will cast from
themselves the shameful German chains and wish to be Russian. Here I have in mind particularly A. Pushkin, whose three
poems, particularly the first, offer great hopes. I haven't hesi-
tated to boldly voice my opinion about his shortcomings either,
in spite of the fact that I am sure he will prefer this to the loud
praises of the publisher of *The Northern Archive*. The public
has little need of knowing that I am Pushkin's friend, but this
friendship gives me the right to think that he, like his worthy
comrade Baratynsky, will not doubt that no one in Russia is
gladdened by their successes more than I!

I will answer the Sayids, who certainly will pronounce me a

Zoilus and envious man everywhere they can, only when I find their attacks harmful for our country's literature, which is precious to my heart. I will gratefully receive the refutations of conscientious and enlightened opponents; I ask them to send these for publication in *Mnemosyne* and I announce in advance to each and all that I will gladly change my favorite opinion for a better one. Truth is dearer to me than anything in the world!

[*Mnemosyne*, 1824]

## N O T E S

1. *V. P. Petrov, S. Bobrov, A. K. Vostokov, V. Kapnist, and S. A. Shirinsky-Shixmatov—ponderous, old-fashioned, neoclassical poets of the latter part of the eighteenth century and the beginning of the nineteenth century.*

2. *Saint Maur (Congrégation Benédictine de)—produced an* History *littéraire de la France (1733–63). Probably Louis S. Auger (1772–1829)—a literary scholar and critic.*

3. *From Lamartine's ode* L'Enthousiasme (Méditations, *No. XII).*

4. *Thomas Gray's "Elegy Written in a Country Churchyard" was one of Zhukovsky's first translations.*

5. *César du Marsay (1676–1756)—grammarian and rhetorician, author of* Traité des tropes.

6. *Semo, ovamo—Church Slavonic words meaning hither and thither.*

7. *Charles Batteux (1713–80)—French pedagogue and esthetician, translator of Horace.*

8. *Pherdousi, Gafis, and Dzhami—classics of Tadzhik and Persian literature (10th, 14th, and 15th centuries).*

# In Place of a Foreword to
# The Fountain of Bakhchisarai

### BY Peter Vyazemsky

---

### Prince Peter Andreevich Vyazemsky (1792–1878)

**Vyazemsky is known both as a critic and as a poet.** The abrasive wit which enlivens his otherwise rather graceless poetry is a characteristic feature of his critical articles as well. He was one of the first and staunchest defenders of romanticism in Russia. As shown by his brilliant correspondence with Pushkin and A. I. Turgenev, he saw the West as the model which Russian enlightenment should follow. But while he was on the side of new movements in the 1820s and 1830s (he wrote one of the few favorable reviews of Gogol's *Inspector General*), Vyazemsky outlived his family, his friends, and his age. He spent twenty years in a civil service job which he disliked, made several disillusioning trips to France and England, and ended his life embittered and generally hostile to contemporary social and literary trends.

Pushkin asked Vyazemsky to write a foreword to *The Fountain of Bakhchisarai* (1824). In his title Vyazemsky alludes to N. A. Tsertelev and others who, in the journal *Well-Intentioned*, signed their attacks on the new poetry with such pseudonyms as "An Inhabitant of the Vyborg Side" and "An Inhabitant of Vasilev Island." Vyazemsky's dialogue stirred up a polemic in which M. A. Dmitriev and Küchelbecker took part. Pushkin's answer to all this is "A Letter to the Editor of *Son of the Fatherland*" (above, pp. 21–22).

The text used for the translation of Vyazemsky's "In Place of a Foreword" is in *Russkaja literatura XIX v.—Xrestomatija kriticheskix materialov*, Vypusk I, ed. M. P. Legavka (Xar'kov, 1959), pp. 148–54.

The selections from Vyazemsky's notebooks cover his readings and thoughts from 1813 to 1848. The text used is P. Vjazemskij, *Zapisnye knizhki*, ed. V. S. Nechaeva (M., AN., 1963).

### A Conversation between the Publisher and a Classicist from the Vyborg Side or Vasilev Island

CLASSICIST: Is it true that young Pushkin is printing a third new poem, a poem, that is, in the romantic sense of the word— I don't know what to call it in our terms.

PUBLISHER: Yes, he has sent *The Fountain of Bakhchisarai,* which is being printed here now.

CLASSICIST: One cannot help regretting that he writes so much; he'll soon write himself out.

PUBLISHER: Prophecies are confirmed by events; one needs time to check them; and meanwhile I will note that if he writes a lot in comparison to our poets, who write almost nothing, he writes little in comparison with his other European colleagues. Byron, Walter Scott, and a number of others write tirelessly and are read tirelessly.

CLASSICIST: You expect to shut the mouths of the critics and their objections by exhibiting these two Britons! In vain! We are not of timid nature. It is impossible to judge a writer's talent by the predilection for him of the superstitious mass of readers. They are capricious, they often pay no attention to the most worthy writers.

PUBLISHER: Isn't it with a most worthy writer that I have the honor to be speaking?

CLASSICIST: An epigram is not an evaluation. The point is that the time of true classical literature has passed in our country. . . .

PUBLISHER: And I thought that it hadn't started. . . .

CLASSICIST: That nowadays some kind of new school has started up, unacknowledged by anyone except itself, one which doesn't follow any rules except its own whims, which distorts the language of Lomonosov, which writes randomly, showing off new expressions, new words. . . .

PUBLISHER: Taken from the *Dictionary of the Russian Academy* and to which the new poets have returned the right of citizenship in our language, a right stolen without trial for I don't know what crime; because up until now we have guided ourselves mainly by usage, which can be replaced by new usage. The laws of our language still haven't been codified, and how can one complain about the novelty of expressions? Will you order language and our poets to submit to Chinese immobility? Look at nature! Human faces, which are all made up of the same parts, are not all molded into one physiognomy, and the expression is the physiognomy of words.

CLASSICIST: Well, at least let's not give Russian words a German physiognomy then. What do these forms, this spirit mean for us? Who introduced them?

PUBLISHER: Lomonosov!

CLASSICIST: Now that's amusing!

PUBLISHER: What do you mean? Didn't he take a survey of German forms in the prosody which he introduced? Didn't he imitate contemporary Germans? I'll say more. Take the three celebrated poets in the history of our literature—you will find a German imprint on each of them. The epoch of reform made in Russian versification by Lomonosov, the epoch of reform in prose by Karamzin, the present movement, the romantic movement (against laws if you want to call it that)—don't these three clearly show the dominating propensity of our literature? Thus our poet-contemporaries follow the direction given by Lomonosov; the only difference is that he followed Guenther[1] and a few other of his contemporaries rather than Goethe and Schiller. And is it just among us that the German muses are spreading their dominion? Look in France too—a country which, at least in a literary regard, has hardly justified its vainglorious dreams of "universal hegemony"; even in France these kidnappers still receive some sovereignty and replace the local hereditary powers. The poets who are our contemporaries are no more sinful than their poet-predecessors.

We still don't have a Russian cut in literature. Perhaps because there isn't one now, there won't ever be one; but at least modern, so-called romantic poetry is no less native to us than the poetry of Lomonosov or Kheraskov, whom you strive to exhibit as classical. What is national in the *Petriada* and *Rossiada* except the names?

CLASSICIST: What is nationalism[2] in literature? There is no such figure in the poetics of Aristotle or the poetics of Horace.

PUBLISHER: There isn't in Horace's poetics, but there is in his works. It is in feelings, not rules. The imprint of nationalism, of the locale—perhaps it is that which is the most essential merit of the ancients and maintains their right to the attention of posterity. It was not in vain that among his sources in his universal history the profound Müller[3] noted Catullus and referred to him in characterizing that time.

CLASSICIST: It seems you already want to recruit the ancient classics into the band of romantics. I suppose that both Homer and Virgil were romantics.

PUBLISHER: Call them what you wish, but there is no doubt that Homer, Horace, and Aeschylus have much in common, more correlations with the leaders of the romantic school, than with their cold slavish followers who strive to be Greeks and Romans at a later date. Can it be that Homer created the *Iliad* foreseeing Aristotle and Longinus[4] and to please some kind of "classical conscience" which had not been invented yet? And allow me to ask both you and your elders whether it has been defined with exactitude what the "romantic type" is, what relation it has to the "classical," and how it contrasts. I confess, for myself at least, that no matter how much I have read about it, how much I have thought about it, neither in books nor in my mind have I yet happened to discover a complete, mathematically satisfactory solution of this problem. Many believe in the classical type because they have so been ordered, many do not acknowledge the romantic type because it doesn't have any legislators who bind one to unconditional and unquestioning faithfulness. They look at romanticism as capricious anarchism, a destroyer of decrees hallowed by antiquity and superstition. Schlegel[5] and Mme. de Staël are not clothed in the armor of leaden pedantry, they don't exude the air of scholastic pomposity, and for some people their rules have no weight because they don't lay on with pomposity; not all of us surrender to allurement and enthusiasm, many are enslaved only by authority. The "herd of imitators" of which Horace speaks[6] is not transferred from type to type. What acts on the minds of many pupils? A good pointer with which teachers pound intelligence into their listeners through the fingers. What does a shepherd drive his herd along the travelling road with? A firm staff. Our brothers love servility. . . .

CLASSICIST: You've calumniated me so much here that I haven't been able to give an appropriate rebuff to you with the following objection: the fact that its very name has no defined sense maintained by a general condition can serve as proof that there is no sense in the romantic school. You yourself acknowledge what classicism is, what it demands. . . .

PUBLISHER: Because its definition has been agreed upon, and there still hasn't been time to agree about romanticism. Its source is in nature; it *is*, it's in circulation; it still hasn't entered the hands of anatomists. Give it time! The hour will come when pedantry will put its leaden brand on romanticism's ethereal clothes too. In some century, Byron, Thomas Moore will fall beneath the scalpels of experimenters, as Anacreon or Ovid have today, and the blooms of their bright and fresh poetry will grow lusterless from the office dust, from the fumes from the lamps of commentators, antiquarians, scholiasts—only if, let us add, in future centuries there are people who live on other people's intellects and who, like vampires, dig in coffins, gobble and chew dead people, not forgetting to bite living ones too. . . .

CLASSICIST: Permit me, however, to remark to you in passing that your digressions are quite romantic. We had begun to talk about Pushkin; from him we were thrown into antiquity and now we've run ahead into future centuries.

PUBLISHER: Sorry! I forgot that such campaigns are beyond the strength of your classicist brothers. You hold to the unities of time and place. For you the intellect is a stay-at-home. Excuse me, I'll settle down; what do you wish of me?

CLASSICIST: I would like to know about the content of Pushkin's so-called poem. I confess that from the title I don't understand what can be suitable for a poem here. I understand that one can write stanzas, even an ode, *to a fountain*.

PUBLISHER: Yes, all the more that Horace already has *The Fountain of Bandusia*.[7]

CLASSICIST: However, the romantics have accustomed us to accidents. Their titles have an elastic quality. All you have to do is wish and it will embrace everything visible and invisible, or else it promises one thing and does something entirely different. But tell me. . . .

PUBLISHER: A legend well-known in the Crimea even today serves as the basis for the poem. It is told that Khan Kerim-Girey abducted the beautiful Pototsky and kept her in the Bakhchisarai harem; it is even supposed that he was married to her. This legend is dubious, and in his recently published *Journey in Tavrida*, Muravyov-Apostol attacks the probability of this story, rather soundly it seems.[8] However that may be, the legend is in the province of poetry.

CLASSICIST: So! In our time the muses have been turned into narrators of all kinds of cock-and-bull stories. Where is the merit of poetry if you feed it nothing but fairy-tales?

PUBLISHER: History should not be credulous; poetry is the opposite. It often values that which the former rejects with scorn, and our poet did very well in assimilating the Bakhchisarai legend to poetry and enriching it with realistic fictions, and even better that he used both elements with perfect artistry. The local color is preserved in the narration with all possible vividness and freshness. There is an eastern stamp on the tableaux, in the emotions themselves, and in the style. In the opinion of judges whose verdict can be considered final in our literature, in the new work the poet showed signs of a talent which is maturing more and more.

CLASSICIST: Who are these judges? We don't acknowledge any except *The Messenger of Europe* and *The Well-Intentioned*,[9] and that because we write in concert with them. Let's wait for what they say!

PUBLISHER: Wait with God! And meantime I will say that Pushkin's story is lively and interesting. There is a lot of movement in the poem. Into a rather tight frame he has put action
full not of a multitude of characters and a chain of different
adventures, but of artistry—with which the poet was able
to depict and add nuances to the main characters of his narration. *Action* depends, so to speak, on the *activity* of talent:
style lends its wings or slows its motion with weights. The
interest of the reader is maintained from beginning to end
in Pushkin's work. —One cannot achieve this secret except
with allurement of style.

CLASSICIST: Nevertheless I am certáin that, according to the
romantics' custom, all this action is only lightly marked out.
In such cases the reader must be the author's apprentice, and
finish saying things for him. Slight hints, hazy riddles—those
are the materials prepared by the romantic poet, and then let
the reader do what he wants with it. The romantic architect
leaves the arrangement and structure of the building to the
whimsy of each—a veritable castle in the air which has neither
plan nor foundation.

PUBLISHER: You aren't satisfied that you see a beautiful building
before you; you demand that its frame be visible too. In
works of art just the general action is enough; why the desire
to see the private production too? A work of art is a deception. The less the prosaic connection between parts extrudes,
the more profit in relation to the whole. Personal pronouns
in speech retard its flow, make the story cold. Imagination
and invention also have their "pronouns," from which talent
tries to free itself by means of successful ellipses. Why say
everything and press everything when we are dealing with
people whose minds are sharp and active? And there's no
reason to think about people whose minds are lazy and dull.
This reminds me of one classical reader who simply didn't
understand what had happened to the Cherkeshenka in "A
Prisoner of the Caucasus" in the lines:

And in the moonlit waters which had splashed
A running circle disappears.

He rebuked the poet for not having made it easier for his acumen by saying straight-out and literally that the Cherkeshenka had thrown herself into the water and drowned. Let's leave prose to prose! The way it is, there's enough of it in everyday life and in the poems printed in *The Messenger of Europe*.

P. S. Here the classicist left me hurriedly and in anger, and I got the idea of putting the conversation we had had on paper. Re-reading it, it occurred to me that I may be suspected of cunning—it will be said: "The publisher purposely weakened his opponent's objections, and purposely concealed everything sensible that he could utter in defense of his opinion!" It's useless to justify oneself to mistrust; but let my accusers take on themselves the labor of re-reading everything that has been said, over and over in some of our journals about romantic works and about the latest generation of our poetry in general: if one excludes the crude personalities and vulgar jokes, everyone will doubtlessly and easily be convinced that my conversant is on a par with his journalistic minions.

(1824)

## N O T E S

1. *Johann Guenther (1695–1723)—German poet.*
2. Narodnost'—*Vyazemsky is usually given credit for introducing the concept of* narodnost' *(nationalism, nationality) into Russian literary criticism. In a letter to Alexander Turgenev (November 22, 1819), he discusses the matter, saying, "Why not translate* nationalité *as* narodnost'*," adding that "the ending* -ost' *is a fine pimp."*
3. *Johann Müller (1752–1809)—German historian.*
4. *Cassius Longinus (c. A.D. 213–73)—rhetorician and philosopher. Best known for his commentaries on Homer.*

5. *August Schlegel (1767–1845)—both of the Schlegels and Madame de Staël influenced Russian romantic estheticians.*

6. *In his* Epistula ad Pisones (*or,* Ars Poetica).

7. The Fountain of Bandusia—*Odes, Book IV.*

8. *Ivan M. Muravyo-Apostol—Pushkin appended part of his travel notes to* The Fountain of Bakhchisarai.

9. *A journal published in 1818–1826 by A. E. Izmailov. In their private correspondence Pushkin and Vyazemsky made the title a phallic allusion.*

# Selections from the Notebooks
## of Peter Vyazemsky

"Do you know Vyazemsky?" someone asked Count Golovin. "I know him! He dresses strangely!" Go, chase after fame! Be a pupil of Karamzin, a friend of Zhukovsky and others like him, write poetry some of which—according to Zhukovsky—can be called exemplary, and in society you will be known by some gaudy vest or wide trousers! —But that's Golovin, you say! All right, but unfortunately society seethes with Golovins.

I don't like people whose *soul* is *intellect:* I want the *intellect* of a man to be *soul.* The first are capable only of shining in society and occupying your bored leisure moments with their witty chatter. The latter is close to you at any time, and while the fertile speeches of the former arouse your attention and only strike your hearing for the time being, often one word of the latter is etched into your memory and into your heart forever. Vauvenargue said: *les grandes idées viennent du coeur.*[1] One may add that they are also accepted by the heart.

We see in women the triumph of *the strength of weaknesses.* Women rule and dominate us, but how? With their weaknesses —which attract and enchant us. They recall the sculpture representing Amour astride a lion. A child bridles the king of beasts.

The war of 1812 was so abundant in saviors of Moscow, Petersburg, and Russia that their real savior was forced to say: *Parmi tant de sauveurs, je n'ose me nommer.*

I think it was Poletika[2] who said: "In Russia there is salvation from the bad measures taken by the government: bad implementation."

The similarity and difference between Moscow and Petersburg is in the following: here stupidity tries to act intelligent, there intellect is sometimes forced to play the fool—in order to be like the other people.

Suvorov used to say: He who everyone says is crafty is not crafty.

He who reveals his cleverness out of vanity is like the skillfully disguised man who out of boastfulness shows himself without a mask and again puts it on in hopes of fooling people.

The success of the comedy *Misanthrope* is the triumph of a perverse age. Molière wanted to please his contemporaries, and he made a fool of an honorable man.

How strange is our fate. A Russian man strove to make Germans out of us; a German woman wanted to make us over into Russians.[3]

Molière drew human portraits with a masterful brush; the same cannot be said of his whole scenes.

Craft is the intellect of petty intellects. The lion crushes; the fox is crafty.

Some people are good *for one time:* like the calendar of some past year, when they outlive their date they outlive their purpose. One can take a look at them later to check things; but if you let yourself be guided by them, you will have to celebrate Easter on Good Friday.

Never use a new word if it doesn't have these three qualities: being necessary, understandable, and sonorous. Especially in Physics, new concepts require new expressions. But replacing an ordinary word with another having only the value of novelty means not to enrich, but to ruin language (Voltaire).

Excessive imitation destroys genius (Voltaire).

Some think that Cardinal Mazarin died,[4] others that he is alive—I believe neither the former nor the latter.

"Close to the Tsar, close to death." Honor to the Tsar if this proverb was born during war! Woe if at a time of peace!

"The sheep were whole and the wolves were sated"—was said for the first time either by a sly wolf or a base sheep. Proverbs, as they say, are the wisdom of peoples: here there is no wisdom, but either a sneer or baseness. Happy is the flock which hungry wolves circumambulate.

How many books there are which you read once just to clear your conscience, in order to say when it comes up: "I have read that book!" As you make some annual visits in order that your visiting card be included in the gateman's list. Not all books, not all acquaintances, are close to the heart. In both the former and the latter we have many hat-tipping acquaintances. A superfluous acquaintance hurts true relations and steals time from friendship; superfluous reading enriches neither the memory nor the mind, it just takes up space in both, and sometimes even outlives something really useful. Now many people study with "economical" *(compactes)* editions of old books; but the economy relates only to the conservation of paper. It would be good if a way were found of extracting the sap of true knowledge and in this way saving the readers' time—which is more valuable than paper. —How vexing is a guest who comes at the wrong time, whom it is impossible to refuse. How vexing is the appearance of a book which you must without fail read when your attention is occupied by other reading or a task which has no connection to it!

It always amuses me to hear how the publishers or the panegyrists of satirists clean their consciences with oaths against being suspected of malice: wouldn't it be the same if surgeons went to the trouble of explaining they are not bloodthirsty cutthroats? A slanderer is a murderer: a satirist is a surgeon who cuts off growths with his knife and lowers a probe into infectious wounds.

When I imagine Kheraskov writing verse, I see an old

peasant woman knitting a stocking: her hands move by themselves while she dozes, but the stocking gets knitted. Could one
write this when awake: "It isn't for us to be timid, but brave
useful."

I think my task is not action, but perception. I must be kept
like a room's thermometer: it can neither warm nor cool the
room, but no one will perceive the real temperature more quickly
or accurately than it does.

The style of one of the ancients which was strong and
robust, but jerky and fragmented, was compared to Minerva's
shield broken into pieces.

Byron was a great lover of horses. Count Ostein, the Vien-
nese minister at the Petersburg court, said of him: "He talks
about horses like a man, but about man or with me like a horse."

"I have noticed that a man whose sentences cannot be corrected without re-doing them completely is a man whose head
one cannot re-educate without replacing it with another."
(Diderot)

Chamfort makes fools of people, La Rochefoucauld debases
them, Voltaire corrects them.

In Catherine's drawing-room Diderot was thundering
against flatterers and in the heat of oration sent them all to Hell.
Catherine changed the subject. After half an hour she asks him:
what are they saying in Paris about the last Russian revolution?
Diderot stammers, tries to get out of this with lame excuses,
answers that in Paris it is called a state necessity, a useful evil
etc. "Be careful, M. Diderot," interrupts Catherine, "you are on
the road to Purgatory at least."

I would like fame, but only to illumine the grave of my
father and the cradle of my son.

Niemcewicz[5] once found La Harpe at a translation of
Camoëns. He asked, "With so much different kinds of knowl-

edge in sciences and languages, how have you had time to learn Spanish too?"—"It's obvious that you are young," he answered, "as if it were necessary to know a language in order to translate it. A good dictionary and intelligence—that's all!"

An intelligent lady used to say, "I love your eldest nephew because he is intelligent, the younger one because he is stupid."

"Experience is not the daughter of time, as is falsely said, but of events." (Pradt)

*Nouvelles de Jean Boccace.* Traduction libre par Mirabeau. Paris, 1802. 8 volumes.

The translation is probably not Mirabeau's—at least in the essay on him in *Biographies des Contemporains* it isn't mentioned among the works left by him. There is a translation by Tiboule published with Mirabeau's name, but that, as the biography attests, was made together with his co-student Poisson de Lachabeaussière, the son of Mirabeau's tutor. It is impossible to judge about Boccaccio's original from this translation. The French, the *old* ones at least, are unbearable with their Frenchifying, nobilifying translations. God knows where they get these chaste apprehensions, this conscientiousness: instead of which they need to know a little more about humility. Either don't translate an author, or when translating submit to him and hide your mind, your opinions. However, it is still hard to understand Boccaccio's fame, which is based on his *Decameron*. It seems his fame would not be so cheap now. Italians are enraptured by the prose of Boccaccio, a writer of the XIVth century; he was for Italian prose what Petrarch, with whom he lived in close friendship, was for its poetry. The description of the Florence plague in the *Decameron* is famous, but the French translator was, it seems, the Eropkin of this plague: he weakened it, and if he didn't stop it altogether he did abridge it.[6] The tale of the three rings translated by Lessing in his *Nathan the Wise* is in the *Decameron*. Boccaccio was an extremely learned man and one of those who introduced love for knowledge and the Greek language into Italy. He was also a poet, but a mediocre one; he left two Greek poems: *Il Teseide* and *Il Filostrato*. He was the inventor of the Italian octave, later adopted by all the Italian, Spanish, and Portuguese epics. *Il Teseide* was translated by the father of English poetry, Chaucer. Later Dryden reworked it. Boccaccio's Latin works are voluminous: among them are *On the Genealogy of the Gods* and others—*On Mountains, Forests and Rivers*. At the end of his life he devoted himself to the spiritual calling. It is strange and instructive to see these contradictions in the celebrated men of middle antiquity. In our time one character is enough for the life of a man (without mentioning political transformations). Boccaccio is a seductive storyteller, also a profound scholar, often entrusted with important business and embassies placed on him by the government, friend of the chaste Petrarch, and, near the end of life, a man of the clergy. His novels are also known: *La Amorosa Fiammetta*, *Il Filocolo*. Princess Maria, the illegitimate daughter of King Robert and object of Boccaccio's love, is depicted in *Fiammetta*. In Sismondi's *Littérature du midi de l'Europe* there is a good account of the contradiction between the calamitous epoch in which Boccaccio sets his story and the playful fantasy of the tales themselves. "Count Nulin" is a Boccaccio tale of the XIXth century. And perhaps our classicists will start looking for romanticism and Byronism here too, when there is simply priapism of the imagination!—The French edition is supplemented with La Fontaine's imitations. The narration is cold, stilted; here and there—but rarely—there are sparks of humor. There is no priapism in these.

*Han d'Islande*, a novel by Victor Hugo, 4 volumes, of the Melmoth type, but with less profound truth.[7] There are the same sins in his prose as in his poetry, but the same beauties too. It is impossible not to admit it is the delirium of a fever, but the fever of a poet. There are many powerful scenes, picturesque characters who are well-drawn, for example the executioner, the guard of the corpses, Spiagudry, Schumaker's daughter.—There is political interest too: the revolt of the miners, their attack, a meeting with the king's army—vivid and realistic. A Russian executioner is discussed.

*Le Corsaire Rouge*, a novel by Fenimore Cooper.[8] Cooper is the novelist of wet and dry deserts, at least in the two novels which I have read, *The Prairie* and this last one. They echo the monotony of the desert a little, but at the same time there is something boundless, fresh and extraordinary in reading him. No one, it seems, is more gifted than he with a sense for the prairie and the sea. He is at home here, and he surrounds the reader in its elements. W. Scott leads you into the din and battle of passions, human emotions. Cooper leads you *up to* look at the same passions, on the same man, but this is outside the drawing of the setting, the cities, etc., with which he surrounds us. With him it is somehow more spacious, his atmosphere is freer, purer; every slight impression which in W. Scott's sphere would not be perceptible works on you more vividly, sensitively. The reader's feelings are refined from the element into which the author transports him. In him there is more of the epic, in Scott more of the dramatic, though in both the shadings merge from time to time. I prefer *The Prairie* to *The Red Corsair;* the end especially is somehow drawn-out and stiff. There is nothing criminal in the character of the Corsair, and therefore there is little moral element in the terror which his name inspires and the punishment which is being prepared for him. This is just a matter of the sea police. We don't know what he was formerly, but in the novel he is just a breaker of the law. But the sea—what free expansiveness in Cooper, you fairly swim in it. The ship, the things associated with the sea, the entire naval part is done to perfection by Cooper. Cooper grasps the sea so well that Peter I would have showered him with gold. In W. Scott's novels one doesn't quickly discern a man in the human crowd unless there are special motives for it, for the most part one makes only hat-tipping acquaintances: all the attention of one's eyes is focused on the externals as in everyday life. On Cooper's empty and vast horizon every being is silhouetted separately and completely; each one arouses one's attention and you follow him until he disappears. The gregarious person will say, "One must live in Scott's world and glance into Cooper's world." The unsociable person (not exactly a misanthrope) will say: "One must live (i.e. it is pleasant to live) in Cooper's world, but for diversion one may glance into Scott's world."

*Canongate Chronicles.* Somnolence of W. Scott and even shameful somnolence. Such books are written only for money, with the assurance that with an already famous signature you can even get away with mediocrity. The first volume is composed of babble; the three following ones of three stories. The first is good. In the second, the duel of two cow herders and the murder of one of them are related. The third is a chain of adventures hastily tied together; there is neither probability, nor naturalness, nor striking supernatural events. The *Canongate Chronicles* are worse than even the history of Napoleon.[9]—The preface is rather complicated.

*Cinq Mars.*[10] A historical novel by Count Alfred de Vigny. French literature has had much success in the last few years in the genre of—what should we call it—romantic, or simply natural, in contradistinction to the classical genre, which is entirely artificial. *Les soirées de Neuillys,*[11] *Les Barricades,*[12] and this novel are all marked by a kind of sobriety of truth which has its vividness and its freshness, like water which gushes from a spring and is drunk on the spot, not the stale saccharine water warmed at a buffet. Alfred de Vigny hasn't the profundity of W. Scott, but there is subtlety, accuracy in the painting.

*The Wild Irish Boy,*[13] a novel by Maturin, the author of *Melmoth*. Maturin, or as the English call him, it seems, *Mefrin*, is an amazing poet in the details. This novel is far behind *Melmoth*, but there are amazing, graceful passages, portraits which are fresh and bright. The episode with Mary—who like a cloudy shadow appears in impalpable, inexpressible charm—slips past you in a minute, and in that minute she loves and suffers so that the impression of her etches itself deeply in one's soul and, having flickered by, "falls into the grave like a sailor into the ocean." All this is enchanting. The author, it seems, knows society poorly, although as an intelligent man he marks it out in sharp features—but, I think, too sharp. However, English society has its own physiognomy; perhaps his observations resemble the truth, though often they contradict general truth or verisimilitude. Moore, Southey, and some English novelists are introduced in it—probably not W. Scott, whom the author judges rather severely, especially with regard to the use of his talents. This classical reproach is strange for the author of *Melmoth* and the *Irish Boy:* he himself is entirely fantastic, and you don't know what remains in your soul after you've read him: impressions resembling the impressions of sunset, a magnificent thunderstorm, mysterious music.

In a little more than a day and a half I gulped down the four volumes of *Le siège de Vienne* de Madame Pichler,[14] traduit par Madame de Montolieu. It's not as good as Walter Scott, although there is a desire to imitate him. The characters of Zrina, Ludmila, her sister Katerina, Sandor Shkatinsky are well drawn, especially the first two. History blends with the novel-story artfully, without coercion; the description of the siege of Vienna is lively. The gypsy scene, the disputes in Leopold's office, Zrina's struggles with herself, Ludmila swimming, her meeting with her mad and incarcerated husband—all are picturesquely sketched. In general there is a kind of coldness, emotion touched but not penetrated. There is an absence of that fever of curiosity, sadness, craving, and fascination which pours over the reader of Walter Scott—the only novelist who knows how to blend all the enchantments of romantic fantasy with history and the historical poetry of an epic, the effectiveness of a drama which is sometimes tragic, sometimes comic, the perspicacity of a moralist, and the eagle eye in a human heart with all the enchantments of romantic fantasy. Walter Scott is perhaps the most perfect writer of all nations and all ages. Karamzin used to say that if he ever lived in a home he would put a monument of gratitude to Walter Scott in his garden for all the pleasure he had partaken of in reading his novels.

(Aug. 12, 1826)

*Les Fiancés*, a novel by Alexander Manzoni,[15] five volumes in small print, but lively ones, not dead. I haven't read a novel which is fuller than this in its conception. The basic plot is the wedding of two fiancés from a poor Italian village in the seventeenth century, a wedding postponed by various obstacles. And just what are these obstacles? The most remarkable historical events—which involuntarily become connected to this wedding or to which it connects itself constantly, and without any strained efforts on the part of the author. It is a vivid picture of the anarchy of Italy during the most despotic and alien rule of the Spanish, a picture of the oppression done by landowners, many of whom were openly and with impunity the leaders of bands of robbers, the so-called *Bravi*, who were always ready for any malefaction at the movement of a hand or at a word from their *patron*; a picture of the famine which dominated the Milan district and the plague which soon followed it. The adventures of the peasant girl Lucia and the peasant boy Lorenzo flow through these grand phenomena; and the reader's attention, greatly aroused by their deep impressions, does not for a moment grow cold in its interest in these humble characters, who, it seems, ought to get lost like small dots in a vast circle. The author's art in reconciling these difficulties is superlative. In the accurate words of the French translator: "Walter Scott reaches the novel through history; Manzoni reaches history through the novel." The Italian novelist does not have the rush of dramatic emotions which the Scot has; for an Italian he has little mimicry. He is a rather dispassionate narrator, but his narration, though rather smooth, is lucid and lively. He has few dramatic episodes in which one facet depicts a character for you, but every line does add to the depiction. How intimately, though not rapidly, you get to know Fra Christophoro, Lucia, Lorenzo, Father Abbondio, Agnesa, Don Rodrigo and his blood-thirsty satellites, the Innominato, Cardinal Federigo Boromeo. How these characters reverberate in your memory, your heart. How good the young fellow Lorenzo, who suddenly and unexpectedly falls, as if from the sky, into the Milan discontent on the occasion of the famine—by the force of circumstances, so to speak, physically pushed by the crowd, he involuntarily comes out in front of all, almost as leader of the discontent, with which he is totally unconcerned; and not without reason the government considers him one of the main instigators of the revolt; and the simple fellow Lorenzo is forced to become a political exile over whom states enter into negotiations. And all this is so believable, so natural; nowhere can one see the needle-marks of an author who has sewn the events together hastily, knowing that an absorbed reader would not discern the stitches of his work. No, the firm hand of fate, which never moves without reason, is visible everywhere here. It is so because it could not be otherwise. And the description of the plague: the imagination is so possessed when reading it, that at moments you want to throw down the book for fear of becoming infected, and at moments you are so tied by sympathy for the poor victims that you regret not being able to go to the hospital jammed with 16,000 patients in aid of the inexhaustible Fra Christoforo, to share his Christian efforts. One thing, it seems to me, does contradict the truth: the rapid turning of the terrible Innominato, the Milanese Izmailov,[16] onto the path of piety. But how touching it is and what a man Boromeo is—a model of Christian virtue, and not an ideal, not a mystic one, but the most practical and at once elevated one.

It was, I think, Osterman[17] who said to, I think, Palluci during a council of war in the campaign of 1812: "For you Russia is a shirt, but for me she's my skin."

Our journals are so dirty that you can only read them wearing gloves.

Could I embody and unbosom now
That which is most within me,—could I wreak
My thoughts upon expression, and thus throw
Soul, heart, mind, passions, feeling, strong or weak,
All that I would have sought, and all I seek,
Bear, know, feel, and yet breake—into *one* word,
And that one word were lightning, I would speak;
But as it is, I live and die unheard,
With a most voiceless thought, sheathing it as with a sword.

(*Childe Harold*, III, XCVII,
quoted in English)

Today I wrote A. Turgenev about his sadness:[18] "Such unhappiness is a banknote. It circulates at home, but abroad it loses all its value and becomes a piece of blank paper. Life can still bring you a few savory fruits. There's no point in expecting magic fruits any longer. The dragons of corporeality have eaten all the Hesperidesian apples of our ancient times, and we are left with the one apple eaten by Eve and which the stomach of the human race has still not managed to digest. We are all exiles in our own country too. Who among us is not more or less a pariah? And it's better to be a pariah under the sun than under the rain and snow!"

I read *Le Cid* with its whole story, Scudéry's criticism, the comments of the academy, etc.[19] There is much that is correct in Scudéry's judgments, but much that is stupid and crude. Of course one cannot believe that Chimène could meet with her father's killer half an hour after the killing, but that is the fault of the classical tragedy. Scudéry interprets, Corneille justifies himself, Voltaire defends him—but they all spin around the truth without touching the sore spot. Galiani is right, Voltaire is unbearable in his commentaries on Corneille. In them he resembles an old French teacher; he notes that such and such an expression, such and such a word is no longer in use. It's a strange thing that Voltaire, who wanted to turn the heavens and everyone living in them upside down, trembles so before some rules and conventions or other, turns pale at a work which doesn't seem current to him, etc. In my opinion the best scene in *The Cid* is Rodrigo's challenge to Chimène's father. All the rest is stilted. Chimène, who shifts in turn from indignation to love, from demands for vengeance to declarations of tenderness, resembles a checker that shifts from a white space to a black on a checkerboard. Of course there is much that is dramatic in the situation; but all this is too abrupt in Corneille. Don Sancho and the Princess are such pitiful creations that it's a shame to look at them. I think it has already been observed by someone that if the classicists permit an abridgment or transformation of 24 hours into 2 hours, why not expand this freedom to a year or two and so on. You say to the spectators: imagine that you have come to sit here for 24 hours; if they submit to this proposal, if their imaginations contribute to your fiction, then they aren't going to argue about a more prolonged period. If you succeed in assuring them that 24 is not 24 but two, or that two is not two but 24, why is it any more supernatural that two might be two thousand or two million? Once you grant imagination in the number, once you grant that two times two is not four—then it makes no difference whether you take 24 hours or 24 years as the total. The classical box is like a coffin: you can't get your hero into it unless he is dead and without movement. While the hero is still free in his movements, he can go to the right and to the left; he is not concerned with the classical coffin. But when the Aristotle mirror is put to his mouth, and it does not fog over from his breath, we welcome a master coffin-maker: his measure will be taken, a coffin will be made, he will be put in and decorated with brocade covers.

(23 November, 1830)

All my little European hopes are turning into smoke. Now B. Constant has died, and I intended sending him my translation of *Adolphe* with a letter.[20] However, Turgenev told him I was his translator.

As Raphaels, Newtons, and Paganinis—especially Paganinis —are born: so it is that one must be born with the ability to pronounce the English "th" and other letters *qui jurent d'être ensemble.*[21]

Krylov said of Shishkov:[22] "He knows how one shouldn't write, but he doesn't know how one should write. One can put trust in his charges, but one cannot follow his advice. He's like a man who would tell you that it's dangerous to cook food in an untinned saucepan and that to avoid harm one must always tin it with red lead."

Salvandi,[23] in answer to a political-academic speech of V. Hugo (in which, incidentally, he praises Danton), said very wittily to him: "Napoléon, Sieyès, Malherbes na sont pas vos ancêtres, monsieur. Vouz en avez de non moins illustrés: J. B. Rousseau, Clément Marot, Pindar, le Psalmiste." (I think David is superfluous here.) This reminds me of my conversation with Hugo, when I visited him in Paris. I kept trying to get him on the subject of literature and he turned everything to politics, the Poles, Emperor Nikolai. "J'aime l'empereur Nicholas, mais si j'étais à sa place, voici ce que je ferais" etc.

Lamartine's "La Marseillaise":

> Chacun est du climat de son intelligence,
> Je suis concitoyen de toute âme qui pense;
> La vérité, c'est mon pays!
> La fumée en courant *léchera* ton ciel blue.

Why give a tongue to smoke? That's what the French call romanticism.

Our literary poverty is explained by the fact that in general our intelligent and educated men are not literate, and our literate men are in general not intelligent and not educated.

The news of Lermontov's death[24] reached me at the same time as an excerpt from a letter of Zhukovsky. What polarities there are in these two fates. But there is a kind of mark of Providence in this. Compare the basic elements from which the lives and poetry of both were formed, and their ends will seem a natural result and conclusion. Karamzin and Zhukovsky: the life of the former was reflected in the latter, just as Pushkin was reflected in Lermontov. This could be the subject of many meditations.

The legislator of French, and consequently almost all European, Parnassus said: "Un sonnet sans défaut vaut seul une long poème."[25]

Now sonnets are no longer written even in schools. Their glory fell along with French kaftans. Arbitrary beauty has only temporary value. A good line in a sonnet is transmitted to posterity as a good line, but the sonnet, no matter how correct it is, is left without esteem. How many *sonnets* one meets among people! A clever phrase uttered by a wit does not soon grow old, but the wit himself outlives himself and no longer has an honored place in society.

What threw our dramatic art onto the narrow road of the French? Sumarokov's bad tragedies. Had he been an imitator of Shakespeare we would have now improved on his bad imitations of the English, just as we have now improved on his pale imitations of the French. How fate loves to give authority to the first-born in all families: their example not only captivates their contemporaries, but their heirs cannot come to their senses for a long time and follow them blindly.

It is in vain that Schlegel says: "If Racine really said that he differed from Pradin only in that he knew how to write, he was cruelly unjust to himself."[26] Of course one must add something to the opinion, but Racine said that in France, and style, which is the first necessity for the French, is (at the other extreme) the last condition among the Germans, if not altogether a trifle. Craftsmanship must be valued in the arts: the Germans buy everything by weight. That's why Schlegel's judgments about French theatre are sometimes incorrect; he judges it not as an expert or lover, but as a pawnbroker. The French place clarity and neatness of style above everything; Corneille has been forgotten in their theatre: the rough verse and the wild phrasing are unforgivable sins in their eyes, and it outlives, i.e., it buries, a whole poem. In general a foreigner can talk about the literature of another nation as an observer, but he should never allow himself to decide about it by means of judicatory sentence—which is always more or less mistaken and prejudiced.

After death there is no falsehood, and to hide anything written by an author, that is from his mental life, is falsehood. I want to know not only the author but also the man: that is why the reading of notes is interesting and instructive.

## N O T E S

1. *Vauvenargues,* Réflexions et maximes *(Paris, 1818), p. 111. "Les grandes pensées viennent du coeur."*

2. *Peter I. Poletika—a member of Arzamas, civil servant in the Ministry of Foreign Affairs.*

3. *Peter the Great and Catherine the Great.*

4. *Cardinal J. Mazarin (1602–61)—first minister of Louis XIII.*

5. *Julian Niemcewicz (1758–1841)—Polish writer, historian, and politician.*

6. *In 1771 General P. D. Eropkin headed the battle against a plague epidemic in Moscow.*

*The "abridgments" to which Vyazemsky refers were praised by the editor of this "translation" of Boccaccio. In the preface he says the plot and main idea are the only essentials—these can be freely rendered. After each re-told tale he includes the fable which La Fontaine had written using that story.*

7. *Hugo's novel was published in 1823. Melmoth is the hero of Charles Robert Maturin's* Melmoth the Wanderer.

8. Red Rover—*James Fenimore Cooper enjoyed considerable popularity in Russia. Pondering the infelicities of bachelorhood, Pushkin complained (in his diary) that "if Scott and Cooper have written nothing new" his typical day is one of idleness or drinking. In 1828 Anna Olenina, attractive daughter of the President of the Academy of Arts and holder of one of the most glittering salons in St. Petersburg, noted that she had nicknamed Pushkin the Red Rover.*

9. Les chroniques de la canongate, *W. Scott,* Oeuvres complètes *(Paris, 1828–33), vols. 71–73, tomes 1–3. Scott's biography of Napoleon (1827) was forbidden in Russia.*

10. *Vigny's novel was published in 1826. See above, pp. 216–219.*

11. *Published in 1827 by August Cavé and Adolphe Dittmer under the pseudonym Fongeray.*

12. *By Louis Vitet, published in 1826.*

13. *By Charles Maturin, published in 1808.* His Melmoth *was so popular in Russia that an enterprising publisher printed de Quincey's* Confessions of an English Opium Eater *under Maturin's name. Among Vyazemsky's other Gothic readings was Anne Radcliffe's* The Italian, or Confessional of the Black Penitents *(London, 1797), translated into Russian (Moscow, 1802–1804).*

14. *Carolina Pichler (1769–1843)—an Austrian writer. The French translation appeared in 1824.*

15. *Alessandro Manzoni (1785–1873)—Italian poet and writer. Vyazemsky read him in French:* Les fiancés, Histoire milanaise du XVII siècle *(Paris, 1830).* [I Promessi Sposi.]

16. *A cruel Russian landowner and general.*

17. *Count A. I. Osterman-Tolstoy to one of the Austrian generals.*

18. *Alexander Turgenev's brother Nikolai had decided to spend the rest of his life abroad because he had been implicated in the Decembrist uprising.*

19. *Corneille's play was attacked by Scudéry* (Observations sur le Cid) *and by the Académie,* Les sentiments de l'Académie française sur la tragicomédie du Cid *(Paris, 1636), edited by Chapelain.*

20. *See above, p. 73.*

21. *Vyazemsky spent the fall of 1838 in England. His diary is full of complaints about the difficulties of learning English.*

22. *A. S. Shishkov—President of the Russian Academy 1824–28, head of the Society of Lovers of the Russian Word (which was devoted to purifying Russian, opposing the reforms popularized by Karamzin and defended by Arzamas).*

23. *N. A. Salvandi (1795–1856)—French politician and publicist.*

24. *Mikhail Lermontov, Russia's best poet after Pushkin, was killed in a duel on July 5, 1841.*

25. *From Boileau's* Art Poétique. *Vyazemsky repeats some of these thoughts in an article on Mickiewicz's* Crimean Sonnets *(in* The Moscow Telegraph, *1827), noting the interest of some Russian romantics (including Pushkin and Delvig) in the sonnet.*

26. *Vyazemsky cites August Schlegel from* Cours de littérature dramatique *(Paris–Genève, 1814), II, 205.*

# A Few Thoughts about Poetry

## Kondraty Fedorovich Ryleev (1795–1826)

(An Excerpt from a Letter to NN)

**"I am not a poet, but a citizen,"** declared Ryleev in his most famous
poem. And in fact, he does belong to political history more than to
literary history. After returning from Germany and France with the
Russian army, he began writing "civic poetry." The political nature
of his historical ballads and poems like *Voynarovsky* now seems
clear, and his agitational songs were openly seditious. He became a
member of the Northern Society, and eventually he was one of the
five leaders who were hanged in the Peter-Paul Fortress for leading
the Decembrist uprising.

He wrote very little criticism, but in "A Few Thoughts about
Poetry" he offers some fairly original opinions on the battle between
classical and romantic poetry.

The text used for the translation is in *Russkaja literatura XIX v.—
Xrestomatija kriticheskix materialov*, Vypusk I, pp. 159–63.

**The argument about romantic and classical poetry has already**
occupied enlightened Europe for a long time, and not long ago
it began among us too. Not only doesn't the heat with which
this argument continues grow cool with time—it keeps increas-
ing. In spite of that, however, neither the romantics nor the
classicists can boast of victory. It seems to me that the reason
for this is that both sides (as it usually happens) argue more
about words than about the substance of the matter, that they
give too much importance to forms, and that in fact there is no
classical or romantic poetry, but there was, is, and will be only
one true self-sufficient poetry, the rules of which always were
and will be the same.

Let's get down to business.

In the middle ages when the dawn of enlightenment was already beginning in Europe, a few learned men termed "classical," i.e., exemplary, the authors they chose for reading in classes and as models for their students. In this manner Homer, Sophocles, Virgil, Horace, and other ancient poets were named classical poets. Teachers and students sincerely believed that only by blindly imitating the ancients both in forms and in the spirit of their poetry could they achieve the height which they had achieved; and this unfortunate prejudice, which became general, was the reason for the insignificance of the works of the majority of the modern poets. The exemplary creations of the ancients, which should have served only as encouragement for the poets of our time, took the place of the very ideals of poetry for them. The imitators could never compare with the models, and besides that, they deprived themselves of their strength and originality; and if they did produce anything excellent, it was, so to speak, by chance; and in almost every case it happened when the subjects of their creations were taken from ancient history, primarily Greek, for here imitation of the ancient was replaced by a study of the spirit of the time, the enlightenment of the age, the human and geographical characteristics of the country where the event which the poet wished to present in his work took place. That is why *Mérope, Esther, Mithridate*, and a few other creations of Racine, Corneille, and Voltaire are excellent.[1] That is why all the creations of these or other poets, creations the subjects of which were borrowed from modern history and molded into the forms of the ancient drama, are almost always far from perfection.

Terming many ancient poets of unequal merit "classics," without differentiation, caused perceptible harm to modern poetry; and to this day it serves as one of the most important reasons for the confusion of our ideas about poetry in general and about poets in particular. We often put a poet of originality on the same level with an imitator: Homer with Virgil, Aeschylus with Voltaire. Having enmeshed ourselves in the chains of foreign opinions and used imitation to clip the wings of poetry's geniuses, we were drawn toward the goal which the ferule of Aristotle and his untalented followers had pointed out to us. Only the extraordinary power of genius occasionally broke a new road for itself, and flying around the goal which had been pointed out by the pedants, soared toward its own ideal. But when a few poets appeared who followed the inspiration of their own genius without imitating either the spirit or the forms of ancient poetry, and gave Europe their original works, it was necessary to distinguish classical poetry from modern—and the Germans called this latter poetry "romantic," instead of simply calling it "new." Dante, Tasso, Shakespeare, Ariosto, Calderón, Schiller, Goethe were termed romantics. To this we must add that the very name "romantic" is taken from the dialect in which the first original works of the troubadours appeared. These singers did not imitate the ancients, because then Greek had already been distorted by mixing with various barbaric languages; Latin had branched, and the literatures of both had become dead for the peoples of Europe.

Thus original, distinctive poetry was called romantic poetry; and in this sense Homer, Aeschylus, Pindar—in a word all the best Greek poets—are romantics, just as the finest works of modern poets written on the rules of the ancients, but the subjects of which were not taken from ancient history, are basically romantic works, although neither the former nor the latter are acknowledged as such. Doesn't it follow from all that has been said above that neither romantic nor classical poetry exists? In its essence true poetry has always been the same, just as its rules have. It differs only in the essence and forms which are lent to it in different ages by the spirit of the time, the degree of enlightenment, and the location of the country where it appears.

In general, poetry may be divided into the ancient and the modern. This would be more well-grounded. Our poetry has more intellectual than material content; that's why we have more thoughts, the ancients have more tableaux; we have more of the general, they have more particulars. Modern poetry also has its subdivisions, depending on the ideas and spirit of the ages in which its geniuses appear. Such are Dante's *Divina commedia*, the wizardry in Tasso's poem, Milton, Klopstock with his elevated religious ideas, and finally in our time, the poems and tragedies of Schiller, Goethe, and especially Byron, in which the passions of men are depicted, their innermost motives, the eternal battle of the passions with a secret aspiration to something elevated, something infinite.

I said above that in general too much importance is ascribed to the forms of poetry. This is also an important reason for the confusion of the ideas of our time about poetry in general. Those who consider themselves classicists demand blind imitation of the ancients and assert that any deviation from their forms is an inexcusable error. For example, in a dramatic work the three unities are, for them, an indispensable law the breaking of which cannot be justified by anything. Romantics, on the contrary, reject these conditions as restricting the freedom of genius, and consider unity of goal sufficient for drama. In this case there is basis for the romantics' view. The forms of the ancient drama are unsuitable for us, exactly as the forms of the ancient republics are. Pure democracy was convenient for Athens, and Sparta, and the other republics of the ancient world, because all the citizens without exception could participate in it. And the form of their government was not purposely invented, not forcibly introduced; it stemmed from the nature of things; given the position that civil societies were in at that time it was essential. In exactly the same manner the three unities of Greek drama, in the works where they are encountered, were not purposely invented by the ancient poets; they were a natural result of the essence of the subjects of their works. Almost all the activities took place in one city and in one place then; this itself determined both the rapidity and the unity of action.

The populousness and vastness of modern nations, the degree to which their peoples are enlightened, the spirit of the time—in a word, all the physical and moral conditions of the modern world—determine a larger field both in politics and in poetry. For us the three unities no longer should or can be an indispensable law in the drama, because not one city, but an entire nation serves as the theater of our activities—and usually the beginning of the activity is in one place, its continuation in another, and a third sees its end. I don't at all want to say by this that we should banish the three unities from our drama. When the event which the poet wishes to present in his work flows effortlessly into the forms of the ancient drama, then of course the three unities are not only not superfluous, but occasionally even an essential condition.

Only it isn't necessary to purposely distort an historical event in order to observe the three unities, because in this case all probability is destroyed. Given the state of our civil societies, we retain complete freedom, depending on the nature of the subject, to observe the three unities or to content ourselves with one, i.e., the unity of the event or the goal. This frees us from the chains placed on poetry by Aristotle. Let us note, however, that this freedom, exactly as our civil freedom, places upon us duties more difficult than those which the three unities demanded from the ancients. It is more difficult to unite various events in one whole, so that they form a perfect drama and harmonize in their movement toward a goal, than to write a drama observing the three unities—given, of course, equally fruitful subjects.

Poetry is also harmed a great deal by the vain desire to set up a definition for it, and it seems to me that those who maintain that one should not define poetry in general are right. At least to this time no one has yet defined it in a satisfactory manner: all the definitions have either been specific ones—concerning the poetry of a certain age, a certain people, or poet—or ones common to all verbal disciplines, like Ancillon's.*[2]

* In Ancillon's opinion "poetry is the power of expressing ideas by means of words; or the free power of representing, with the help of language, the infinite in finite and defined forms which in their harmonic activity will speak to the emotions, the imagination, and the judgment." But this definition also fits philosophy; it fits all areas of human knowledge which are expressed in words. Also, many (taking the teaching of modern German philosophy into account) say that the essence of "roman-

The ideal of poetry, like the ideals of all other subjects which the human spirit strives to comprehend, is infinite and inaccessible; and therefore a definition of poetry is impossible and, it seems to me, useless. If it were possible to define what poetry is, then it would be possible to reach its highest summit; and if it were reached in any age, what would be left to future generations? Where would the *perpetuum mobile* be put?

The great labors and superb creations of some of the ancient and modern poets should inspire us with esteem for them, but not at all piety, because this is contrary to the laws of the purest morality; it lowers the worth of man, and at the same time settles a kind of fear in him which prevents him from getting close to the exalted poet and even from seeing faults in that poet. Therefore, let us respect poetry and not its priests; and leaving the useless argument over romanticism and classicism, let us try to destroy the spirit of slavish imitation and, turning to the source of true poetry, let us employ all efforts to embody in our writings the ideals of elevated emotions, ideas, and eternal truths which are always close to man and always insufficiently well-known to him.

[1825, *Son of the Fatherland*]

## N O T E S

1. *Racine wrote* Mithridate *and* Esther, *Voltaire* Mérope.

2. *Johann P. Ancillon (1767–1837)—German writer, historian, and political figure. Ryleev had read a volume translated as* The Esthetic Opinions of Mr. Ancillon *(St. Petersburg, 1813).*

---

tic" (in our terms, "old") poetry consists of the aspiration of the soul to perfection, which is unknown to it itself, but which is an essential aspiration for it—one which possesses every emotion of true poets of this kind. But isn't this the essence and philosophy of all the arts?

# A Critique of an Essay on Eugene Onegin
## Published in The Telegraph

---

### Dmitri Vladimirovich Venevitinov (1805–1827)

**In spite of his youth, Venevitinov was the center of a circle known** as the *Lyubomudry* (Lovers of Wisdom), a group of talented men devoted to the study of German idealistic philosophy. Mirsky describes Venevitinov as "a man of dazzling abundance of gifts—a strong brain, a born metaphysician, a mature and lofty poet," but he does not note that Venevitinov's early death was apparently a suicide.

His works include some fifty poems, translations from Goethe and Hoffman, a few essays on philosophical themes, and several critical essays, mostly on Pushkin.

His "Critique of an Essay on *Eugene Onegin*" was an answer to Nikolai Polevoi's review *(Moscow Telegraph,* No. 5, 1825) of the first chapter of *Eugene Onegin.* Venevitinov's critique was followed by a long answer from Polevoi and a final reply by Venevitinov again. Pushkin is reported to have said of Venevitinov's critique: "It is the only article that I have read with love and attention. All the rest are either abuse or cloying nonsense."

The text used for the translation is D. V. Venevitinov, *Polnoe sobranie sochinenij* (Academia, 1934), pp. 220–28.

**If talent always finds the measure of its perceptions and its** impressions in its own self, if its lot is to scorn the usual prejudices of the crowd (which is one-sided in its opinions) and to feel more vividly than others the creative power of those rare sons of nature on whom genius has put its mark, then what thought struck Pushkin when he read the essay about his new poem in *The Telegraph,* where he is presented not in comparison to himself, not in relation to his goal, but as a faithful comrade of Byron on the field of world literature, standing on the same spot with him?

*The Moscow Telegraph* has such a number of readers and such curious essays are found in it that any unjust opinion promulgated in it will certainly have an influence on the evaluations made by, if not all, at least many people. In such a case it is the obligation of every conscientious person to correct the errors of the editor and resist, as far as possible, the deluge of delusions. I am sure that Mr. Polevoi will not be offended by criticism written with this aim: in his soul he will admit that in the critique of *Onegin* his pen was perhaps guided partly by a desire to enrich his journal with the works of Pushkin ( a desire which, incidentally, is praiseworthy and doubtless shared by all the readers of *The Telegraph*).

And can one fight the spirit of the time? It always remains unconquered, triumphing over all efforts, enclosing in its chains even the thoughts of those who not long before had sworn to be faithful fighters for objectivity!

Mr. Polevoi's first error, it seems to me, is that he intends to raise Pushkin's worth by excessively lowering the critics of our literature. This is an error against the most ordinary prudence, against the politics of getting along with people—which requires always assuming as much intellect as possible in others. It is difficult to fight with opponents whom you make talk without sense. I confess it is an unenviable victory. Let's listen to the critics invented in *The Telegraph:*

"What is Onegin," they ask, "what kind of poem is it that has chapters like in a book," etc?

I don't think anyone has asked, nor probably will ask such a question; and so far no literary person except the editor of *The Telegraph* has tried to note the difference between *a poem and a book.*

The answer is worth the question.

"*Onegin*," answers Pushkin's defender, "is a novel in verse, therefore it is permissible to use a division into chapters," etc.

If Mr. Polevoi permits himself this kind of conclusion, won't I be right in concluding, in the same way, the opposite and saying:

"*Onegin* is a novel in verse, *therefore* in verse it is not permissible to use a division into chapters." But our bold syllogisms prove nothing either in favor of *Onegin* or against it, and it's better to leave it to Mr. Pushkin to justify his work by the division which he has used.

Let us leave off the picayune critique of each sentence. How can one avoid mistakes of this kind in an essay in which the author did not posit a *single* goal for himself, in which he discussed things without resting on *a single fundamental idea*? We are going to speak only of those errors which can spread false conceptions about Pushkin and about poetry in general.

Who denies Pushkin has *true talent*? Who has not been enraptured by his verses? Who will not admit that he has gifted our literature with fine works? But why always compare him to Byron, to a poet who in spirit belongs not just to England, but to our time, who concentrated the aspiration of a whole era in his fiery soul, and who would forever remain in the chronicles of the human mind even if he could be effaced from the history of the special sphere of poetry?

All of Byron's works bear the imprint of one profound idea —an idea about man in his relation to the nature which surrounds him, in a struggle with himself, with the prejudices which have engraved themselves in his heart in contradiction to his feelings. It is said: there is little action in his poems. True— his aim is not the *narrative tale;* it is *the character of his heroes,* the *connection* between descriptions. He does not describe objects for the sake of the objects themselves, not to present a *series of tableaux,* but with the intention of expressing the impressions these have on the character whom he has put on stage. A truly poetic, creative idea.

Now, Mr. Editor of *The Telegraph,* I repeat your question, "What is *Onegin*?" You *know* him; you *love* him. So! But in your own words the hero of Pushkin's poem is a "prankster with wit, a flibbertigibbet with heart" and nothing more. Like you, I am judging just by one chapter, the first; perhaps we will both be mistaken and justify the caution of the experienced critic who, fearing his ideas would be cockeyed, did not wish to utter his judgment prematurely.

Now, dear sir, allow me to ask: what is it you call the "new inventions of the Byrons and the Pushkins"? Modern poetry is proud of Byron, and in a few lines I have already tried to point out to you that the character of his works is truly new. We are not going to question his fame as an inventive person. The singer of *Ruslan and Ludmila*, *A Prisoner of the Caucasus*, and so forth has the unquestionable endorsement of his fellow-countrymen for having enriched Russian literature with beauties hitherto unknown to it; but I confess to you, and to our poet himself, that I do not see inventions in his works which, like Byron's, "do honor to the century." The lyre of Albion has acquainted us with sounds entirely new to us. Of course no one could have written Pushkin's poems in the age of Louis XIV, but it is not that he is better which this proves. Many critics, says Mr. Polevoi, assert that *A Prisoner of the Caucasus* and *The Fountain of Bakhchisarai* are in general taken from Byron. We do not assert so definitely that our poet borrowed the structure of his poems, the character of the protagonists, the descriptions from Byron; but we will say only that Byron leaves deep impressions in his heart, ones which are expressed in all his works. I am speaking boldly about Pushkin, because among our poets he stands on a level where truth is not hard to swallow.

And Mr. Polevoi pays his due to current fashion. How can one not make a dig at Batteux in an article on literature?[1] But is it magnanimous to use the superiority of one's age to abase old Aristarchs? Isn't it better not to disturb the peace of the deceased? We all know that their worth is only relative; but if one is going to attack prejudices, isn't it more useful to harass them in the living? And who is free of them? In our time one does not judge poetry according to a book on poetics; one doesn't have an arbitrary number of rules according to which the levels of works of art are defined. True. But isn't an absence of rules for judgment a prejudice too? Aren't we forgetting that there should be a positive foundation in poetics, that every positive science borrows its strength from philosophy, that poetry too is inseparable from philosophy?

If from this point of view we cast a dispassionate look at the development of enlightenment among all nations (evaluating the literature of each as a whole by the level of philosophy of that age, as separate parts according to the relation of the ideas of each writer to contemporary concepts of philosophy), everything, it seems to me, will be cleared up. Aristotle will not lose his claims to profundity of thought, and we will not be surprised if the French, subordinating themselves to his rules, have no independent literature. Then we will judge the literature of modern times according to the right rules too; then the reason for romantic poetry will not consist of "an indefinite state of the heart."

We have seen how the editor of *The Telegraph* judges poetry; let's listen to him when he talks about art and music, comparing the artist to the poet.

"The sketches of Raphael show an artist capable of the great: it is his will to take up the brush, and the great will amaze your eyes; unless he himself wants to, no threats of a critic make him paint what others want." Further:

"In music there is a special type of work called the *capriccio* —and they exist in poetry. *Onegin* is one."

What! In Raphael's sketches you see only the capability of the great? Must he *take up* the brush and complete the painting to amaze you? Now I'm not surprised that Onegin pleases you as a *series of tableaux;* but it seems to me that the first merit of any artist is strength of thought, strength of feelings; and this strength is revealed in all the sketches of Raphael in which one can already see the size of the subject. The artist's ideal and of course, the coloring, which is essential for detailed expression of feeling, also function toward the beauty and harmony of the whole; but these only spread the main idea—which is always reflected in the character of the subjects and in their arrangement. And what kind of comparison is this of an epic poem to a painting and *Onegin* to a sketch?

"He doesn't wish to write what others wish and no threats of the critics will make him."

Do Raphael and Mr. Pushkin enjoy the exclusive right of not submitting to the will and threats of their critics? You yourself, Mr. Polevoi, will not renounce this right; and, for example, if you do not wish to agree with me about the mistakes I have noticed, surely threats will not force you to.

There is also a constant rule in the special genre of musical composition called the *capriccio*. The *capriccio*, like every musical work, must contain a complete idea, without which art cannot exist. "Such is Onegin?" I don't know and I repeat to you: we have no right to judge it until we have read the whole novel.

After all the noisy praise which the publisher of *The Telegraph* heaps on Pushkin, and which, incidentally, is perhaps more dangerous than "silent thundering," who would expect this in the same essay: "Pushkin stands in the same relation to the earlier writers of comic Russian poems as Byron stands to Pope."[2]

One musn't forget that on the preceding page Mr. Polevoi says that in our country "nothing at all bearable has been written in this genre."* We remind him of I. I. Dmitriev's "Fashionable Wife" and Bogdanovich's *Dushenka*.

A few words about the nationalism which the publisher of *The Telegraph* finds in the first chapter of *Onegin*: "We see what is our own," he says, "we hear our native sayings, we look at our own oddities—to which we were not always alien."[3] I don't know what there is that is national here except the names of Petersburg streets and restaurants. In France and in England, too, corks pop to the ceiling, devotees go to theaters and to balls. No, Mr. Publisher of *The Telegraph!* Attributing the superfluous to Pushkin means taking away that which truly belongs to

---

* Mr. Publisher of *The Telegraph!* Allow me, for the sake of clarity, to give the equation for the two aspects you have chosen in the accepted form. We will call the letter "X" the sum of all the unknown (in your opinion) Russian writers of comic poems, and we will say: Byron : Pope = Pushkin ; X.

him. In *Ruslan and Ludmila* he proved to us that he can be a national poet.

To this point Mr. Polevoi has spoken decisively; he has defined the merit of the *future Onegin* without any difficulty. His review poured out of his pen by itself and, it seems, without the author's knowledge—but here is the keystone. His effusion stops: "Where is a reviewer of Pushkin's poems to find mistakes?" Dear sir! Sometimes a whole work can be one mistake; I am not saying this about *Onegin*, but only to assure you that mistakes too are defined only in relation to the whole. However, let us be just, even in the chapter of *Onegin* which has been printed, strict taste will perhaps note a few lines and digressions which are not completely consonant with the elegance of poetry —which is always noble, even in a joke. Concerning the expressions you have called "imprecise," I am not agreed with everything. In poetry "the lyre sighs" is fine; "to waken a smile" is good and correct; one can hardly express one's idea more clearly.

It remains for me to point out to Mr. Polevoi that instead of making such decisive conclusions about the novel from the first chapter, which has something whole and complete only in one respect, i.e. as a picture of Petersburg life, it would have been better to dilate on the poet's conversation with the bookseller. In the poet's words one can see a soul which is free, ardent, capable of powerful efforts. I confess, I find more true poeticalness in this conversation than in *Onegin* itself.

I have tried to point out that poets do not fly without a goal and solely to spite the poetics, that poetry is not an indefinite fever of the mind but (like its subjects, humor, nature, and the human heart) has in itself its own permanent rules. Our attention has been turned now on the critique of the publishers of *The Telegraph*, now on *Onegin* itself. Now, what will I say in conclusion?

Of Mr. Polevoi's essay—that I would like to find in it criticism based more on positive rules, without which all judgments are shaky and inconsistent.

Of Mr. Pushkin's new novel—that it is a beautiful new

flower in the field of our literature, that in it there is not a description in which one cannot see an artful brush guided by a lively, sportive imagination; there is hardly a line which does not bear the stamp of either playful wit or enchanting talent in the beauty of expression.

[1825 *Son of the Fatherland*]

## N O T E S

1. *Polevoi makes fun of Batteux's formalistic listing of rules for the epic.*

2. *Polevoi complains that Russian comic poems are filled with dirty taverns, card players, and cachinnating drunkards. Pushkin is above this, and:* "In general recent poets have discovered new aspects of works in this genre, aspects unknown to the old writers."

The *Rape of the Lock* is monotonous, the poet just makes you laugh. But Byron doesn't just make you laugh, he goes much further. In the middle of the most joking descriptions, with a penetrating stanza he displays the heart of a man, his gaiety blends with dejection, his smile with a sneer; and Pushkin stands in the same relation to the earlier writers of comic Russian poems as Byron stands to Pope.—N. Polevoi, *The Moscow Telegraph*, No. 5, 1825.

3. *Polevoi writes:* "The same philosopher says that national (nationale) literature takes from the imagination that which speaks most strongly to the mind and character of a nation [narod, people or nation], and Pushkin has expressed this nationalism, this harmony in the description of contemporary manners, in a masterful fashion. Onegin is not copied from the French or English; we see what is our own. . . ."

# INDEX